The Office Romance

The Office Romance

playing with fire without getting burned

Dennis M. Powers

AMACOM

American Management Association

New York · Atlanta · Boston · Chicago · Kansas City · San Francisco · Washington, D.C.
Brussels · Mexico City · Tokyo · Toronto

This book is available at a special
discount when ordered in bulk quantities.
For information, contact Special Sales Department,
AMACOM, a division of American Management Association,
1601 Broadway, New York, NY 10019.

This publication is designed to provide accurate and authoritative
information in regard to the subject matter covered. It is sold with the
understanding that the publisher is not engaged in rendering legal,
accounting, or other professional service. If legal advice or other expert
assistance is required, the services of a competent professional person
should be sought.

Library of Congress Cataloging-in-Publication Data

Powers, Dennis M.
     The office romance : playing with fire without getting burned / Dennis M.
Powers.
         p.   cm.
     Includes index and bibliographical references.
     ISBN 0-8144-0464-2 (alk. paper)
     1. Sex in the workplace.   I. Title.
HF5549.5.S45P69   1998
331.2—dc21   98-27074
                                                                         CIP

Printing number

10 9 8 7 6 5 4 3 2 1

To my wife, Judy,
Whose independence, love of life, and presence
Has made the difference in my life.

092142

Contents

Preface   xv

Acknowledgments   xix

Chapter 1   The Matchmaker   1

     Karen and Frank   2
     Some More   3
     What's Really Going On at Work   5
     It's About Relationships   5
     Why Romance Thrives   6
     But What About Sexual Harassment?   7
     Pro-Interactive or Not?   9
     The New Rules of Romance   12
     Joint Partnering   13
     When Good Things Come to an End   14
     When Good Things Continue   15
     Then There Are the Attorneys   16
     What's a Company to Do?   18

Chapter 2   Close Encounters of a Natural Kind   21

     Why?   21
     All the Work-Related Romances   24
     Women Have Changed the Rules   25
         Roberta   27
     It's About Friendships and Relationships   28
     It Happens to the Best of Them   28
     The Pluses of Office Relationships   29

Chapter 3   **But What If?**   31

What the Surveys Say   32
The Motives Are Important   33
It Depends on Where You Are   34
The Major "Watch-Out" Areas   34
    Damaged Professional Reputations   35
    Unhappy Coworkers   35
    Productivity Changes (Both Yours and Others')   36
    Dating the Boss   37
    Conflicts of Interest   38
    Corporate Game Playing   39
    Sexual Harassment Charges   40
    Extramarital Affairs   40
    The Relationship Doesn't Work Out   41
    Factoring in Your Career   41
Making the Decision   42

Chapter 4   **The Law of Romance**   44

What Is Illegal Sexual Harassment?   44
    Quid Pro Quo Harassment   45
    Hostile Environment Harassment   46
Other Legal Considerations   49
The Company's Liability (and Its Defense)   51
So What Is Sexual Harassment?   53
People's Reactions Aren't the Same   55
The Fears of Management   56
And Then There's Romance   58
The Law of Romance   58
    The Courts   60
    The Stages of a Relationship   62
There's Much More Love Than Hate   63

Chapter 5   **Where Romance Ends and Harassment Begins**   64

The One-Size-Fits-All Problem   64
Persistence or Harassment?   67
Unequal Power, Favoritism, or Just People in Love?   71
    Suzanne and Jeffrey   71
    Attorney Golden and Anita   72
    The Extramarital Affair   72
    The Horror Stories   73
    Flings and "Just Plain Sex"   74

Despite the Rules, It Still Depends on the Person   75
The Minefield of Legal Rights   76
   The Lovers Against the Company   76
     Right to Prohibit Dating   76
     Regulating Married Employees   78
     Regulating E-Mail   79
   An Ex-Lover Against the Company   80
   Ex-Lovers Against Each Other   80
   Coworkers Against the Company   80
   Third-Party Relationships   81
   Professionals and Their Clients   82
   Educational Institutions   84
Where Do You Go?   85
   The Buck Stops Here   85
   Inside and Outside the Company   86
Men on the Other Side   87
When the Accused Fights Back   88
How Do the Sexes Differ?   90
What About Cultural Differences?   91

Chapter 6   How Cold's the Climate?   93

The Corporate Climate   94
A Few Cases   97
   Bill and Vicki   98
   Steve and Alice   100
   Alex and Samantha   100
   Terry and Marlene   102
Climates Vary   102
   Randall   102
   Autodesk   103
Pro-Interactive Companies   104
   S. C. Johnson Wax   105
   Delta Air Lines   106
   Johnson and Johnson   106
   And All the Others   107
It's an Attitude   108
How Does Pro-Interaction Develop?   109
Where Would You Work?   110
Ask Before Drinking at the Well   111
The Trend   111
Which Is Best?   112
   A Written Dating Policy or Not?   113

Don't Confuse Harassment With Love   114
Don't Police the Workforce   115
Maintain an Open Door Policy   115
Emphasize Solving Problems, Rather Than Punishing   116

Chapter 7   Getting to Know You   118

What's Great at Work   120
Lia and Rick   122
Some of the Stories   122
And Some of the Ways   124
    At Work   124
    The Commute   125
    The Business Trip   126
    Customer, Client, or Candlestick Maker   126
    Friends of Friends   128
The Fears of Men and Women   128
To Flirt or Not to Flirt   130
But What's Permissible?   131
Dating Etiquette   133
But Be Aware of Miscommunications   134
What People Do   137

Chapter 8   The New Rules of Romance   139

Know What You Want   139
Start Out as Friends   141
Date Because You Like Each Other—Not for Power   142
Check Out the Corporate Climate   144
Evaluate the Career Pros and Cons   145
Create a Mutual Partnership   147
    Joint Partnering   147
    Decide on the Rules in the Beginning   148
    Keep It Quiet and Discreet   148
    Keep Your Confidences to Yourself   149
    Don't Hold Hands by the Fax Machine   150
Exit Routes   151

Chapter 9   Running From the Blocks   152

Starting Off   152
E-Mail and Romance   154
Problem Situations   155
    Rejections   155

Office Hyenas, Office Wolves, and Black Widows   158
Mike   159
Debbie   160
The Ferrari   161
People Are People   162

Chapter 10   Partnering the Relationship   164

It Starts in the Beginning   165
What Each Receives   165
What Each Gives   166
When to Go Public   166
This Doesn't Mean You Stay Together   167
What if the Romance Dies?   168
Bob and Betty   169
Work Considerations   170
Maintain a Professional Image   170
Create Safe Communication Channels   171
Your Own Code   171
Act the Same as Before   172
Keep Love Separate From Work   172
Consult Frequently With a Work Buddy   173
Think Ahead   173
But Enjoy the Romance   174
Working Together   175
Tommy and Nicki   175

Chapter 11   Dealing With Those Around You   178

The Signs of Love   179
Restrain Yourself   179
When to Go Public   180
Don't Wait Until the Word's Out   181
The Decision Might Not Be Yours   182
Suzanne and Jeffrey   183
Soul Mates or Not?   186
Selling the Boss and the Company   186
Donna   187
Christian and Amy   187
Put Yourself in the Boss's Shoes   188
Paula and Chuck   188
Working With Coworkers   189
The Reporting and Complaining Coworker   190
How Committed Are You?   191

        Lyle and Vi   191
        Office Hyenas, Busybodies, and Hatchet Men   192
  Hell Hath No Fury   192
        Alex and Samantha   193
        The Five Airplane Transfers   194
  Enjoy Your Romance   195

Chapter 12   When Love's in Full Bloom   197

  There Are Challenges   198
  But Look at All the Benefits   199
  There Will Be Ups and Downs   200
  How Do They Do It?   201
        All Work and No Play Makes . . .   201
        Make Romance a Priority, Just as You Do Work   202
        Do Those "Unexpected" Things   202
        The Little Things Do Count   203
        This Is Your Day   204
        Both Count   204
        Have Some Fun   204
            The Two Programmers   204
            Steve and Alice   205
        Think About the Other   206
  Enduring Relationships   206
        What Do You Really Want?   206
        What's Your Partner Really Like?   207
  The Test of Time   208

Chapter 13   Good Things Do Continue   210

  Married Couples in the Workforce   211
  The Trends   212
  The Irony of Becoming Married   213
  Some of the Situations   214
        It Depends on the Company   214
        Tommy and Nicki   216
        Christian and Amy   217
        Bernie and Lucy   218
        Suzanne and Jeffrey   219
        Lyle and Vi   219
        Jennifer and John   220

Chapter 14   When Good Things Come to an End   224

You Can't Hide   225
    Sue   225
    Marianne   226
More Than Work Is Involved   227
    Bob   227
    Donna   228
Endings Don't Have to Be Earth-Shattering   229
    Carrie   229
    Vincent   231
Why Did It End?   232
When It Happens to You   234
    At First   234
    A Cooling-Off Period   235
    Working It Out   236
    If It's Interfering With Work   236
    Damage Control   238
    Not Taking "No"   239
Nonwork Considerations   240
What's the Company's Approach?   241
    Pete and Peggy   242
    Fraser   242
    Transfer, Leave, Demotion, or Promotion?   244
Who Loses More?   244
More Stories   245
    The "Burnout"   245
    Going "Postal"   245
    The Chutzpah of the Year Award   246

Chapter 15   Read This (Before You Hire a Lawyer)   247

The Role of the Media   247
The Procedures   248
    The Statistics Are Against You   251
A Few Cases   254
If You Want to Go Further   256
    Don't Make the Decision When You're Upset   256
    Have You Done All That You Could?   256
    What Do You Really Want?   257
    You Have to Prove Your Case   258
    Talk to Several Attorneys   258
    About Attorneys   259
    Mediate, Don't Litigate   259

An Overview   262
Making the Final Decision   263
Who's the Real Winner?   264

Chapter 16   Companies Are People, Too   265

It Starts With the Company's Climate   267
A Reasonable Office Romance Policy   269
Using the Policy   274
A Strong and Enforced Sexual Harassment Policy   276
Communicate, Communicate, Communicate   277
Mediate, Mediate, Mediate   279
Keep the Channels of Communication Open   281
Follow Basic Concepts of Fairness   282
Respond Promptly and Reasonably to Problems   282
Balance Employee Privacy With the Company's Interests   283
    Employee Privacy Rights   283
    A Reasonable E-Mail Policy   283
Arbitration Clauses   284
Effectively Training Supervisors   285
Employment Practices Liability Insurance   285
Office Romance Agreements   286
The Best Company Defense   287

Chapter 17   The Twenty-First Century   288

A Different Workplace   289
The Competitive Pressures   289
The New Rules of Romance   290
The Law of Romance   291
Pro-Interactive Companies   291
Bankers Trust Company   292
Romance vs. Harassment   292
Harassment vs. Gender Discrimination   293
Ford Motor Company   293
It's About People   294

Appendix 1   Sample Office Romance Guidelines   296

**Appendix 2   Working Mother's 1998 "100 Best Companies
for Working Mothers"**   302

Selected Bibliography   305

Index   313

Preface

When I think about *The Office Romance*, I journey a few years back in time to when I was searching for a book idea. Writers love to write, and I'm no exception. For me, however, the hard part is to find a project that seizes me, makes sense, and can contribute in a way to helping some people with their lives. I had looked at numbers of areas previously, including sexual harassment. As a lawyer who has known clients and friends ending up on both sides of these complaints, I was acquainted with this area and its limitations. I soon discarded this subject when I discovered the numbers of authors who had written on this subject and the stark polarization of their positions.

One day, I mulled over with myself: just what about the positive side of relationships at work? Not the negative side as to how men and women relate in the workplace under current sexual harassment laws, or better yet, how the sexes don't relate at all. This "flip side" involves the enjoyable romances that spring up between people at work, complete with all of their strengths and fragility.

I started with the somewhat heretical assumption, opposed strongly by some, that men and women basically like each other— that there's something to this underlying attraction between the sexes that dates to the very beginnings of civilization. And that this magnetism continues even when men and women march into work in the morning, regardless of whether it is a department store, hospital, oil rig, Fortune 500 company, or farm.

The number of relationships starting at the office, I thought, had to be more than the abject, quite separate incidents of sexual harassment—even with unwelcome advances at work (and I'm talking about relationship advances, not sexual requests or innuendoes) that can become sexual harassment under our laws (and which isn't a consideration in many foreign countries). The fact that this attraction takes place at work has created different rules, somehow here, at least as to dating and romance under our current one-size-fits-all sexual harassment philosophy. This didn't make any sense: the law of romance had to be separate from that of sexual harassment. I discovered most researchers agreed there is a huge difference between being asked out nicely at work (even if you're not interested) and being subjected to not-to-be tolerated sexual innuendoes or requests.

Common sense told me that men and women spend much more of their time at the office working together and falling into relationships than harassing each other. A 1988 Bureau of National Affairs study, seemingly years old now, concluded even then that one-third of all relationships started at or from work. Given the tens of millions of couples who are married, dating, or in relationships, this is a sizable number. There are some 135 million Americans in the workforce, split nearly fifty-fifty between the sexes. When you reviewed the statistics, there were multiples of positive relationships over sexual harassment charges, even at the same office and involving the same people (once the target of harassment and now in a later work romance with another). See Chapter 4, "The Law of Romance," for more.

Millions of women are working now over the numbers present in past decades, including in managerial and executive positions. More women are being teamed up with men on projects and traveling together. The huge time demands placed on everyone by their employers have made work the only place to meet people for vast numbers of Americans. When you add in the opportunity to work closely with someone at no risk, view them in all types of settings, and be with someone of similar expectations and education, then you easily see why work has become the meeting and dating place of choice. This phenomenon will continue and increase into the next century.

However, I still wasn't satisfied. Were we talking about relationships, or were we just talking about sex? Sex is fine, but relationships are so much better and bring such quality and joy to one's life. It made sense that these office encounters had to be more long term in nature than outside affairs, given the risks that couples were taking in these politically correct, at times socially engineered, working environments. I discovered then the 1994 American Management Association survey which reported 80 percent of the replying managers said that they either had been aware of, or had been involved in, an office romance—and that one-half of these relationships had ended in a long-term relationship or marriage. Other surveys supported these conclusions. Bingo, I thought, this was a worthwhile subject.

I talked to my wife, Judy, and she agreed that there was something here. I called my agent and friend, Jeanne Fredericks, and talked with her about it. Jeanne also felt positive, and that's all I needed to jump into this area.

However, I asked myself about the impact from the continuing march of women into the workforce and managerial positions. I began calling companies to discover what was indeed happening in today's economy. I was quite surprised to learn that there were businesses that encouraged a freely interactive environment—not the restrictive, "don't let a pin bounce" attitude. These companies wanted their employees to work together; in fact they encouraged it, and their philosophy was based on a feeling of mutual trust. In turn, relationships in the workplace were subject to a policy of "benign neglect," and that as long as their workers were professional and discrete, management didn't concern itself with those relationships. Supervisorial relationships were managed, not banned—in essence, keeping the people but eliminating the evaluation functions and other "favoritism" problems by transferring, changing functions, and other managerial options. They weren't listening to the fears of the attorneys and shouts of the opposing philosophies.

These are "nineties" relationships as well, based on joint partnering and mutual decision making on careers. There are tacit rules of romance for both, not based on any sexual prerogatives or wedded to discarded assumptions such as "let the boss have his way." Given the fact that careers are important, today's couples establish their own road maps when inflexible corporate rules stand in their way. When the corporate climate is cold, couples tunnel underground to buy time and find more progressive companies, then leave—putting their relationships over their present jobs but not their careers.

It was my telephone call with JoAnne Brandes, the senior vice president–general counsel of Johnson Wax, that clinched it. Here was a company that years ago, like nearly all at the time, had banned married couples from its staff. This isn't the case now, and employees work together in a positive atmosphere. Workers are encouraged to socialize and meet new friends at its company facilities and extensive recreational areas. It, like other companies, has strong sexual harassment policies in place that are consistently followed—but it isn't receiving the harassment complaints that others do, even with these relationships flowering and at times ending at work. Johnson's employees are productive, and company goals are being exceeded. It was from this conversation that I coined the term "pro-interactive."

I discovered that companies oriented toward attracting and keeping their female employees and supervisors tend to be pro-interactive ones. As I randomly interviewed firms, I discovered that "pro-interactive" companies are listed not only on *Working Mother*'s "100 Best Companies for Working Mothers," but also on *Fortune*'s "100 Best Companies to Work for in America," in essence supporting the idea that a positive management attitude toward women also means accepting that personal relationships do arise at work. These firms don't want to lose well-trained managers and supervisors over what's a basic fact of life.

Meanwhile, I was interviewing couples and employees in various fields who had or were experiencing office romances. I had interviewed previously numbers of people for past books, including an unpublished manuscript on singles and dating. What couples want is different from what companies allowed in the past, and employers are now eliminating this difference. Pro-interactive companies are out to keep the best employees in a competitive market and regardless of the state of the economy.

I began writing the manuscript before a publisher was secured. I would have self-published this book, even if a well-known and recognized publisher like AMACOM hadn't come along. It's fascinating to me to see how romance flourishes at work, despite the bad press and political opposition. People meet and mate for life every day in America, whether it's in the glass towers of Los Angeles and New York City, or the small-town police and fire departments of Kansas and South Dakota.

While explaining his university's opposition to his romance and subsequent marriage to a younger student, one professor confided to me: "The only people who believed in us were ourselves." They are still together, years after their first meeting.

My hat is off to all of you who have taken and will take this journey despite the difficulties. I congratulate, as well, the employers who will make your path easier, recognizing that your romance and relationship will happen regardless of the obstacles placed in your way.

Dennis M. Powers
June 1998

Acknowledgments

Although the opinions in this book are solely my responsibility, I thank Lloyd Pearcy for his time in reviewing and commenting on portions of the manuscript. Lloyd, a long-time attorney and friend whom I first met in law school many years ago, reviewed the legal portions of this text. I thank Chuck Pierce, Lisa Troyer, and Michael Karpeles for their comments with respect to certain portions of this book.

I also wish to thank wholeheartedly all of my friends and "new" friends who so willingly gave their time to contribute their stories on such a delicate subject. These stories help to form the foundation for this book and were wonderful. You are too numerous to mention in person—but you know who you are.

This is to acknowledge the efforts of my agent, Jeanne Fredericks, for her usual professional, cheery, and optimistic support for this project—thanks again, Jeanne and Wes. I also want to thank the many people at AMACOM for their unstinting help and belief in this project, especially Ellen Kadin, Irene Majuk, Stephen Arkin, and Hank Kennedy.

Above all, I want to thank all of my friends, whether in this country or abroad, for their stories, friendship, and support to me over the years. On a recent trip to Panama, I met a new friend, Raul, and as authors we swapped books. His notation on the book presented to me was: "To the newest of my old friends." I borrow this in turn and say the same to all the new friends I met by researching and writing this book—which is what life and living is truly about.

Chapter One

The Matchmaker

Yes, romance at the office is flourishing, and you can count on this phenomenon to continue with widespread implications. The sexes are attracted to one another everywhere—at Fortune 500 companies, small businesses, hospitals, publishing companies, law offices, even fire departments, post offices, and in fact any place where the sexes can mingle. The pairing-off is equally noticeable in the professions, ranging from architects and dentists to doctors, lawyers, and their staffs. When people spend long hours together, even sharing intense times, *L.A. Law* and the soaps have nothing over what actually happens in the real world.

A December 1994 survey of 485 managers by the American Management Association (AMA) underscores the extent to which today's romances are thriving. Nearly 80 percent of the managers surveyed said that they either had been aware of or had been involved in an office romance—one-quarter had experienced a romantic relationship with at least one office colleague. Three-quarters of the respondents believed it was okay to date a coworker.

Sharing coffee breaks, lunches, business travel, elevators, and late nights at work are ideal relationship starters. This "togetherness" occurs naturally and whether or not someone's even looking at becoming involved. Whether it's carpooling, chatting by the copy machine, playing on the company softball team, or just plain working together on a project, the numbers of opportunities to meet and mate simply increase at work. Then add in as many women as men in the workforce, high divorce rates, worries over AIDS, and no time to date elsewhere, and there's no question why romance at the office is here to stay. A Bureau of National Affairs (BNA) study in 1988 concluded at that time that one-third of all relationships started at work.

With the influx of women into the workforce, winning executive and managerial positions in exponentially increasing numbers, romance has thrived and been nurtured. This revolution in the workplace includes their relationships, as well, and all under new rules. Let's take a look at what's happening.

Karen and Frank

"I met Karen at work," said Frank.* "I was forty years old, newly divorced, and not interested in dating. My attempt at owning my own software company had failed, but I was able to convince the hospital that my programming skills were still sharp. They placed me in Karen's department. She was a little older than I was, and I liked her from the start. She was attractive and didn't order me around, working with me as if I was a long-term team member and showing me shortcuts on how things could be done.

"We worked together on a project, then I was reassigned by her boss to another project. It wasn't until after the employee picnic that we started seeing each other socially. We kept our relationship a secret, and eventually I told her that she was more important than what I did—that jobs could come and go, but there would only be one Karen. Our marriage six months later surprised a few people at work, although I learned later that some had already figured us out.

"She had the better chances to be promoted, and I couldn't see both of us rising upward in the company at the same time. A few years later, I started looking around, then took a better paying job with another company. That was five years ago, and she'll always be the most important person in my life."

Karen: "I was impressed by Frank when we began working together. He knew his software programs and was good with people. He was confident but not arrogant. And I knew I wanted to share my life with someone, especially after breaking off a long-term relationship. I thought about asking Frank out, especially after he transferred away from my department, but I just wasn't sure about mixing work and personal matters. We'd see each other at times in the hallway or coffee shop and keep each other up on what the other was doing.

"After the picnic, we ended up at another employee's house and

---

*The names of individuals have been changed, or composites used, to protect privacy and assure anonymity.

started talking. You know, about what people talk about when you're not at work, such as . . . family, movies, and life in general. He was a good conversationalist and I liked his sense of humor. When it was time to leave, I mentioned we should stay more in touch with each other, perhaps over lunch. He took the cue.

"Work has always been an important part of my life, especially the advancements I've received in the last five years. It makes up for the time I spent waiting for positions to open up. We make our career decisions together on what's best for us as a couple, as well as individually. It was Frank's decision to leave, but we agreed that I had the better opportunity here between the two of us."

Some More

A TV sports announcer met his wife who was then a news editor for the television station. A shoe saleswoman bet ten dollars with a friend that she could get a date with that cute stockbroker who had returned to buy a pair of expensive shoes—they're now engaged to be married. A man in his twenties met his wife at barber school; the two now are married, have four children, and run together the most successful operation in town. The senior vice president of a life insurance company's legal department began dating one of the outside lawyers who represented the company; her boss gave her permission to continue the romance, and she subsequently married the attorney.

Mack, a single professor at a small northeastern college, began dating the department's secretary. At first, they tried keeping it quiet but one of his psychology colleagues spotted them holding hands at a restaurant. People in the department weren't too happy about this, especially since Kim, at thirty, was fifteen years younger than Mack. He would tell Kim matter-of-factly: "Although you're not working for me, or here as a student, you could really screw me if we broke up and you complained to the administration. It wasn't that way before, but this place is really uptight about anything that could possibly resemble sexual harassment now." They stayed together for two years, breaking up over "the little things." It was uncomfortable when they worked together afterward and tensions between them ran high. However, Kim simply looked for another job outside the university that paid better and took it. They haven't talked or seen each other since then.

Beth is a bright, attractive, petite woman in her late forties who now runs a collection agency. "Office romances?" she laughed. "Funny you should ask me about that. My first office romance wasn't great. I dated a coworker at a large company and we were an item at first, but we really didn't have anything in common except for work. Then, I decided after two months that he wasn't as hot as I had first thought. It was tough breaking up, especially when he didn't want to. By then, I thought he was a real Dufus. But we talked one day over lunch and decided that our jobs were more important. It was a little tense for a while but everything finally worked out.

"A few years later, I was working as a temp for a large computer company. Ed was a manager, and he was cute. Tall and cute. We didn't work together, but we'd say Hi in the hallways. On my last day temping for the company, his secretary ran up to me and began asking a lot of questions. Questions like Are you married? Do you have children? Do you like the outdoors? She said Ed liked me, and I answered, 'If he does, then he has only three hours left to ask me out, because I'll be gone forever by five o'clock today.' After the secretary reported back, Ed asked me out for lunch and we started dating, then lived together. We married, are happy, and have been together now for twelve years."

Steve: "I was the vice president of a small real estate development company, and Alice worked for me as a leasing coordinator. We worked closely together for nine months, sharing lunches and coffee breaks while talking shop . . . but nothing else as I was married. Her marriage had ended a few years before then. My marriage was running on the rocks, but I didn't want to leave my wife because of the children. One night, we headed over to a local bar with some employees, ending up both drunk and wildly kissing each other in the parking lot.

"Alice invited me to dinner that Friday night at her home, and I went, telling my wife that I was working late at the office. We left later for a nearby beach, ending up making love by a secluded cliff. I spent the night on her living room sofa, trying to get the sand out of my hair, and left my wife the following day. Alice and I stayed together and shared a lot for eleven years before breaking up, although both of us worked for other companies during this time, and I raised my children as a single parent."

It is a fact of life. Love in the workplace is prospering, despite the laws, attorneys, and opposing philosophies. It may be heresy to say, but the fact is that men and women still like and love one another, and they're not all out in the workforce spending their time harassing each other. The American people have been socialized into thinking about intimacy and work as separate compartments of life. And that is simply not true.

What's Really Going On at Work

How high is the interest between people at work? Very high. The surveys generally indicate that anywhere from 25 to 33 percent (one survey concludes 70 percent) of the employees at a given company have had an office romance at one point in their careers. Nancy, a senior manager at Ford, commented: "It's interesting to find out who's really going out with whom. There's a couple in the department next to me who've been together for several months, although they think it's a secret. The cute little financial analyst down the hall is now dating the burly janitor in the next building. She does a good job at work, meets him discreetly, and works more overtime at the office than you could believe. And as I think about it, her attitude now shows a definite improvement."

Complementing the AMA report is *Training & Development's* 1994 survey. It reported that three-fourths of those surveyed believed that a romance at the office was just fine, and that one-half of the respondents knew about an office liaison that was then going on at their workplace. This and other reports consistently support the general level of romance that's been occurring in the workforce over the years. For example, a *Personnel* magazine survey taken back in 1986 found that 80 percent of the employees had either observed or been in a romantic relationship at work. So love marches on.

It's About Relationships

And this isn't about sex at the office—it's about relationships. As Helen Gurley Brown wrote in *Sex and the Office:* "The people who think it (the affair) consists of dirty little half-hour episodes—people sneaking off to a motel and that sort of thing—are fuzzy observers. Many an affair is grounded in friendship and mutual respect and has deep emotional and intellectual rapport going for it." That's exactly right, although she wrote this over fifteen years ago.

According to the AMA survey, one-half reported that their romance resulted in marriage or a long-term relationship. These are better odds than for nonworkplace romances. To say that one out of two office relationships are long term is significant. Just look at what's happening outside the workplace. Various surveys indicate that nearly one-half of all first marriages in the nineties will have ended in divorce. A 1995 Council on Families in America report states that the chances that a marriage will break up today are a "staggering 60 percent."

The numbers of relationships people experience in a lifetime are increasing dramatically. According to the U.S. Census Bureau, the proportion of women never married by their late twenties tripled from a 1960 low of 11 percent to 33 percent by 1993, and there are 4.5 million unmarried couples now living together. A University of Chicago study conducted in 1992 indicated that one-half of all Americans have had up to three different partners in a lifetime, with men reporting a median number of six.

Work relationships also involve friendships without sexual intimacy. These involvements are a natural occurrence because people are constantly interacting with one another. Employees who work together, whether it's on an assembly line or in an office, become friends because they're spending time together working toward common interests and goals. "Fred and I are real buddies. Neither of us tells our spouses, because they'd get jealous. But Fred and I can talk about anything, whether it's on break or in the back breaking down parcels. We're both careful not to cross the line and become romantically involved. We have the best of both worlds—good relationships at both work and home," said Diane, a postal worker in her thirties.

Why Romance Thrives

As developed later in this book, office romances are inevitable regardless of the laws, regulations, or opposition. The Families and Work Institute of New York concluded that 45 percent of all workers put in more than forty hours per week *and* that over one-third of all romances now start at work. Managers encourage interdependence and working together in teams. With the proportion of women in the workplace now 46 percent (for managerial and professional specialties, the percentage has increased from 40 percent female in 1983 to 50 percent now) and growing, the increase in the age for first marriages (24.5 for women and 26.5 for men), and the rising time demands at work, the workplace has now become the dating place of choice.

Judy Kaiser, a twenty-eight-year-old administrative assistant, says: "Singles bars are too chancy and superficial. Personal ads take a lot of work and just plain luck. How can you afford to waste time at a museum trying to find somebody when you're always at the office? Now, you can check people out there before making a decision to ask them out. You're getting paid to be there any way. So why not make the most of it? Most of my single friends have dated, are dating, or are interested in someone at work. In fact, I'm going out for drinks tonight with one of my coworkers. It's supposed to be about work, but I know better than that."

Work offers any number of magnetic social benefits: being with people of the same economic, social, interest and educational levels; the opportunity and time to get to know one another; continued closeness with one another on projects; the ability to share emotionally intense and even exciting times; and the best background checks available. It beats singles' bars, blind dates, and personal ads, and any chemistry is given the time to become hotly seasoned. These benefits are not one sided: businesses now are recognizing the direct link between employee job satisfaction and company profits with pro-interactive policies. See Chapter 2, "Close Encounters of a Natural Kind," for further details.

Romance flourishes despite the risks: the affair can be used against one or both workers politically; coworkers fear a loss of power or otherwise aren't supportive; there can be career damage (both for having the relationship and for an awkward breakup if it ends); and there's the potential for later sexual harassment charges. Although the consequences depend on the business, the workers, and how the couple manages their relationship, surveys indicate that 60 to 70 percent of all employees and CEOs believe an office romance has no effect on the participants' standing in the company. Chapter 3, "But What If? . . . ," focuses further on this topic.

But What About Sexual Harassment?

A negative side of romance is perceived by some to be included under the general concepts of sexual harassment. The media bombards us with sexual harassment complaints from the workforce, ranging from the U.S. Army training grounds to automobile assembly lines. These instances clearly don't involve romance, and when proven, they're un-equivocally harassment. We read about the $1.185 million Equal Employment Opportunity Commission (EEOC) settlement of sexual harassment charges at Del Laboratories and wonder about the $7.1 million jury verdict against the law firm of Baker & McKenzie in San Francisco.

But this is abject harassment and the type that must be prohibited. The EEOC filed its complaint against the president at Del on behalf of fifteen women employees, mostly from his secretarial pool, who testified that he fondled, conducted business with an open fly, and made degrading comments for years. The jury found that the partner at Baker & McKenzie had forced himself on several female subordinates while the firm turned a blind eye. Proven harassment like this deserves punitive awards, and office romance is unquestionably not this.

Then there are the statistics you read or listen to concerning sexual harassment. For example, a 1992 poll conducted by the National Association of Female Executives (NAFE) reported that 53 percent of those responding said they had encountered or knew someone in the workplace that had been sexually harassed. Yes, there is sexual harassment at work and that's not romance. What's interesting is the 80 percent of all workers who either have been in a romance or know about one—all occurring in the same workplace along with the harassment complaints that involve different people and separate issues.

Soured affairs result in a minuscule share of the sexual harassment charges actually brought, although owing to the media, they can become highly visible—such as the widely publicized problems of Oracle's Lawrence J. Ellison and Staples's Martin Hanaka. The EEOC's own statistics indicate that only 5 percent of their sexual harassment charges are brought owing to a failed affair. This is covered in greater detail at Chapter 4, "The Law of Romance."

We will see that asking a person out for a date and being refused isn't legal sexual harassment. Asking a second time isn't either. Sending a valentine to a coworker who doesn't accept it, doesn't meet the test. Not even if that person is offended, and especially not if he or she's one of those who take offense to just about anything. Complimenting a person on their appearance, even if they take offense at that, isn't harassment—although you might not receive a good evaluation if that person's the boss. Nor is buying a gift for someone who then returns it, even if one of you is working for the other. And the courts have been consistent in holding that a relationship by itself isn't sexual harassment, nor can an affair by any stretch of the imagination indicate a hostile working environment.

Kim said: "Mack asked me out a few times, but I said no because I was seeing someone else at the time. I liked him then and the attention he gave me. I was glad he asked me out again when I was available, although after we broke up, I had my doubts as to why I had accepted in the first place. That usually happens if it doesn't work out." Mack reflected that he knew he "could get in trouble by my pursuit if she complained, but she didn't seem to be too put off by our conversations. She even laughed lightly when she first told me that 'she just couldn't.' So I said to myself 'what the hell' and asked again. She then accepted and off we went."

An overardent suitor, a pursuing ex-lover, an especially persistent boss, as you would expect, can all be guilty of harassment if there's a complaining worker who wants no part of this attention. And most companies, especially the small minority that discourage office romances, try to avoid having one lover supervising the other. The factual question becomes just when does such pursuit, either to initiate the romance or to try to keep it going, run past romance and end up as harassment? See Chapter 4, "The Law of Romance," and Chapter 5, "Where Romance Ends and Harassment Begins," for these distinctions.

Pro-Interactive or Not?

The question becomes, Why don't companies crack down on office romances? The answer is simple: you can't legislate against love. Owners, managers, and shareholders alike have concluded that it's none of the organization's business *and*, given the very nature of people, that they would become involved anyway.

In a survey of two hundred chief executives by *Fortune* magazine in the mid-1990s, nearly three-quarters of the executives agreed that office romances were "none of the company's business," 80 percent concluding that an office romance between discreet, unmarried couples was not a proper company concern. This opinion was held despite the belief by three-quarters of these same CEOs that office relationships could expose their company to the danger of sexual harassment suits. The great majority of these companies had a formal policy in place prohibiting sexual harassment.

AT&T, one of *Working Mother*'s "100 Best Companies for Working

Mothers," exemplifies the emerging view in corporate America that even romances between bosses and subordinates are relationships to be managed and not banned by corporate edict. Burke Stinson, AT&T's senior public relations manager, said:

> To understand why companies are taking this flexible stand, you need to understand the history. At AT&T and in corporate America, the management workforce in the late sixties was a white male in a gray suit with a company that valued the past and traditions. And this past and traditions weren't necessarily all that bad.
>
> As you entered the seventies, the workforce was in tumult, as women, men, and minorities in their early twenties joined these businesses and wanted conditions to be different. Affirmative action loosened things up as well, and by the mid-eighties, this class of 1970 found itself in positions of responsibility and power. They started by saying, "Let's make some changes."
>
> And changes they did. Spurred by the demands of women in the workforce who wanted more flexible arrangements, we had the first rumblings in the eighties for child care assistance, flexible hours, work at home, elder care, and other benefit changes. They weren't interested in just medical, dental, and pension plans. As the eighties ended, it became apparent that with the numbers of women working with men, that complete changes had to be made in order to keep your best employees from leaving.
>
> These benefit changes were made—along with changes in the attitudes to personal relationships at work. In the seventies, if a workplace romance was discovered, then at least one person was transferred. This generally was the woman, because she usually had a lower position and it was assumed that the man would have the career. By the nineties, this had changed entirely—and as it should have. Now, you don't want to lose your best employees because they're having a relationship.
>
> At AT&T, eight thousand of our employees are married to one another and countless others have and are dating one another. Our one condition for people dating is they should come forward and tell us. They won't have to shift to another state; in fact, they can stay within the same department, but they can't report to one another. We're not going to fire well-trained people, as that makes no sense.
>
> We have a strong, sexual harassment policy and enforce it strongly. As a matter of fact, when the Justice Clarence Thomas and Anita Hill controversy surfaced, the *New York Times* printed a por-

tion of our sexual harassment policy as an example of a strong but fair one. We don't have a written policy on office romances, other than a general approach of "benign neglect" and the unwritten rule that we don't want spouses or lovers reporting to one another. We know that numbers of our employees have had and are enjoying romances with their coworkers and that does not concern us. We have had very few problems as to sexual harassment allegations, regardless of how a relationship ends.

The CEO of a financial conglomerate subsidiary commented: "I'm fast-tracking one manager now. She's quite talented and moving up quickly. She told me a few months ago that she's been dating seriously one of the guys who reports to her. This didn't make me happy, but she's good. So what am I supposed to do? She's complied with our policy: disclosure of reporting relationships, no public displays of affection, and she recommended a departmental transfer for herself. The move made sense for her career-wise, so I approved it. I told her to keep me advised if they break up, monitor the effects on her coworkers, damage control, and all that."

Alice commented she liked the environment of the small company where she and Steve first worked. "If we had worked for another company, some people might have really complained that I was trying to get ahead by sleeping with the boss. But I loved him and we were trying to make our relationship work. The company we worked in had a lot of company activities and the people were encouraged to mix and enjoy each other's company. There was a company picnic, Christmas party, weekly breakfast meetings, and drinks after work. There was a lot of camaraderie, and other people were dating in the office. It was a fun time."

Steve observed: "I probably would have gotten some flack if I had worked somewhere else. And if we had broken up while at work, I could have been in trouble just because I was her supervisor. That doesn't mean it would have been right, but it didn't happen. Even with the company's approach, there was a time or two when I felt a little insecure about mixing work with our relationship." We will visit Alice and Steve again, as well as many others throughout this book.

A *Human Resource Management* survey in 1991 indicated that 98 percent of all companies permit coworkers to date (28 percent permit but try to discourage it). In fact, the AMA study concluded that only 6 percent of companies had a written policy on employee dating, most preferring not to get involved in matters of the heart. The surveys support the general finding, as expected, that relationships with supervisors, extramarital affairs, or clear conflict-of-interest romances with third parties (such as suppliers and vendors) are not in favor. Nearly three-fourths of the AMA managers, for example, didn't think it was okay for an employee to date a superior or a subordinate.

Despite the litigating attorneys and possibility of harassment lawsuits, various companies nurture the corporate "fringe benefit" of socialization. They have decided that guiding employees to work together toward corporate goals as a team is good for business. Pro-interactive companies abound, and a clear trend is emerging to let romance flourish in the workplace, even between bosses and subordinates—provided that they don't continue working for one another. Some companies require the supervisor to transfer, some let both decide, and others handle this on a case-by-case basis. This is exactly opposite to what used to be the case.

It also seems clear that the more "pro" a company is toward women and their careers, the more flexible that company is with personal relationships at work. Companies on the well-known annual *Working Mother* survey of the "100 Best Companies for Working Mothers" lead the pack not only as to women's support groups, advancement, child care, work at home, job sharing, compressed workweeks, and the like, but also as to the underlying philosophy of shared respect between employer and employee, including a tendency to a flexible approach toward workforce romantic relationships.

We'll look at some pro-interactive companies and the continuing business trend toward utilizing the benefits of this approach. Businesses are better off taking a positive approach to office socializing, rather than looking the other way or worrying about but not following their legal departments' narrow legalistic warnings. The benefits of employees' becoming more involved in company goals and objectives are just too valuable to pass up. See Chapter 6, "How Cold's the Climate?" for more on this topic.

The New Rules of Romance

Joanne, a thirty-five-year-old accounting manager, recalled: "I met my future husband at work. He was in another area, but would meet with me over how my 'number crunchers' were going to treat his budget. He was good at his job, but he seemed to be distant, as if he'd rather be working with a man. That turned me off. Then, we were put together on a team evaluating a potential acquisition. After the first meeting, I decided we needed to get our working relationship straight.

"I suggested a lunch meeting. Once there, I asked nicely but directly if he had any problems working with a woman. He seemed surprised, stumbled a bit, then said he really liked working with me but didn't want to appear too friendly. I started laughing and that broke the ice. We began working late at night, then having dinners out. What I liked was that Tom made me laugh . . . and his eyes sparkled. We ended up spending a night together at his place.

"That morning, we discussed how we could be both lovers and workers. We talked about our mutual fears, wants, and needs. It was the first time either of us had been involved with someone at the office. We decided to keep everything quiet, then decide when and how we would tell our bosses. It was that talking together, that joint decision making, that set our relationship on the right course from the very beginning."

The influx of women into the workplace, particularly into management and executive positions, has been one of the most dynamic sociological changes in this country in the past several decades. This integration of the sexes has brought about their interaction as peers. Gone forever are the black-and-white images of a male supervisor behind a metal desk with a younger, smiling secretary in a long dress holding her steno pad. Work romances have changed along with the work relationships. Office romances now are more communicative and managed by equals. Although covered more fully in Chapter 8, "The New Rules of Romance," here are a few of the rules:

- Know what you want from the relationship.
- Start out as friends, whenever possible.
- Date because you like each other, not because one's afraid to say no.
- Evaluate the pros and cons for your career.
- Create a joint partnership.
- Decide on the rules in the beginning.

Joint Partnering

The new rules now include "joint partnering" the relationship. This isn't as formal as it might first sound. What this means is that if there ever was a "male prerogative" in romance, it's now long gone. The key to any romance is jointly deciding on the nature of the relationship and where it's going. For example:

- Discuss together the rules of the relationship (for example, what one's prepared to give up for the other and the relationship),
- Decide when to go public, if at all,
- Determine when and how to sell, or at least tell, the boss, and
- Agree on what to do if and when the romance dies.

Polly, a forty-year-old police dispatcher, said: "Ken's out on patrol. What's great about a lover in the same field is that we speak the same lingo. We know the pressures and time demands. The problem is what to do if we break up. We talked about that before we got too involved. We concluded that we're not working directly together, so that shouldn't be a big problem. We haven't had any problems being professional with our work. Nor do we anticipate them."

Vicki is a thirty-year-old management consultant. "When Bill and I started dating, we had more problems to overcome than most. He was my supervisor and I was advancing at the company. We felt like conspirators when discussing how we could both be together winning promotions. It's been six months now. We may be lucky in that our company has a new president and he does seem to be less rigid than the old one. But it's still wait-and-see right now, as this company doesn't have many transfer options. We are keeping a very low profile."

Good communication starts at the very beginning, both about the good and the bad. This is what sets the foundation for a lasting relationship. See Chapter 10, "Partnering the Relationship."

When Good Things Come to an End

Just as in the nonbusiness world, relationships also end. The breaking up of a work romance has all the emotional and practical problems of any ending, but with one complication: you can't just stop seeing one another. As Beth observed, "I didn't like the first guy I dated in the office after breaking up. I'd say to myself 'What did I see in that jerk?' I had to get that under control and finally did."

Most people work something out, but it can become complicated if you work in the same department, report to one another, or see each other a lot. "I decided that if I was ever going to become involved again at work," said Beth, "I would locate the exit doors *before* getting involved. And whether that new one was worth it. With Ed, those problems didn't exist, and I liked that."

Persistence isn't a virtue when one person wants to stay together and the other doesn't. "I was miserable when we broke up," said Katherine. "We shared so much in common, from being in bed at night to facing offices during the day. The first day after breaking up, we stayed in our offices and only ventured out when we thought the other person wasn't around. Coworkers began talking, and later that day, the executive vice president called us both in. We were told to work things out and get along, or one of us would have to transfer.

"I couldn't handle talking with Eric," she continued. "So I sent him long E-mail messages pleading to get back together. . . . I'm embarrassed about all that now. He always kept his feeling to himself, so he never answered back. The executive vice president found out about them, and it had to have been from Eric. I was transferred to another state within the week. I hated that transfer and eventually left the company. I'm back in this area again, but it took time to find another job and it pays less." See Chapter 14, "When Good Things Come to an End."

Even if the relationship is solid, the work climate may not be. The chief inspector for a utility became romantically involved with one of his female inspectors. He was single, but she was married with young children, although she had just separated from her husband. Unfortunately, they were seen embracing in a company truck at a secluded park during their lunch break. Another inspector (it was suspected that this coworker was following them) saw the amorous couple and reported the incident to a higher-up. The chief inspector was fired for breaking the company's rules against dating (one of the few that have such "antifraternization" rules) and the woman inspector was demoted. Six months later, the former chief inspector and his subordinate married and are still together.

When Good Things Continue

Karen and Frank, even after marrying, needed to watch over their work environment. "Our company didn't have a policy on dating or married couples at work," she said. "Unofficially, it depended on whom you reported to. Eventually, it became clear that Frank would more likely be promoted if he worked somewhere else. However, this wasn't a big problem with us. A friend of mine married about the same time, but they divorced later because they couldn't blend in the stepchildren. Other couples have problems with finances, in-laws, children, you name it. Working around work is just another problem you handle and solve to keep a relationship together."

The considerations were different with Steve and Alice. "At first," said Alice, "we were careful about the feelings of other workers . . . to be sure no one would be threatened. In fact, no one was. Two other couples had met there and were serious. I was put on commission at my request, feeling I could make more money and not needing a lower salary floor. Leads brought to Steve's attention were fairly distributed, just as before. When I left one year later for another real estate firm, my leaving didn't make any difference as to our relationship. That was a hard decision because I liked that office, but the other real estate company had a stronger reputation in my specialty." Steve echoed those thoughts. See Chapter 13, "Good Things Do Continue," for more.

Then There Are the Attorneys

The position of the nonromantic lawyers can be summarized as "Today's fling is tomorrow's filing." Keep in mind the following:

> If you have turned down any discrimination suits recently because you didn't think they would pay for themselves, you should reconsider, because the new law (1991 Civil Rights Act dealing with sexual harassment) makes these suits much more economically worthwhile than they were previously. (January 1992 issue of *Lawyers Alert* [known now as *Lawyers Weekly USA*], a newsletter for attorneys)

Since then, bar association articles, trial lawyer seminars, and newsletters (both defense and plaintiff) multiplied in this area, as the legal profession grabbed onto the golden goose of sexual harassment litigation—and remember that what the lawyer makes, the complainant doesn't get. However, they haven't been able to mint the same dollars in the ex-romance area.

You must be careful when deciding whether a broken romance has crossed into the sexual harassment area. Look first with a cool, objective eye at the entire situation before making any final decision to hire a lawyer. Don't make this decision when you're angry or upset.

It's important to know first what you really want when a romance has ended. Do you want space from your ex-lover, the conduct stopped, or money because there was unfair or unequal power (as when the ex-lover is your boss)? If you want monetary damages, then remember that you could lose. In fact, the surveys indicate that the complainant loses up to 60 percent of all harassment cases (including the sexually explicit, hostile working environment ones). However, it is comforting to know that 90 percent of all cases are settled before trial. Remember that attorneys get paid from the proceeds (if on contingency, the fee can range all the way to one-half if trial has started), *and* the expenses of court filings, expert witnesses, depositions, and investigating expenses must also be paid from the proceeds.

These cases also aren't the "dialing for dollars" you might first think—regardless of what the media reports on large awards. The large awards do happen to somebody else and getting one is akin to winning the lottery.

Litigated cases can take years to resolve (one took twelve years), and even EEOC investigations of harassment complaints can average one and a half years just for starters. This federal agency will only sue on your behalf less than one-half of one percent of the time, generally utilizing this alternative for class action lawsuits against companies with situations such as Del Laboratories and Mitsubishi. For practically all other cases, you'll need to hire your own attorney.

Whether you're suing in court or complaining to the EEOC, you have to prove your case—being wronged is not enough. This means you have more outside evidence than just relying on your word against someone else's. The EEOC's own statistics show that three-quarters of its sexual harassment complaints are rejected for lack of proof, continuing interest, or legal insufficiency—and keep in mind that these statistics involve *all* sexual harassment charges, not just the broken romances that are on the low end of the "win" scale. And to get a win, you need not only to prove the facts, but also to have the law on your side. It also depends on the attorney you hire, how good he or she is, and how the other side reacts, among other intangible factors.

Let's look at one sexual harassment case to get an idea as to the problems inherent in this one-size-fits-all procedure. Dawn, a thirty-year-old cocktail waitress, was sexually harassed at her job. She was propositioned on several occasions by the owner who used sexually explicit language, and another waitress experienced the same "hostile working environment." Dawn quit, quickly found work at another restaurant, then looked for an attorney. After she hired one, my advice to her was that she had a provable case of sexual harassment, and that she should pursue her case. She had felt this way from the start.

Her observations were: "I hired a lawyer on contingency [there's no attorney fee until the other side pays some money] whom I thought was the best sexual harassment lawyer in the state, and I would even drive the five hours to Portland, Oregon, where her offices were located. I've learned a few hard lessons since then. First, it's been three years since that first meeting, and I don't know if I'll ever get any money. Second, we filed a complaint with the EEOC, finally receiving a consent-to-sue letter [where the EEOC won't sue for you, but says you can but using your own lawyer]. This was a win because the EEOC usually doesn't do this. We then filed a lawsuit against the owners. However, the lawsuit just seemed to sit there.

"Third, my first law firm lost interest in my case. At first she said I had a 'good case'; then she wanted to send a letter saying we'd settle for $30,000. I'd get about $15,000 after the expenses and the lawyer's cut. However, I couldn't bank on that because the owners said they were broke. Then, my attorney left her firm and the law firm said that they didn't want to represent me any further—plus, they said I owed them some $1,500 for costs. I finally found a local attorney who will represent me, and we're preparing for trial. It still remains to be seen if I'll ever get any money out of this."

Imagine the problems in using this procedure with the broken romance or overardent suitor situation, which isn't the same as abject sexual harassment. This doesn't mean that every case will be this way, but remember the problems of time, costs, and the other side's reaction. See Chapter 15, "Read This (Before You Hire a Lawyer)," for more information.

What's a Company to Do?

The company is caught in the middle. Employers, whether they're businesses, fire departments, or architects, don't want to interfere unduly with their employees' rights to privacy and a social life. On the other hand, they don't want to allow a "hostile working environment" or to become another victim of a sexual harassment complaint. The great majority of businesses want a motivated workforce that's working together as a team to meet the company's goals. So what can they do? There are clear-cut effective strategies:

- Establish a reasonable office romance policy and educate all employees on the guidelines and effects.
- Encourage a pro-interactive work environment.
- Keep confidential channels of communication open for all.
- Have in place a strong policy against sexual harassment and enforce this policy strongly but fairly.
- Emphasize mediation as a conflict resolution technique.

Michael D. Karpeles, a partner and the head of the employment law group of Chicago's Goldberg, Kohn, Bell, Black, Rosenbloom & Moritz, Ltd., states:

> Every company should have a realistic written policy that applies equally to all of its employees, whether they are senior or lower level, married or single, gay or straight. It's important to remember that you can't treat married workers differently, due usually to applicable state, county, and local laws that ban discrimination on the basis of marital status. Thus, you can't allow single employees to be romantically involved, then turn around and say that married people can't—regardless of issues of morality.
>
> Written standard guidelines should be in place to create a sense of fairness for a company's workers, that they know there are guidelines that apply equally to everyone, and this also reduces the potential for ugly sexual harassment charges. These guidelines should not be lengthy, should be communicated to all employees, and should be brought to the attention of the workers by continuing education programs.
>
> Employers should require employees in close personal relationships to report these involvements as part of their job to their supervisors on a confidential basis, especially when employees work closely together. Employers should generally prohibit romances between people who work together in supervisor-subordinate roles due to the potential sexual harassment and employee morale problems. If the employees cannot be transferred or their responsibilities changed, then noninvolved supervisors should be appointed to handle the performance reviews of the subordinate. The subordinate employee should be clearly advised that he or she has the option to talk with the highest level supervisor to discuss any aspect of the work relationship. Employees also should be made aware of their

responsibility not to make excessive public displays of affection or spend time at the workplace on personal issues.

What is important over the past several years has been the strong change in emphasis by employers from firing love-struck workers to working with them. Given the dollars invested in the training of a typical company's employees, you manage these relationships—you don't try to ban them. Remember that you can't stop love, and even if a business uses a policy of benign neglect for them, it must develop written guidelines as another management tool to protect both the company and its workers."

Businesses need to bring office romances out into the open by designing reasonable policies of confidential disclosure that are then communicated to all employees. These policies would include eliminating the reporting aspect of boss-subordinate romances but striving to retain the lovers in their existing responsibilities with the company. By doing this, the company is taking charge so these situations can be dealt with before they fester into larger problems through inaction. Documenting that the relationships were in fact welcome and voluntary can preclude later harassment charges alleging that they weren't.

Tom Davidow, a principal with Genus Resources, a family business consulting firm in Needham, Massachusetts, advises:

> Companies should educate their workers about these relationships and bring them out of the darkness. They should communicate what their policy is, what could happen practically between workers, and the pluses and minuses of workplace romances. It appears that companies with open communication lines and a relaxed environment do seem to do better in the areas of romances and low sexual harassment problems.

See Chapter 16, "Companies Are People, Too," and Chapter 17, "The Twenty-First Century" for the final details, as well as Appendix 1, which contains model office romance guidelines.

Chapter Two

Close Encounters of a Natural Kind

Four-fifths of all workers have either been involved in or observed an office romance during their working years, as documented by numbers of surveys (including the ones we've already discussed). Anywhere from 25 to 33 percent of us in any given industry or at any time (depending on the survey) have been in a workplace relationship—some surveys head even higher, depending on the target audience, questionnaire wording, and numbers of responses. And, as the AMA survey indicated, one-half of all workplace romances wind up in marriage or a long-term relationship.

Why?

The answers are easy. Ten years ago, nearly one-half of the respondents to a Gallup poll for *Newsweek* magazine said that work was the best place for single people to meet dating partners. Nearly 80 percent (again, the magic number) said they knew or thought someone at their office had had a work romance; over one-fifth answered that they personally had enjoyed an intimate relationship at work. And this was before the crush of longer work hours, the requirement that both spouses or significant others work to make ends meet, and large downsizings that decreased even more the ability to have any quality personal time away from work.

The more you are around someone, the greater the chances to become friends, if not to form a deeper, lasting relationship. The very nature of numbers of industries leaves little room for socializing except at work. One financial services managing director said, "Single men and women who are asked to work such long hours are looking at this demand as harassment in and of itself."

The long hours expended in high-tech Silicon Valley have become legendary. This technology-driven industry spins so fast that sleep is viewed as a luxury. Employees are grouped in teams, and when deadlines approach, extraordinarily late nights become part of the expected workday. Socialization between employees isn't discouraged, and late night dinners among men and women working together are viewed as a necessity. As John, a highly paid software programmer said, "If you work twelve hours a day and sleep eight, plus eating, commuting, and those silly personal errands, then there isn't much time left over for socializing."

People attract one another—and rarely in a sexually harassing way. Regardless of the obstacles, romance wins out. Laurel, a forty-five-year-old bank manager, said, "Let's face it. The sexes love each other, and there's a natural attraction between us, going back thousands and thousands of years." Karen said, "The great love stories of the centuries, whether it's Romeo and Juliet or Adam and Eve, are played out every day in corporate America. You get paid to work with someone you like, and there's time for the chemistry to become seasoned."

Lisa Troyer, an assistant professor of sociology at the University of Iowa, has studied workplace romances. She comments:

> Attraction is a basic process between the sexes. There is the studied concept of "propinquity," or that the more contact two people share, the greater the liking that tends to characterize their relationship—which basically means that the more you hang out with someone, the more you like them. And this is exactly what happens in the workplace, no matter what type of job you have or where you work. So it's not surprising to see the vast numbers of people who are meeting and having nurturing relationships that occur where they work.

It's also safer. People feel more secure and knowledgeable dating a coworker than meeting someone for the very first time on a date. "Where are you going to find people your age if you're living in the suburbs, or working those crazy hours at your job. There, you don't have to worry about a serial killer, like you're thinking about in the bars. It's the best background check available, better than personal ads, social functions, or even community meetings. You can be with like-minded people. There are similar interests, income, and social levels," said one thirty-one-year-old hospital fund-raising manager who recently married.

It's easy to get to know someone, and you don't have to make excuses for why you're spending time with them. Two weeks after "rooming together" in the same cubicle, two software engineers started dating—they married two years later. As Laurel observed: "If spouses tire of their partner, it's easy to check out the people at work. They don't have to make excuses for why they're out so late at night— they're honestly at work with people they have common interests with."

The gender revolution at the workplace has created mutual respect. Working with someone on an interesting project can create the same mutuality as being on a date; there is closeness in working toward common goals and interests. Anne married the man she worked with on a company merger project one year after meeting him. "You not only have the chance to get to know someone," she said, "you also have the time to overcome any initial dislikes or prejudices that would have quickly turned you off in a social scene."

Laurel said: "You're both dressed up every day with the woman wearing her best clothes, not slopping around the kitchen in a 'Don't Mess with Me' T-shirt. The man's clean-shaven, smells great, and is wearing neat clothes. Now, your girlfriend or boyfriend, or your spouse, was left that day yawning and scratching in the bathroom before shaving or putting on any makeup. They're not a pretty sight then, as you know. Once you're at work, you're at your mental best all day. You have your best face on, because being a bitch doesn't last very long."

When you're working with someone, this closeness gives you the excuse, even the reason, to get to know that person better—your employer wants you to get along with the people you're around. They're a captive audience and can't leave even if they want to. You have the time to overcome initial problems or personality conflicts. Gina, a thirty-two-year-old marketing survey project leader, said, "There's an excitement when you work together toward meeting your goals. The pressures of going for it, then winning creates a close tension. You celebrate later with a win." As Laurel stated, "You can use business as an excuse to get to know someone. If you've had a fight with your lover at home, there's always a willing ear to listen to your complaints at work. Not to mention you can create close professional bonds with whomever you're working with. You can talk about starting up your own business. I frankly think there's more going on in the workforce than people let on to their friends."

With the extensive downsizing by businesses over the years, neither companies nor their employees have the loyalty they used to share. According to U.S. Department of Labor studies, the average American will have over eight jobs and somewhere between three and four different careers (3.5, to be exact) over their lifetime—and this may be on the low side. So it shouldn't be a surprise that people are choosing relationships over their jobs, regardless of the corporate attitudes, policies, and opposing philosophies.

And this is happening worldwide. One British survey indicated that fifty-eight out of seventy-six young executives knew about an average of six workplace romances. Office romances include same-sex relationships, as well: a survey by Mobil Europe, covering nearly two hundred companies, discovered that almost 25 percent of those businesses were prepared now to recognize same-sex partners (whether both were at that company or not) when recruiting for jobs in Europe.

There are the problems, of course—whether it's the reaction of coworkers, what happens when the affair ends, or even the potential for sexual harassment charges. The problems will be covered in Chapter 3, "But What If? . . ." Suffice to say, romance at work is here to stay and growing stronger everyday.

All the Work-Related Romances

The workplace is large and diversified, ranging from large and small businesses to law offices, hospitals, police departments, and the post office. You name a business, and you'll find romance. A college professor kissed a student for the first time in a hallway underneath a sexual harassment sign that severely warned about the consequences of this behavior; we'll visit more with Alex and Samantha later in this book. A man and woman in their thirties worked together in the back office for the post office—they left their spouses for one another and are still married five years later. A manager for a Fortune 500 company dated a man in her department clandestinely for several months; although they broke up, the higher-ups still don't know about this (although they had their suspicions). Two assembly line workers paired off, married, then divorced after a couple of years. Volumes of books could be written about the different relationships created at work and still not scratch the surface of all the experiences.

Office romances involve more than people who work at the same company. It includes patients, customers, and clients as well. A plumbing contractor was called to clean the kitchen drain; he asked the owner out for a date, and they married six months later. A female telecommunications specialist dated one of her customer representatives for months before they decided to go their separate ways. A doctor married a patient for his third wife. The list goes on and on— just think about situations you know about from your own friends and experiences.

Women Have Changed the Rules

As recently as twenty years ago, most companies enforced antinepotism and antifavoritism rules that prohibited married couples from working together. The business world operated on the assumption that married couples at the same company had an unfair advantage over employees who weren't so attached. The approach basically perpetuated the "husband works, wife stays at home" concept.

This has all changed, as you would expect. With the large numbers of married couples working for the same companies, it's clear that business has done a complete turnabout from what was acceptable practice before. A 1993 survey by the Society for Human Resources Management reported that 84 percent of the reporting human resources executives said that their company employed husband-wife teams, while an earlier study indicated that 88 percent of the reporting companies believed that employers should not discourage dating between coworkers. Talk about change.

As women entered into the workforce in historically unprecedented numbers, they demanded full participation, and that meant being treated equally when they were married. In fact, as we will see later in this book, companies are taking pro-interactive approaches to retain husband-wife teams owing to the large investment that they have in their workers, not to mention their focus on the women they're grooming for greater responsibilities.

Few companies have detailed, formal policies that govern fraternization or dating among their employees, electing to stay out of the area—and no policy by itself is taking a position on this subject. It is a widespread practice, however, for businesses to prohibit one spouse from working for the other, simply because the risk of bias is too great in job evaluations and termination situations. Companies understandably don't want spouses working where collusion could spell disaster for the firm, as in financial areas such as check writing, cash disbursing, and investing.

This doesn't mean people can date and marry at any company that they want as long as they avoid conflict-of-interest situations. Wall Street firms, for example, have been categorized as frowning on coworkers' dating and marrying—but it happens all the time. Anne and Wally, for example, met at a New York City investment banking firm. They kept their dating a secret, at least as best they could. It was after Anne left to work for another company last year that they went public with their relationship.

As we shall see throughout this book, women have been the catalysts behind a number of important changes in the workforce. Moreover, the increase in the numbers of women employed overall at work, rising numbers of women in management, increased travel by members of the opposite sex, more use of opposite-sex work teams, and increased average numbers of hours worked per week have combined to support the increase in romance and long-term relationships at work.

This also has kept businesses from generally cracking down on romance, if love even could be regulated by fiat. Nancy, a thirty-year veteran of Ford's corporate wars, said: "I've seen about as much change as you could imagine over the years I've been here. From where women were only secretaries to where I could now, if I wanted to, 'eighty-six' a man out just on my word that he sexually harassed someone in my department who had complained. But women are now choosing whom they want to date at companies, primarily because they tend not to marry until later in life. They've become more aggressive not only in their work relationships, but also as to their career paths and objectives."

Harry, a retired, ex–general counsel of a Fortune 500 company, observed: "The good old boy network has been severely changed and for all time. Women are now doing the same thing we used to do ten years ago with strong corporate ties and networking. The office wolf is dying out, if not yet extinct, owing to the sexual harassment laws and women's attitudes. In its place, I've seen women become much more aggressive and some are now chasing the men, when they decide they want to."

These changes have transformed the rules of romance, as we shall see at Chapter 8, "The New Rules of Romance." At the same time, women are demanding more access to child care facilities and more pro-interactive approaches by companies to keep their employment. See Chapter 6, "How Cold's the Climate?" and Chapter 17, "The Twenty-First Century."

Roberta

Roberta is an attractive and pleasant woman now in her late thirties. Having worked in her career over the past two decades, her story reflects some of the trends being seen with women in the workforce. "Gals are becoming more aggressive than the men," she said. "This doesn't mean that they're out looking for affairs, but it means they will go out after what they want, just like the guys. I was sexually harassed at one job when my supervisor made some off-the-wall comments and sexually offensive comments that I didn't like. He was suspended for a few days and given a warning. I didn't feel comfortable there any longer, so I took a job next at Pacific Telephone, a large phone company in the San Francisco and Northern California area. I met Vic there when he was married and we became good friends.

"We were friends for two years, laughing a lot and going out for drinks with others after work. Then we started dating when he and his wife broke up. It was so easy, because we already were friends. We kept it quiet because it was our own business and we wanted to keep it to ourselves. I had decided already to look for a job with more opportunities, and this also would make it easier for us than always trying to keep everything secret. So I located a job in Napa, a good hour's drive from where Vic worked, and he moved in with me. Although he was a cable installer, Vic was a genius when it came to figuring out how people could work together and get things done. I kept saying 'Vic, you should go into management.' Well, he applied for an opening, and a female manager picked him for her department.

"They worked together closely for several months. Then she began inviting him to dinner and drinks to talk about different department problems. They went to different training sessions, and some were held out of state. The next thing I knew was that he wasn't coming home when he should have been. He then told me that he and his manager were romantically involved. We were having problems then anyway, but we might have kept it together if that hadn't happened. Women today are very aggressive—but I'm not like that. I've always been shy."

It's About Friendships and Relationships

Work friendships can ripen into sexual relationships when the time is right, as we've just seen. It's also obvious that having work friendships doesn't necessarily mean that the people will be lovers. Far from it.

Social intimacy at work brings positive benefits such as mutual support for careers, greater commitment to the company, and the bottom line of more enjoyable working conditions. Companies support these friendships, especially those between managers and their subordinates. "It's equally true that businesses become wary if the boss and their top people are always off skiing with one another, square dancing three nights a week, or becoming too close," said one human resources specialist. "There's a concern about favoritism. However, they realize that people who get along with one another do better jobs than those who don't. There is better teamwork, people communicate more honestly and directly, and it aids career advancements, whether you're male or female."

It Happens to the Best of Them

One of the most publicized recent marriages was between multibillionaire Bill Gates and Melinda French, whom he met at his company. Susan Molinari, the Republican representative from New York, married Bill Paxon, another Republican representative from the same state; he proposed to her on bended knee on the House floor in 1993. Vidal Sassoon married Rhonda Holbrook who designed packaging for Sassoon's products. Federal Reserve Bank of Boston president Cathy Minehan and former New York Federal Reserve Bank president Gerry Corrigan, her one-time boss, became a twosome. Richard B. Fisher, chairman of Morgan Stanley (the Wall Street investment banking firm), met his wife at the company—she at the time was his assistant. In the early nineties, the chairman of Citicorp, John S. Reed, met his wife who reportedly was a flight attendant on the company's jet. Jane Robelot, CBS morning anchorwoman, married the cameraman whom she met on a shared network assignment in Cuba. From Robert (and Elizabeth) Dole to Leona Helmsley and Pablo Casals, important men and women have met their love partners through work.

Then I remember my grandfather who was widowed at the ripe age of eighty-four. He told me he wanted to hire a housekeeper to cook and help with the household tasks. What I couldn't believe was how long it took him to find one. He interviewed over twenty women over a four-month time span. He took his time and made lists of questions. When I asked him why it took so long to do such a simple task, he'd just smile and say, "It takes time to find someone you can trust with an old man like me." He married the one he hired three months later.

The Pluses of Office Relationships

Charles A. Pierce, assistant professor of psychology at Montana State University, has studied workplace romances extensively. "In certain circumstances, workplace romances can be quite beneficial. Employees often channel romantic energy to work tasks, and they bring enthusiasm and energy to their work." Other experts note that stable workplace romances can benefit the employer, as the couple works harder to make the company successful because both having important interests at stake.

Workplace romances can energize individual workplace morale, improve attitudes, soften work-related personality conflicts, and improve the teamwork of the involved workers. The individual pluses and minuses depend entirely on the people in the relationship and their attitudes, the corporate climate, whether any coworkers feel threatened, whether it's a boss-subordinate relationship, and whether the romance lasts. In short, the advantages of individual work romances are just like the disadvantages—they depend on the parties and their individual situations. If you've been in a workplace relationship, or have seen one, think of what you observed; however, remember that others may reach different conclusions—people tend to generalize from their own experiences.

The emotions vary, depending on the person. For example, Carla is a thirty-eight-year-old marketing manager. She observed, "At first, I was elated by my romance. Although my lover was in another department, I couldn't wait to get to work and do my thing. If my subordinates suspected anything about it, they were clearly keeping it to themselves. I felt renewed because I was in love. I didn't worry too much about the negative aspects of my job, because when things were good, they were good, and I received the best marks of my career. Joshua felt the same way.

"It was midway through our relationship that I settled into my usual work pattern. Although my boss continued to grade me with good marks, it was now business as usual. When we broke up, my attitude suffered as well. My marks weren't as high, and it took time for me to become grounded again and get my motivation back up. Joshua left to work for another company, and we didn't stay in touch. It was a tough time. It would have been even tougher had one of us been working for the other. In that case, I would have asked for a transfer, had my ex-lover not left first."

It's axiomatic that the advantages of a work romance depend on whether or not the relationship works out. Joanne, the accounting manager we observed in Chapter 1, was as productive before as during the course of the relationship with her to-be-husband. Steve and Alice worked together fine, although they were in a reporting relationship, because their coworkers were supportive. Even though Beth's first office affair didn't work out, she seemed to handle the ending well. She also wasn't the one who broke it off either.

There is no simple answer. As we shall see in the next chapter, there are numerous pros and cons from both the employer's and the employee's viewpoint with the motivations of the partners being a key factor.

Chapter Three

But What If? . . .

There are risks, of course, when having a workplace affair. The romance can be used politically against either person; coworkers may fear a loss of power, if not being downright jealous and suspicious of favoritism; there can be career damage, both for having the romance in the first place and then if it ends; work productivity for the lovers and coworkers, depending on the circumstances, can be affected. There's always the concern over potential sexual harassment charges. Also, professional reputations can be threatened, again dependent on the situation. Breaking up is hard to do; and a broken relationship can lead afterward to self-doubt, just like any nonbusiness ending.

There have been over seventy academic treatises in recent years that deal with office romance—the pitfalls, problems, and draconian solutions—not to mention the hundreds of magazine and newspaper articles that have appeared. Corporate attorneys are on record that their clients must avoid these troublesome office romances like the plague. Some authors feel that "productivity plunges," "reputations are destroyed," "office romances end without any benefits," "sexual harassment increases," and "80 percent say that office romances are a lousy idea."

Should romance be allowed in the office? The answer is a resounding no from some. After reading or hearing their words you wonder why on earth anyone would even blink at a coworker. *They miss the point. It is basic that opposite sexes attract naturally and they've been doing this since history was recorded. The office romance is here to stay, and businesses must accept this fact in a positive way.*

What the Surveys Say

The respected AMA survey indicated that 74 percent of the responding managers said it was okay to date a coworker but only 23 percent approved of dating a superior. *Although 68 percent of those whose romance became known said that this didn't affect their standing in the company, 25 percent said it adversely affected them, and 6 percent said it actually had a positive affect.* Of those who had a romantic relationship with an office colleague, 62 percent said that their coworkers knew about the relationship (despite their efforts to keep it quiet), while 37 percent said that they had managed to keep it a secret.

What's striking is that 49 percent of the romances resulted in marriage or a long-term relationship (11 percent of those had ended). Women reported happier outcomes, with 56 percent saying their affair led to either marriage or a long-term partnership, compared with 47 percent of the men.

In the survey by *Fortune* magazine of two hundred CEOs, 79 percent agreed that if an unmarried couple was discreet, an office romance was not the company's concern. This held despite these same executives' saying that affairs increased the possibility of favoritism (86 percent), created an unbusinesslike appearance (78 percent), and exposed the company to the danger of sexual harassment suits (77 percent). *Fully one-third said that the incidence of office romances had increased at their company over the past ten years*—and that was in 1994.

Another set of respected surveys on this subject is compiled by Strategic Outsourcing, a division of Romac International. One was completed in 1996 with 427 companies responding; the latest was completed in 1997 with 592 companies responding. Both surveys reached the same conclusions with the later results following: 91 percent of those responding said that they didn't have any policies in regard to dating among coworkers, most feeling that it was impossible to legislate and enforce any rules without the employees feeling that their liberties were being infringed upon. Surprisingly, 62 percent said that they allowed a supervisor to date an employee within the organization. *Fully 75 percent said that they had never had a "serious problem" with consensual office romances that ended in an unfriendly manner,* 88 percent taking steps to reinforce their policies prohibiting sexual harassment. Nearly 70 percent said that they had not had a formal sexual harassment complaint in the past year (although this narrowed down to 57 percent for companies having over 500 employees). A follow-up telephone survey was completed in January 1998 of two hundred companies that had replied previously to the past two surveys; Jack Erdlen, vice president of Romac, commented that the results of this latest survey "mirrored" what had been discovered previously.

The bottom line: what's feared generally with office romances by firms is not in fact the reality. However, whether or not there are problems from a broken romance will depend on the individuals' motives in the first place. It does make a difference whether love or "less pure" reasons are present.

The Motives Are Important

Why someone enters an office romance is a crucial factor: whether it's due to "pure" motives of love or "impure" ones of career advancement, gaining power or reduced workloads, or sexual gratification. Affairs entered into for less salutary reasons are more likely to end with hostile results when they end. This factor also makes a difference as to whether coworkers support the participants or not.

Professor Charles A. Pierce at Montana State University has researched this area. He states:

> It's why coworkers feel people are involved in an affair that brings about their negative or positive perceptions. Employees perceived as participating for love are less likely to receive the negative gossip associated with work-related objectives such as acquiring more power or reduced workloads.

> When a relationship goes bad, the problems can start for the individual partners, and that can depend on their motives for entering the relationship in the first place. Sometimes they can end up as friends; however, if the romance ends on a sour note with an impure motive in the beginning, plus a boss-subordinate relationship, you have an extremely volatile mixture. For example, if a subordinate goes out with the boss just to get a pay raise, and the boss breaks off the relationship before that can happen, then that worker is perhaps more likely to bring a sexual harassment complaint. One who enters a romance more for romance factors is less likely to complain later.

> Mutuality is a big factor here. If I ask someone out for a date because I like her, then that's one consideration. However, if it's job or money related, then that's another and the problems can be there at the start. Breakups, when they occur, are always difficult. This is

compounded when there may be impure factors for being there in the first place.

One woman became involved with a man to whom her boss reported. When the secret got out, her boss became worried over how he would manage her. He was afraid that she would tell her lover (and his superior) in bed what she thought was wrong with his decision making. Although she felt her comments about her working relationship with her boss were accurate and made in good faith, in retrospect they were interpreted by her lover as being critical. She and her lover broke up several months later. Her ex-lover continued their working relationship as before; however, her immediate boss did say he would have appreciated "a bit more team loyalty." She realized that he was referring to her bedroom conversations.

Later, her boss transferred her when he consulted with her ex-lover over her job performance. She stayed with the company but always wondered if what she had said and the breakup had contributed to that transfer—and they more than likely did. As it turned out, the transfer in retrospect proved beneficial to her career, although this couldn't have been predicted.

It Depends on Where You Are

The decision to get involved depends on your specific situation. You must anticipate the response of your company and coworkers (see Chapter 6, "How Cold's the Climate?"). Jacqueline, the assistant director for a major hospital chain on the West Coast, said: "We have a clear policy: what you do on your own time is your own business, but you can't work for someone else. When you do, then either one, or both of you, will transfer, resign, or leave. With enough discretion, you might get away with it; but someone will see you at the supermarket, arm in arm, and the word gets out. Then all hell can break out if you haven't given some thought to what you're going to do about it."

The Major "Watch-Out" Areas

An office romance, whether it survives or not, has risks. Depending on your situation, you need to think about these in advance, if at all possible. At least by then, you will have made a conscious choice.

Damaged Professional Reputations

Whether the romance works out or not, one potential problem can be damaged work reputations. However, keep in mind the surveys in which two-thirds said their romance disclosure by itself didn't affect their corporate standing. The best approach is to scout out what the company's reaction would be before you begin (including if your romance doesn't last). This would include discussing all possible "exit doors" with your potential partner if it doesn't work out (as Beth advised) and trying to keep it discreet to see if the romance is a solid one. See also Chapter 8, "The New Rules of Romance."

If you're becoming involved in a boss-subordinate relationship, then the situation becomes more complex. Transfer, realignment of reporting or reviewing relationships, relocation, or finding another job are definite alternatives, depending on your work environment, but career advancement and coworker reaction can be also problematic. Deciding whether your particular job is as important as your love can become the major consideration.

Unhappy Coworkers

A major consideration is the reaction of your coworkers and whether they will support the relationship or not. Cindy, the assistant to the president of a shipment brokering company, ran into problems when her coworkers learned about her romance with a vice president. When the president of the company discovered that they were involved, he "made more than twenty telephone calls that night to his top people, worried about the sexual harassment risks." Their coworkers worried about what they talked about at night, especially because "between them they had all of the sensitive information about where the company was going, even more than the president." The workers complained to the president that this alliance would benefit Cindy unfairly. At one time, Cindy decided to leave and the times were tense; however, she stayed on. One month later, the two announced their engagement. Although this action calmed the waters somewhat, their coworkers still are concerned over their joint access to the company's secrets.

The consistent approach used by lovers is: "run silent, run deep." The great majority of workers in office affairs go to extreme lengths to keep their relationship hidden. However, coworkers can pick up that something's going on—it's only a question of time. The company's climate will be important to their reaction, as well as whether they think you're obtaining an unfair advantage or favoritism from the relationship. If in fact you are gaining work advantages, be prepared for the flack or be ready to find another job or department. Consider these alternatives *before* the problems occur.

Productivity Changes (Both Yours and Others')

Productivity basically means whether you are as effective in your job after the romance begins (or ends) as you were before it started. The change in productivity for your coworkers depends on whether their morale is adversely affected by your relationship: whether they spend time complaining to others, gossiping, or trying to sabotage you, or really aren't affected by it.

The studies go all over the map on this. At least eleven studies indicate that workplace romance can sometimes have an "enhancing" effect on how well those in a work romance perform at work; some seven other studies indicate that there's an "impeding" effect. What's interesting is that the view twenty years ago was that performance decreased owing to workplace romances, starting with Quinn in 1977. However, the modern viewpoint is quite different: researchers now believe that participants are easier to get along with, experience less tension, and enjoy being at work more—which is what you would expect (Brown and Allgeier (1995); Pierce, in press; Pierce et al. (1996); and others). The consensus of the experts is that "chain of command" or boss-subordinate affairs carry the greatest risks to productivity, whether they work out or not. This makes sense: the greater the contact with your partner, the more likely it is your work decisions can be influenced by personal agenda items and the greater the potential reporting problems if the relationship ends. It will, however, make a difference whether the company reassigns performance reviews and compensation assessments to a third party so that these concerns diminish.

Professor Pierce comments:

> As to productivity and morale, you need to consider the particular stage of the romance. Although individual reactions can differ, participants might eventually become more energized, motivated, and with higher job satisfaction. However, some researchers feel that there can initially be a lessening of work performance, owing to the time taken off from work or personal moments to be together.

In the middle of the relationship, the participants are back into their usual work efficiencies and motivations. Toward the end, there can be a downturn for those that are more emotionally involved. However, it's important to research these romances over time before you can make meaningful conclusions here. It also depends on the individual participants.

Tom and Eileen worked at a car repair shop, Eileen in the office and Tom as a mechanic. The owner didn't like that they were dating, no matter how good they were. He thought the other employees were bothered by their relationship, although they didn't appear to be so concerned. The owner cut down Tom's time and eventually fired Eileen. The couple stayed together and eventually married, which makes you wonder about these types of business policies in the first place.

Dating the Boss

The type of romance considered most disruptive is one involving a supervisor and a subordinate. It's the one most likely to create hostility among coworkers (unless you have a Steve and Alice environment) and, if not handled right, with the greatest potential for later problems. The statistics discussed previously indicate the lack of support this relationship receives in the workplace.

"A prime problem in boss-subordinate relationships is the perceived work benefits for the subordinate and favoritism concerns," commented Professor Pierce. "There's a fear that power is being exchanged for the relationship. Even when companies don't have written policies prohibiting these relationships, responsibilities are changed or workers are transferred, demoted, or leave on their own accord."

Carrie is a manager in her mid-forties with a U.S. Government "troubleshooting" agency. She said: "I turned down many overtures from my subordinates. I don't mean to sound egotistical, but I am attractive and fairly smart. I turned them down because I was afraid of the possible hassles if we broke up and especially the potential sexual harassment charges. As to superiors, at one time I started going to the office without wearing any makeup to discourage one boss. I started also wearing long skirts and bulky tops before I transferred to another office. As a rule, I dated only people who were around my own level, not anyone whose job was lower or higher than mine. My concern with a few bosses who learned about my latest romance was their becoming upset because I wouldn't be accepting their standing offer to get together. I never accepted any of them."

This doesn't mean that you shouldn't date your boss if this is right for you. People at work become involved each day, regardless of their reporting relationships. What it means is that you must go into the relationship with your eyes open and know the risks at your company in advance, deciding at first how important the relationship is and how both of you will handle your work at the firm. It will be important to determine both of your likely career paths—once your relationship is public (which it will become) and including your company's reaction—along with potential outside career alternatives.

Conflicts of Interest

Although part of the boss-subordinate problem, conflicts of interest can exist in other situations as well: for example, one participant has access to sensitive company personnel or financial data; or both are in the check-writing or financial disbursement area; or the couple can make together sensitive decisions, even when in different departments. Financial institutions obviously have a concern over this area, as they don't want even a hint of collusion between two people who could transfer money inappropriately.

Dating a customer or a client has come lately under increasing scrutiny. For example, a growing number of states allow lawsuits to be brought by clients against their attorneys when the two have had a personal relationship (plus the affair ends, for example, and the lawyer dumps the client). One attorney said, "Basically, if the relationships work out, then you'll never hear about this problem. It's when they end that the recriminations begin."

Various professions, from psychiatry to medicine, have enacted their own professional codes of conduct regulating relationships between their members and clients. Psychologists and psychiatrists are especially sensitive to this issue (and have strong prohibitions in place), owing to concerns over the particular influence that the professional has over a client in therapy. For example, one woman entered into a love affair with her California psychiatrist. They lived together for six years, as she continued her therapy with her lover. When the female professional broke off their relationship, the client brought ethics charges and a lawsuit against the psychiatrist. It was settled out of court.

Embarking on an affair with a customer representative does occur frequently, but you need to consider what you'll do if you break up and still work together. Another factor is how other people will view such a relationship, especially if you own your own business.

Bob, a realtor in his early fifties, began dating Betty, a mortgage broker who arranged real estate loans for some of Bob's clients. As Bob said, "Even though we were with different companies at the time, we tried to keep our relationship low key. I would include her name with a couple of other mortgage brokers, then tell my clients that we were seeing one another. It was a dilemma for us. Betty did the best job in town, but it wasn't a good idea for people to think that there was more than a professional relationship between us. However, there were some people who thought they'd get even better service because they knew we were related. Later, the problem went away when we moved in with one another and opened up our own brokerage company."

Another real estate broker said that his girlfriend, also in bank lending, had made him three owner-occupied loans (it's impossible to live in more than one house). She was called on the carpet for doing this, and the boyfriend had to refinance the loans. This is the type of situation you should try to avoid.

As with Bob, the best idea is to disclose conflicts of interest. A manager became involved with a department head in a different area. To her horror, she was told she would be transferred to work under her lover. She told her boss that she would work for anyone, but couldn't accept that transfer because they were involved. Her boss appreciated being told in advance, and the company respected her wishes. She's still happily working there and has been promoted on schedule.

Corporate Game Playing

You need to look around and determine who could benefit if your relationship was discovered or ended. It is an unfortunate fact of corporate life that there are players who want to advance at your expense—and in any way possible. You need to factor this into your decision before heading full steam into a relationship.

One corporate vice president told his secretary that he would date her if she worked for another company. Their firm's policy flatly forbade reporting relationships, and he decided he couldn't afford that risk. When the secretary left eventually for other reasons, she and her ex-boss began an intense relationship.

Sexual Harassment Charges

Soured affairs result in a minuscule share of all sexual harassment charges, as most parties understand that this is a relationship problem and not a legal one. In fact, less than 5 percent of all EEOC sexual harassment charges involve an ended affair.

However, an "injured spouse" or ex-lover also can get riled up and bring charges. For example, a talented female surgeon had a relationship with a male patient. His ex-girlfriend brought sexual harassment charges against the surgeon, alleging breach of the doctor-patient relationship. The hospital cleared the surgeon, but only after investigating all of the facts. It determined later that the patient had called for the first date, three months after the minor surgery had been performed and all formal treatment had ended. However, these facts did not deter the ex-girlfriend from filing her complaint. The surgeon and her boyfriend ended their relationship after the complaint had been tossed out—which might have been the ex-girlfriend's purpose in filing the complaint in the first place.

Extramarital Affairs

Extramarital affairs do occur, although the studies are inconclusive as to their extent and whether they lead in turn to long-term commitments between the new partners. They're obviously risky if your company is conservative (for example, the president may look at the affair as a sign of a basic character weakness). However, extramarital affairs happen every day in America when relationships at home run into problems, and not necessarily just at the office. It is an unfortunate fact of modern-day life that commitments end and divorces happen: more than half of all married men and more than one-third of married women claim that they have been in at least one adulterous affair, according to numbers of surveys.

Steve's affair with Alice didn't cause problems, because of where they worked. However, if they had been working at a less liberal place, they would have had to decide how important their relationship really was. One woman surfaced with her divorce papers filed and dating a coworker at the same time. Her supervisor wondered, "All of a sudden she was divorcing her spouse and dating someone else. The waters were muddy, because we didn't know which came first, the chicken or the egg. But she was doing a good job, so we went along with it."

The Relationship Doesn't Work Out

What are you going to do if you're reporting to your lover and the romance ends? One worker had an office romance with his officemate. It worked fine until they split up. After a few days of jarring confrontations, he was able to transfer to another department. Coming to work to earn your living each day of the week, only to face an ex-lover, can be traumatic. You and your partner need to discuss what you will do if things don't work out, along with the exit doors.

We discussed Kim and Mack in Chapter 1. Kim had a real problem once they broke up. As one coworker said, "I spent a lot of time with her, giving her boxes of Kleenexes and consoling her. It was a heavily charged environment, until she found another job." Although discussing this doesn't necessarily mean that you will have solved the problem, it is a necessary first step.

There is more to consider than the fact that you can't stop seeing an ex-lover at work (at least before someone makes a change or you work it out). Sometimes you need to factor in what someone might do in retaliation. Although many people seem to be able to control their emotions outwardly, we have seen the case where an ex-lover sent continual E-mail messages pleading to get back together. The overzealous ex-suitor can begin sliding over the line into sexual harassment.

Factoring in Your Career

People do decide their careers are more important. However, if you meet the "right one," you may decide that you can always find another job. Jacqueline, the hospital chain executive, observed: "Although it depends on the industry, my experience was that higher level managers were more likely to take the chance with a prohibited work relationship. The lower staff was more conservative; however, the higher levels felt they'd have no problems finding another job. They wouldn't want to, but they could, if they had to." A vice president of a retail chain said the opposite, "Many of our people are in lower paid sales jobs. They'll accept a transfer, even leave, because lower paid jobs are easier to find." Regardless of position, some workers willingly take their chances.

You need to decide how your boss will react. "Remember that your boss has different job objectives from yours," said Carrie. "They don't want their job to be endangered or made more difficult by your relationship choices. In the end, you'll need that person's support. So start thinking about how to get this. You'll have to think about what could happen to your career, not only if you break up, but also if you continue in a work-related romance with someone in the company."

Making the Decision

Matt, an executive with years of experience, said: "I had four office romances that came to my attention over the years. In two involving reporting relationships, one had a partner transfer to another department, while a second pair switched groups to separate themselves. Both couples married and are still together with the company. In the third case, the people divorced their spouses, didn't remarry, but are living with one another and working in different company areas. A fourth involved two singles, where one stayed at corporate and the other moved on. What we're seeing is that employees, whether lower staff or higher level, are choosing their partners over the possible problems at work. They are evaluating whether the risks outweigh the benefits. We, as a company, have had to work within this framework to retain the most talented people."

"Balancing the relationship versus my career," said Frank, "was easy when I thought about Karen. It was true for me that she was more important." That is an admirable thought; however, Frank's decision turned out to be the right one. If it hadn't been, then what? "I would have taken the luck of the draw," he said. "That was where I was at that point in time."

Organizations today are acting as filters, in effect becoming dating pools, because they hire employees who are similar in terms of work-related and other personality attitudes. Accordingly, work relationships can last because "birds of a feather flock together," and the lovers enjoy a foundation of respect, common experiences, and mutuality—but don't bet your wallet that both of you will be staying with your first company. Remember that romances even at work have all the joys and frailties of any other relationship (before adding in the pluses or minuses of the work element). As Karen said, "You will always have differences over who cleans the house, where you spend your money, in-laws, and vacations. Just like any other couple. Partners stay together and break up for the silliest of reasons. The work factor can affect people differently. Some love the common bond when you're at home; others get tired of only talking about work, day in and day out. Both of you are subject to how well the company does over time. Frank and I agreed that as long as we were together, it didn't make much difference where we worked. We would just manage whatever turned up."

Although considering all of the factors at first is an excellent start, in fact, many of those in office romances don't do this. "People are optimistic that love wins out. They feel they can overcome anything and at times don't care about the risks. I was that way, until my breakup," said Carrie. "It's after the breakup occurs that you find out people can get angry and create unexpected problems."

Chapter Four

The Law of Romance

The emerging law of romance has a clear and straightforward basic tenet: a free and voluntary relationship, whether between co-workers or a boss and a subordinate, cannot amount to sexual harassment by itself and is not prohibited by law. Further, conduct that people don't appreciate in their personal lives doesn't necessarily become sexual harassment just because it occurs in the workplace. Even "unwelcome" conduct in the office, depending on its severity, is not prohibited sexual harassment.

There are a number of offshoots from the law of romance. For example, the fact that the object of a romantic advance doesn't welcome the pursuit is not, by itself, enough to constitute a violation of sexual harassment laws. The termination of a relationship, even though one or both of the ex-participants are emotionally hurt by the breakup, also is not a violation of harassment laws.

The law of romance can only exist with the strong enforcement of sexual harassment laws and policies. Sexual harassment of any kind should be prohibited and dealt with severely—this book does not advocate dismantling any of the current prohibitions against harassment. Although the problem is to define "sexual harassment" under various fact situations, it is clear that both the law of romance and sexual harassment prohibitions exist side by side. To understand one, we must understand the other, and this means starting with a discussion of what constitutes sexual harassment under current law.

What Is Illegal Sexual Harassment?

The basic law stems from Title VII of the Civil Rights Act of 1964 (generally called "Title VII"). This law prohibits discrimination against any individual as to his or her compensation, terms, conditions, or privileges of employment on the basis of some protected factor, such as race, color, sex, religion, or national origin. This law has been broadened and interpreted by thousands of court and administrative decisions, from decision makers such as state and federal courts to the EEOC and state human rights' commissions. There are many state statutes prohibiting sexual harassment, in addition to the Title VII mandates and EEOC regulations. As an outgrowth of the Senate hearings involving Clarence Thomas's U.S. Supreme Court nomination, the Civil Rights Act of 1991 was enacted. As one experienced attorney said, reflecting back, "After the Clarence Thomas hearings and the 1991 act was passed, my phone nearly rang off the hook with people looking for lawyers to take on harassment cases. It was as if someone had cranked on a faucet full blast, and there's been a lot of work since then."

The provisions of the 1991 act resolved conflicting court decisions on the required legal standards of proof, as well as permitting jury trials. Juries can be more sympathetic to individual plaintiffs than to corporate defendants, thus this change widened the exposure of businesses to monetary damages. The act not only allowed plaintiffs to recover lost wages (both back and prospective) as under prior law, but it also permitted compensatory and punitive damages (monetary awards to "punish" prohibited conduct) and allowed the recovery of attorney fees. All of these decisions and acts are generally referred to by the legal profession as being under the canopy of Title VII—which we will also use for this book.

The courts historically have defined two basic types of sexual harassment as actionable under Title VII: *quid pro quo*, or "this for that," sexual harassment and *hostile environment* harassment. Although the U.S. Supreme Court held recently that the labels "quid pro quo" and "hostile working environment" are not controlling for the purposes of establishing employer liability (we will discuss that later), they are quite helpful in understanding this area.

Quid Pro Quo Harassment

A quid pro quo action involves unwelcome conduct owing to an employee's sex that affects a term, condition, or privilege of employment. This action arises when a person is forced to choose between suffering some economic penalty at work or submitting to sexual demands. For example, a boss tells the employee that a few nights of sex with him (or her) would do wonders for their upcoming job evaluation. Cases have uniformly held that unlawful sexual harassment was committed when a worker was reprimanded, demoted, discharged, or adversely affected by a supervisor's sexual advances, whether the subordinate participated or not in the requested sexual conduct.

The simple demand for sexual favors by someone with authority over your job in exchange for his or her assistance to promote, hire, or retain you violates this concept—however, if nothing else happens after your response, the occurrence of the demand can be difficult to prove. The demand can either be the sleazy "sleep with me, and get your raise; forget it, if you don't," or can be implied by unwelcomed physical conduct such as touching, grabbing, or fondling.

Quid pro quo harassment can *only* be committed by people who have the power to affect your job. Only a supervisor, manager, or executive who can affect the tangible benefits of your job can violate this concept when making a "sex or else" demand. A coworker without this power cannot by definition commit a quid pro quo violation and, thus, create liability for the company under this concept. Employers are held *strictly liable* (without regard to fault) to employees if the harasser had the actual authority to affect the harassed person's work environment—and this liability will exist whether the employer knew about the harassment or not. It's a tough standard, but accusers also have difficulties in proof.

Clearly, if a supervisor asks a subordinate for a date and the subordinate accepts willingly due to a mutual attraction, quid pro quo harassment is not present. The problem, of course, is the difficulty in determining another person's mind or reasons for doing something. The danger with boss-worker relationships is that if they do break up, it's all too easy for the subordinate to say, "I was forced into sleeping with the boss." Yes, this isn't ethical; but when people feel hurt and raw due to the ending of a relationship, their minds can justify nearly anything for why the relationship started in the first place—such as that there was no choice because the ex-partner was their supervisor. Yet people still take their chances in romantic attachments all the time, whether they are the boss or the subordinate.

Hostile Environment Harassment

Although a coworker's unwarranted sexual advances cannot create quid pro quo harassment, a coworker's conduct can create a hostile environment action under the second circumstance. Victims must prove that a sexually hostile environment existed by showing: (1) they were subjected to unwanted harassment based on their sex and that this affected a term, condition, or privilege of employment; and (2) this conduct by the coworker (whether a supervisor or not) was sufficiently pervasive or severe to adversely alter the victim's work conditions and create a hostile working environment.

Vulgar language, sexual slurs, innuendoes, and insults clearly indicate a rancorous work situation. Employees clearly do not have to tolerate demeaning sexual inquiries, requests for nonconsensual sexual relations, or demands to wear revealing clothing in any situation, whether this occurs at work or not. Stark examples of hostile working environments were presented in the Mitsubishi, Astra USA, and Del Laboratories cases: these situations involved accusations of multiple cases of women being fondled, sexually catcalled, degraded, or groped and led to large, negotiated settlements with the EEOC.

Meritor Savings Bank v. Vinson, a 1986 U.S. Supreme Court landmark case, is generally credited with carving out the hostile working environment concept. *Meritor* involved a bank teller who said she had engaged in sexual relations with her branch manager out of a fear that her refusal would lead to reprisals—all in all, some "forty to fifty times" over a four-year period. When she was discharged on the grounds of taking too many sick leaves, she filed suit.

Although the complainant alleged outrageous conduct by the bank manager (he fondled her in front of other employees, followed her to the women's room and exposed himself, among other allegations), the teller didn't present a case for quid pro quo harassment. Because she actually had received various job promotions based on merit alone during that time, the only applicable cause of action at that time was based on a hostile environment theory. Ms. Vinson never complained to a superior or an officer of the bank. Although she argued that the manager's advances were "unwelcome," the teller admitted she had engaged in sex with the manager "voluntarily"—at least part of the time.

The district court held that she couldn't prevail because she had engaged in a voluntary sexual relationship. The court of appeals reversed on grounds that the Supreme Court later generally upheld. The Supreme Court held that Title VII granted employees the right to work in an environment free from discriminatory intimidation or insult. It barred conduct that was so severe or pervasive as to create an objectively hostile work environment and one that the victim perceived subjectively as being abusive. The decision held that liability could ensue from even "voluntary" behavior, the question being whether the manager made the employee's tolerance of the sexual acts a condition of her employment.

The complainant also didn't need to prove that the harassment had caused her economic injury. However, not all workplace conduct described as "harassment" necessarily affects a term, condition, or privilege of employment within the meaning of Title VII. For a sexual harassment case to be actionable, it must be "sufficiently severe or pervasive" to alter the conditions of the victim's employment and create an abusive work environment.

The *Meritor* decision held that employers could be held liable for the acts of their employees for sexual harassment, whether or not they received actual notice of the illegal conduct. It also held that employers could reduce their liability by establishing a specific policy prohibiting sexual harassment that was consistently followed and installing procedures that encouraged victims to come forward. This concept would be expanded later to form a strong legal defense for the companies. This defense also in turn became the argument and foundation for the restrictive behavioral policies that are seen today in numbers of companies and entities.

Harris v. Forklift Systems, Inc., decided in 1993 by the U.S. Supreme Court, reaffirmed the concepts in *Meritor* but added more elements. The *Harris* decision held that the complained actions didn't need to "seriously affect the employee's psychological well-being." Liability for harassment required an objectively determined standard that the environment was abusive (using a "reasonable" person's point of view), as well as the victim's subjective perception that the workplace was indeed hostile. To determine whether the working conditions were hostile involved looking at all of the circumstances, not just isolated incidents. This meant considering the severity of the complained conduct, whether it was humiliating or threatening, or a mere offensive statement; whether the conduct continued for long periods of time, was frequent, or isolated; and whether the actions unreasonably interfered with the worker's job performance. The Court decided that cases must be judged by weighing *all* these factors to determine whether the workplace was permeated by behavior that was "sufficiently severe or pervasive" to create a discriminatorily hostile environment and that altered the terms or conditions of the victim's employment.

Other Legal Considerations

Most important, the complained-of actions must have been *unwelcome* to the complainant for any harassment causes of action. If they weren't unwelcome, then a subsequent complaint would not be sustained. For example, if a drunken friend made a pass or two at Carrie, who thought it was funny at the time, didn't take it further, and kidded the drunk when he sobered up, there isn't a case for sexual harassment. However, if the same drunk made the same passes at Debbie, who reacted hysterically, there's a problem and we go to the next steps of the test.

Both objective and subjective standards must be met to create liability. Conduct that the complainant perceived as unwelcome (subjective) may not be found so by a reasonable person (objective)—and therefore no valid claim would exist. The conduct must also affect a term or condition of employment and be "sufficiently pervasive or severe" in its effect on the workplace. Although inappropriate conduct might not rise to the level of these legal tests, it still can be grounds for discipline by the company pursuant to its internal policies and procedures.

Consequently, many times a single incident won't meet the legal test of sexual harassment. Why? you might ask. "Because," as one defense attorney commented, "the courts ask how else can a person know that this conduct is unwelcome to that person. This implies that people get one free pass. You can't keep someone in the dark and then nail them for doing something they have no idea might be a problem to someone."

Additionally, to violate Title VII, the behavior must unreasonably interfere with the employee's work or create a hostile environment—and this implies a continuing or frequent series of events. However, one-time episodes aren't per se ruled out as a potential hostile workforce charge, because it's the severity of the episode that counts. As one human resources executive said, "If it's verbal like a bad joke or innuendoes, then you'll get a second chance. If it's a physical attack or groping, then I'll escort you out the company door that very day."

Although most federal, states, counties, and cities don't prohibit same-sex harassment by specific statute, the trend is definitely toward prohibiting such behavior. The U.S. Supreme Court in March 1998 ruled that sexual harassment law applies to cases where both the harasser and victim are of the same sex. As lower courts previously held, sexual advances by gays toward nongays clearly are prohibited under Title VII, because these advances were made owing to the victim's gender. The same reasoning was applied by the U.S. Supreme Court to make same-sex harassment actionable when it takes the form of unwanted physical touching, threats, actions, or intimidation. Thus any unwelcome sexual behavior should be prohibited now, regardless of gender.

Depending on the state and the court, judges use different tests to determine objectively whether an environment is hostile. Some courts employ a "reasonable woman" test, or whether in the eyes of the reasonable female the workplace is abusive. This assumes that men and women look at what's acceptable conduct from differing points of view, and the academic studies confirm this commonly held position. More courts and the EEOC at this time employ a "reasonable person" analysis that balances the facts from the viewpoint of both sexes.

The complainant's apparent voluntary submission to sexual relations doesn't mean that the actions were welcome, and the court must weigh whether the consensual sex was consistent with any later arguments that they weren't welcome after all. It's easy to see the practical and legal difficulties when a boss-subordinate affair ends with an angry subordinate around. However, complainants do find it more difficult later to establish that the conduct was "unwelcome" if they previously had engaged in consensual sex with the accused.

For example, June ended her love affair with a coworker. Her ex-lover reacted to the breakup by making negative comments about her to June's supervisor, and the supervisor subsequently fired her. June doesn't have a Title VII complaint under present case law, however, because the comments were accurate and her ex-lover didn't threaten her with that exposure for refusing to continue their relationship.

The complainant must prove the existence of an abusive environment that alters the terms or condition of the victim's employment before the company has any liability. Some courts have extended this liability to include the actions of nonemployees such as vendors or customers, provided the third-party employers of the perpetrators knew or should have known about the harassing conduct and failed to take proper corrective action. This area is discussed further in Chapter 5, "When Romance Ends and Harassment Begins."

Coworkers also may have a case for harassment if favoritism occurs as a result of a reporting relationship. If a supervisor's lover receives additional work benefits (for example, higher pay, better working hours, or more time off), workers in the same class may have a case against the employer for the denied benefits. There isn't a clear trend among the cases in this area, but remember that this is a potential employer liability. See Chapter 5 for further discussion.

A "gender discrimination" argument is used to include conduct that is not overtly sexual or of a sexual nature as sexual harassment. Thus actions that are based on gender differences can also be included as harassment. Examples are cursing, blowing cigar smoke in another's face, spitting, you name it—provided it's directed at the opposite sex—but the courts don't always buy this.

The Company's Liability (and Its Defense)

Any harasser is individually liable for his or her conduct, even if it occurs in the workplace. The liability of the company is a different consideration, and the U.S. Supreme Court in two June 1998 cases set down the parameters. Basically, employer's aren't "automatically" liable for harassment, even when committed by a supervisor (but depending on the circumstances), and employees don't have to prove that they suffered adverse job consequences as damages in order to prevail. The Court held in *Burlington Industries v. Ellerth* and *Faragher v. City of Boca Raton* that an employer is subject to strict liability without regard to fault for an actionable hostile environment that's created by the victim's supervisor. When no adverse employment action (such as a demotion, bad evaluation, or some penalty) has been taken against the plaintiff by that supervisor under the complained about circumstances, the defending employer has an affirmative defense that allows the employer to escape liability. This defense is that (a) the employer exercised reasonable care to prevent and correct promptly any sexually harassing behavior and (b) that the plaintiff employee unreasonably failed to take advantage of any preventive or corrective opportunities provided by the employer or to avoid harm otherwise. This defense isn't available (and the organization is liable), however, when the supervisor's harassment ends in unfavorable employment action being taken, such as a forced resignation, demotion, or some penalty.

The Supreme Court in these case retained the difference between quid pro quo and hostile working environment cases to distinguish between threats that are carried out and offensive conduct in general; it also held that these labels aren't controlling for the purposes of establishing employer liability. Thus, the employer is vicariously liable when a plaintiff proves illegal harassment—provided that if the plaintiff didn't experience a job penalty (which is usually the case in hostile working environment cases), the employer has the affirmative defense that it took reasonable precautions, such as antiharassment training and workplace monitoring, and that the victim of the conduct unreasonably didn't avail himself or herself of these procedures.

The Supreme Court stated that *Meritor's* statement of the law is still the "foundation on which we build today" (although it changed some of its reasoning as to employer liability); it affirmed *Harris* and still relies on the twin objective/subjective tests derived from that case. The court also is on record that its standards for judging hostility are to be sufficiently demanding to ensure that Title VII does not become a "general civility code." Prohibited conduct still must be extreme in that it must cause an adverse change in the terms and conditions of employment. The *Burlington* and *Boca Raton* cases considered only the question of employer liability and did *not* change the standards upon which sexual harassment conduct is defined.

The bottom line: a company has a strong defense when it has in place a written, reasonable policy against sexual harassment; follows that policy consistently and promptly, investigating as soon as it discovers prohibited acts; confidentially informs the involved employees about the results of its investigations; takes appropriate disciplinary action pursuant to that policy; and implements other actions necessary to promptly end and correct the complained-of harassment.

For example, the president and ex-president of a telephone company were held not liable for the actions of their subordinates in sexually harassing another worker. As soon as the employee complained, the officers promptly hired an attorney to investigate the complaints; they transferred the complaining employee to a location away from the harasser; and the harasser was directed to cease any contact with the complainant. They brought an administrative complaint against the harasser, although it was dropped when the complainant refused to cooperate further.

In another case, a woman complained to her supervisor about a coworker's sexually harassing remarks. The supervisor quickly investigated, reprimanded the coworker, placed a warning letter in his file, and transferred the coworker. The woman still brought a lawsuit and, not surprisingly, lost.

Another employer learned about a supervisor's alleged sexual harassment of an employee. It promptly investigated and issued a stern warning to the supervisor, admonishing him that any future instance of inappropriate activity would result in his immediate termination. The alleged sexual harassment ceased from that point forward. In case after case, the company wins on this point, provided it acts in a reasonable, fair, and prompt manner. The prompt remedying of the problem is a strong defense both legally and practically.

What experienced attorneys puzzle over are the number of lawsuits still brought when the company has "rectified the wrong"—a plaintiff seldom prevails when the company has promptly acted pursuant to its enforced policy and the complained conduct has stopped as a result. The ensuing effect, however, is that businesses can overreact to perceived problems, just so that they will have this legal defense in place. Unfortunately, what gives excellent legal protection can have a chilling effect to employee morale. Thus pro-interactive companies make a basic business decision that morale is more important than restrictive legal strategies, and that open, progressive policies that form a trust with their employees provides an even better defense—problem harassment situations that fester with potential legal defense costs simply don't occur as often.

So What Is Sexual Harassment?

The EEOC says:

> Unwelcome sexual advances, requests for sexual favors, and other verbal or physical conduct of a sexual nature constitute sexual harassment when submission to or rejection of this conduct explicitly or implicitly affects an individual's employment, unreasonably interferes with an individual's work performance or creates an intimidating, hostile or offensive work environment.

As you can see, even this definition is vague—and that's the point. How do we really know that an advance is sexual in nature? How many advances meet this definition? What really is "physical conduct of a sexual nature"? When does conduct "explicitly or implicitly affect an individual's employment"? What is an "unreasonable" interference with an individual's work performance? What facts constitute an "offensive work environment"? It's a lawyer's dream but everyone else's nightmare.

Depending on the circumstances, a wide variety of behavior may or may not constitute *illegal* sexual harassment. A joke in bad taste doesn't make it; a physical assault or attack defines the far extreme of what does. The test is absolutely met if the complainant was reprimanded, then terminated for refusing to submit to a supervisor's sexual demands.

Having to endure questions of a personal, sexual nature, then being propositioned by drunks at a company party also clearly makes it.

The problem is deciding when much lower level actions enter into this prohibited, illegal harassment ground. For example, sending a birthday card with an obscenity, assigning a menial task, and reacting coolly after having a sexual solicitation rejected was held by one court not to create a hostile environment. A federal district court decided that a female employee didn't perceive her work environment to be hostile, because she asked the supervisor who allegedly harassed her to reemploy her after she had turned in her resignation.

A male supervisor's alleged sexual harassment of a male employee (which included a congratulatory kiss at the employee's wedding, staring at him in the bathroom, bumping into the employee, positioning a magnifying glass over the employee's crotch, commenting on his appearance, and making inappropriate sexual comments) didn't meet the objective standard for a hostile or abusive environment. The alleged acts occurred over a seven-year period, and several of the incidents occurred in groups of employees although the complainant subjectively perceived them to be directed solely at him.

Unquestionably, sexual harassment was present, as a court held, when an employee's supervisor subjected her to extreme questioning of a sexual nature and repeated propositions. But what if a coworker propositioned her (which is not romance) twice in six months, then backed off and never did it again? What if the coworker inquired discretely about "heading to a motel," accepted the rejection without any response, then followed up a second and last time one year later, accepting a second rejection with the same lack of response? Remember we are talking about whether something is *illegal* sexual harassment, not whether it's in bad taste or shouldn't be present in the ideal workplace.

Suppose a man says to a woman, "Tight buns, baby." This clearly would be in bad taste and bad behavior, but it wouldn't rise to the level of illegal harassment. Similarly, if a man calls a group of women "you feminists," this also isn't harassment—although it might bring him a quick conference with a supervisor. However, the fact that behavior isn't illegal harassment (not in violation of the legal tests) doesn't mean that companies can't discipline employees for inappropriate behavior in accordance with their policies. They do. The problem is that some go overboard—and, again, such conduct does not involve romance.

When companies formulate their sexual harassment policies, they often attempt to stamp out any trace of harassment, whether the conduct meets the applicable legal standards or not. This is a very laudable objective—unfortunately, these policies also trample on the employees' sense of freedom, security, and knowledge as to what they can or can't do. Firms are motivated to avoid lawsuits and the attending high costs, as if that is possible in today's litigious world. They bow to the most sensitive employee's definition of what is or isn't acceptable conduct, and this clearly chills the rights of everyone else in that working environment.

For example, on February 17, 1994, the National Association of Scholars placed a full-page ad titled "Sexual Harassment and Academic Freedom" in the *New York Review of Books*, saying in part:

> Academic freedom and the rights of individuals can be—and have been—violated by misguided efforts to combat sexual harassment. Too many institutions have adopted vague definitions of harassment that may all too easily be applied to attitudes or even to a scholar's professional views. Not surprisingly, a chill has descended on academic discussions of sensitive but legitimate topics. . . . Worse, procedures have been widely adopted that violate *the canons of due process.*

No kidding—and this also applies to the business world.

People's Reactions Aren't the Same

Part of the basic philosophy of sexual harassment law is that an act alleged to be harassment is judged by its impact, not by the actor's intentions. In fact, what the actor thought at the time isn't considered: saying that "I was only joking," even if it is true, becomes irrelevant. Apologizing with a downcast face that "I was drunk" after having made an errant pass, might soothe the recipient's feelings, but it won't be a defense legally. This is a strong legal sword, because the intentions of the actor are held most important in many other legal arenas, ranging from criminal law to personal injury and intentional torts.

On the other hand, a two-part test is used with both subjective and objective components. The victim's subjective feelings do count as to whether there's a hostile environment. In fact, that perception matters more than any litany of excuses from the perpetrator. However, an objective or "reasonable person" test is used to assess actions and safeguard against problems caused by the supersensitive complainer. Let's say Debbie was an overly sensitive woman who went ballistic over two bad jokes told six months apart: Her inner reaction would meet one part of the test. The "reasonable person" or objective criteria might not reach that same result—hence, she wouldn't have a case. This doesn't mean that the joke teller shouldn't be warned, just that Debbie hasn't met the *legal* definition of harassment.

The fact that one woman might shrug off a situation, whereas another falls to pieces over the same thing, creates a nightmare of legal problems and a quagmire of administrative decisions. For example, Arlene is a postal worker in a large metropolitan city. She said: "There's this young worker. He's a nice guy and tries to be friends with everybody. He came over one day and rubbed one woman's back; she loved it and loved the attention. Then he came over to me, rubbed my shoulders as a gesture, and then walked away—and it only happened for a few seconds. I knew it wasn't a sexual thing, but I got mad and shouted: 'Don't you ever do that to me again! I'm not that other woman.' I know I hurt his feelings because he never came around to me again. But that's okay. . . . I don't see why that other woman thought it was so much fun and okay for her." People do react and reach differing conclusions about the same event.

The Fears of Management

What management fears at times may not be actionable under the law. What is "unwelcome" may not in fact be illegal. We have seen that people's feelings and reactions to the same event can be entirely different, because they're different people with differing personalities. The fact that they reacted differently isn't legally material, except to the extent that one reaction can be eliminated as unreasonable under the objective "reasonable person" test.

Workers are disciplined over "unwanted" conduct under sexual harassment complaints at the workplace that would never pass these legal tests. Companies should keep the workplace free from impolite and disrespectful conduct, but at what price and penalty? Vague policies simply create uncomfortable working conditions.

For example, let's say a company's policy states that "sexual harassment is any kind of behavior that is deemed inappropriate or unwelcome for the workplace by any worker. You must take into account the reactions of the most sensitive person in the workforce before taking any action." You would say that's a silly policy, and yet, that's what happening with some companies in today's business world.

This "fear factor" has been causing some firms to handle the "problems" of relationships with nonfunctional and repressive managerial policies. For example, there are corporations that discourage employees of opposite sexes from traveling together on business. At a few companies, male supervisors aren't allowed to give performance reviews to female subordinates unless another supervisor, or even an attorney, is present. At various universities and some companies, meetings between men and women can't be held unless the door to the office is always kept wide open—and it's these types of policies that also impede the upward track of women in management. Chase Manhattan Bank some ten years ago had a policy that forbade employees to ever touch one another, even to give a pat of congratulations on the back; this policy was reversed in the nineties.

There will always be wrongs for which there's no legal remedy—even in a country with a surplus of litigating attorneys. Not every inappropriate or boorish behavior is against the law, and you can feel humiliated without being sexually harassed in a legal sense. As we've seen, what's lurid is not necessarily illegal. When a worker is unhappy over an innuendo, touch, arm stroke, or bad joke, a supervisor must balance the office disruption from the upset employee against the reaction from the to-be-disciplined actor or joke teller.

As one vice president observed: "The sensitive employees seem to be winning more than they're losing. Businesses are running scared from the threats of lawsuits and the lawyers, and they don't want to say what they think is fair, only what gets them out of the problem with the least dollars or time spent. There are public image, employee morale, and 'politically correct' factors that they consider, in addition to the legal considerations. What happens is that people in these environments eventually leave to work for someone else."

The vice president of a large, publicly traded company was sacked the day after his assistant complained that he had put his arm around her waist without her consent. This was the only complaint, there were no other incidents, and the act occurred in his private office. This could have been the excuse that the president was looking for to fire this person; the senior vice president who described this incident left soon afterward, saying that the company's reputation was one of bad management and executive turnover. The problem is that these incidents cheapen the laudable concept of eliminating true sexual harassment incidents.

Six-year-old Jonathan Prevette became a headline sensation when he was charged with sexual harassment for kissing a little girl on the cheek. This first grader was isolated from his class and banned from an ice cream party as his punishment. For once, some feminist and men's rights groups agreed that this was ridiculous. Unfortunately, life has become way too serious to be fun for some.

And Then There's Romance

The good news is that romance is still in the air. It's such a positive and refreshing subject after discussing sexual harassment. Matt is in his late fifties and a twenty-five-year veteran of the pharmaceutical industry. He said: "Romance thrives because you have people working so close together. Let's face it, there's a basic attraction between them. Although the harassment laws, corporate attitudes, and policies affect what employees can do outwardly, workers still form couples and do it anyway. There is a difference between sexual harassment and romance. The problem is that people can get confused between the two, although they're as different a concept as anyone could think."

Two employees met at a company picnic, and they began sharing lunch together. The man began slipping discreet notes under the woman's office door, commenting on what they had discussed at their last lunch. He won her over on Valentine's Day with a card asking for dinner that night and signed "Love . . . Daniel." She went and they're still together.

Regardless of whether you are trying to show quid pro quo or hostile environment discrimination, the test is primarily sexual in nature. Sex, power, and control are the objectives, not a meaningful relationship. Instead of receiving flowers, the recipient is getting sexual innuendoes and bad jokes. Instead of being bought dinner, the recipient is getting a drunken proposition. None of this is romance.

The Law of Romance

The law of romance is not the law of sexual harassment. It is separate but complementary. There are no statutes, codes, or specific regulations in this area. It is created by what sexual harassment is not and was never intended to be. Many academic researchers clearly believe that sexual harassment and romance are two distinct areas, not related, and this law simply reflects this commonsense division.

For example, a coworker asks for a date and is turned down.

He or she accepts the response and doesn't ask again. Whether that coworker is the boss or a subordinate, clearly this isn't sexual harassment. If that person asks again later, discreetly and politely—again being refused and accepting it—it still isn't sexual harassment. Even if the recipient didn't like being asked out. Technically, you can ask, send a nice note, even give flowers, receiving a no response to all without committing illegal sexual harassment—up to the point where the recipient is reasonably made uncomfortable by these acts.

An insurance account executive said: "I've been asked out by men at work, some more than once, and I've later gone out with them. A friend of mine feels 'no means no' and that means no more asking out. I've asked her back, 'Does that mean forever and ever?' . . . Of course not. Asking for a date and dating isn't a 'one strike and you're out' ballgame. Take a look at how many relationships develop: people, feelings, and situations change. It's *how* a man, or a woman, asks someone out that's important, along with how they react to the response." The law agrees, provided the approach is relationship-oriented, not sexual or with innuendoes, and any subsequent approach is reasonable after receiving a refusal. Taking time before making another request makes sense, as obviously badgering someone to go out isn't going to meet with success. It's all in the approach, although this can depend on the personality of whomever's being asked.

As part of this law of romance, men and women should relate to each other respectfully and politely—whether at work or not. You don't say to one another "Nice, tight body," or "Sexy, sexy, sexy . . ." You don't call each other "girls," "Macho Man," "Sweetie," "Hot Stuff," or any other slang words, regardless of the sex of the recipient. Nor is this romance.

Reading *Playboy* in the company cafeteria isn't sexual harassment, no matter what some want you to believe. However, if someone complains, this shouldn't become a cause célèbre because workers shouldn't be reading personal material (at least if controversial) at work anyway—not to mention that this isn't romance either.

A man or woman can take the risk and compliment someone on their dress. If the person objects, then simply don't compliment them again and go on to someone who's more approachable. You can compliment men and women, no matter where they are (even at board meetings), and you aren't guilty of harassment under even the most conservative of policies. A person might be offended, but that's a different consideration.

Buying a valentine for someone, then writing "Best" and your name, isn't unlawful. Even if you sign it "Love," this by itself doesn't meet the tests. Nor is buying a gift for someone who returns it.

It is true that what's on and off limits can depend entirely on how close a working relationship you've developed. For example, if you've known each other for years, then the other person will be more understanding or flexible. If you've met someone only once, then compliments, gifts, and the like may not be welcome. They aren't harassment either, but you'll be taking your chances.

A consensual affair even between a boss and a subordinate isn't sexual harassment by itself, although it could be portrayed this way after the fact. As part of this, firms are applying a *standard of reasonableness* to the conduct of supervisors involved romantically in reporting relationships. If supervisors violate this standard, then the companies discipline them. Otherwise, companies will work with the supervisors (such as facilitating a transfer or eliminating review responsibilities), given that there are no indications of bad motives or control. This is an important concept, as these firms are recognizing that reporting relationships by themselves aren't the problem—it's the conduct, motives, and actions of the participants.

"One-night stands" aren't sexual harassment either, provided both participants are willing. A thirty-five-year-old marketing manager in New Jersey said: "I had a one-night stand with my boss when I was leaving the company. I had accepted a position with another firm, and they threw me a 'going-away' party. He drove me home afterward, and I was drunk . . . dead drunk. We made love in the parking lot of my condominium complex, and I don't remember much of that. It was just one of those nights." With that, she started laughing to herself.

Then there are the just plain "physical relationships" with nothing more at stake. A paralegal at a prestigious New York City law firm had an affair with her supervising paralegal. She didn't care whether either one loved the other or where it was going. "It was just a physical thing," she said. "It only lasted a few months, and that's all I wanted at the time." A friend of hers said, "When she's interested in someone, she makes it known." Not exactly romance, but not sexual harassment either. Would it be harassment, if the man were the actor? To embrace true equality, it shouldn't be.

The Courts

Court decisions don't address the law of romance—the cases rely on whether elements of the legal tests for harassment are missing or the fact patterns don't constitute it. The following cases illustrate aspects of the law of romance, all involving decisions where sexual harassment was not proved:

- A male employee testified that none of the female president's actions made him feel harassed, except for thank you notes from her signed "Love" or "Much love." The man said he felt uncomfortable, rather than harassed. There was no evidence that the man communicated his feelings to the woman, and he gave her an expensive, personal Christmas gift during the same time period.
- A white supervisor asked a black employee how she would feel about dating a white person, stared at her during the elevator ride, and said that he had a crush on her and would "kiss her face" (although he didn't make any attempt to do so). He never touched her. Although this made the employee feel uncomfortable, the supervisor's actions didn't establish a hostile work environment.
- A supervisor and his subordinate had a romantic relationship. The court held that this relationship did not, without more being present, give rise to a sexual discrimination or sexual harassment claim.
- A supervisor's flattering remarks about a coworker, his favoritism toward her, and the kiss that she blew back at him weren't sufficiently pervasive conduct to create a hostile working environment for a coworker. The court held that favoritism by itself, absent evidence proving a sexual relationship existed between the two, didn't meet the test.
- Female coworkers told other female workers that they looked "hot" and one woman's dress and buttocks were complimented by those workers on several occasions. The former employees said that they never interpreted the comments as indicating that their coworkers wanted to have sex with them. There was also no proof that the alleged harassers were lesbians.
- The female plaintiff needed to prove that she neither solicited nor incited the harassment and that she considered the conduct undesirable and offensive. The court held that she didn't prove this.
- A former female employee admitted that she was never threatened or disciplined by her supervisor, nor did the supervisor use his position to affect adversely any of the terms and conditions of her employment. His motivation for touching her was held to be solely personal.
- Another case revolved around trying to decide whether the alleged harasser's invitation to the plaintiff was to go out on a date or to

have sex with him. The court held that if it was to go on a date, then there couldn't be any harassment, regardless of what her response was.

Some companies argue that they don't want any lawsuits brought that could put them in an unfavorable light—whether the alleged behavior is illegal sexual harassment or not. They don't want the expense and therefore take strong actions to guard against any hint of "unwelcome" conduct. The problem with this approach is that they can't insulate themselves from lawsuits, even spurious ones. In return, restrictive companies buy wrongful termination lawsuits and bad morale for their heavy-handed policies. Having a nonrestrictive working environment, open communication channels, and clear but reasonable policies is a better defense. Pro-interactive companies don't have the same numbers of these problems.

The Stages of a Relationship

There are relatively few problems in the beginning or middle of work affairs, provided the participants don't bring their personal arguments into work with them. Although the vast majority of ended relationships don't end up as sexual harassment complaints, it's the breakup that creates the potential for legal trouble. Management must step in and work out the problems when difficulties occur. As one human resources executive said, "Usually, all we say is that your staying employed here depends on the two of you working out your problems, or deciding who transfers or leaves. If you can't decide, then both of you must leave. Our experience is that the parties fairly quickly work out their difficulties." See Chapter 14, "When Good Things Come to an End."

It isn't unreasonable for an employee to begin a discreet quest to win over another person's heart, provided the actions don't interfere with either's work performance. A company shouldn't be surprised if those efforts continue in the face of rejection. However, it isn't easy to decide when a pursuit taken delicately, in good taste, but persistently falls into the gray area of sexual harassment.

When one person has had it with the other's pursuit, the company has to decide what to do about it. The same human resources executive observed, "We've had little problems here, as well. We will tell the one pursing that he or she needs to stop and reconsider their actions. We'll say, 'You can apply for a transfer, stop and work out a truce, or leave. If you don't, then you leave.' We may recommend that they see a therapist or go into counseling, because we aren't interested in buying lawsuits." What's important is that companies are managing these personal, human relationship issues, just as they do any other human resources area. See also the following chapter, "When Romance Ends and Harassment Begins."

There's Much More Love Than Hate

The overwhelming number of broken workplace romances, whether involving boss-subordinate relationships or not, don't wind up in the hands of the lawyers. Companies counsel, mediate, transfer, and separate responsibilities to solve the problems. The ex-lovers work out their difficulties, leave, or change departments: they put the broken romance behind them and go on to better things. The EEOC's response to charges in most cases doesn't get too far; historically, the commission has turned down three-fourths of the harassment complaints it receives (due to lack of proof, facts that don't meet the legal tests, and other reasons).

Firm upon firm, survey upon survey, all report there are many more office romances than sexual harassment cases. This shouldn't be too surprising when you look at the overall statistics. Given that the workforce is 135 million strong (nearly one-half women) and climbing, there are millions of workplace romances occurring every year. The EEOC had nearly 16,000 sexual harassment cases filed last year, of which the great majority involved sexual innuendoes, sleazy comments, and tasteless conduct—not broken relationships.

A total of 54,000 cases involving sexual harassment were filed with the EEOC over the past six years, of which only 5 percent (or some 3,000) dealt with quid pro quo (boss-subordinate and sex-for-services) harassment filings. In fact, the American Management Association's survey reported that 84 percent of those managers profiling an office romance said there was *no* official action taken against the participants (not even an "informal" talk by the boss)—only 7 percent reported "other action" taken, ranging from an "informal" talk with the boss to voluntary transfers or resignation by one partner (another 3 percent received a warning; 3 percent reported an involuntary transfer; and 3 percent gave no response). Few firms need to take even official action against one or both romantic partners, and this includes when romances breakup.

Any continuing connection between romance and harassment is wildly exaggerated. Cupid must somehow find a better press agent.

Chapter Five

Where Romance Ends and Harassment Begins

On one side of the equation stand romance and people in love; on the other squat sexual harassment and inappropriate, not-to-be-tolerated behavior in all its squalor. It's the difference between asking someone, "Would you like to have a lunch today and take a break?" (then accepting the response with grace), and saying, "Hey, baby, let's head out to the parking lot and neck." It's the difference between giving a bouquet of flowering wildflowers and handing over a clump of thistles and poison ivy. However, what if the conduct is more tolerable, but the recipient is supersensitive? Or the conduct is simply colored unfavorably by an employee who is looking for political control or is simply having a bad day?

The One-Size-Fits-All Problem

We've briefly discussed the six-year-old who was punished for kissing a little girl on the cheek. As Meg Greenfield wrote in *Newsweek* at the time:

> The count against young Jonathan Prevette for kissing a little girl on the cheek told you where we have come to in the culture of counterintuitive and bloodless, not to say pointless, rulemaking in our civic life today. By its very nature this creation of one-size-fits-all rulings and prohibitions manages not only to create preposterous incidents of this kind, but also to free responsible authorities from dealing, in the normal, human community way, with the odd kid who is truly disturbed and needs to be singled out for attention. . . .

What I worry about . . . is that the whole thing [the Jonathan Prevette case], in a short while, won't seem as utterly preposterous to me as it does now."

No sooner had the media trucked away from Lexington, North Carolina, where school officials had suspended little Prevette for one day (and banned him from the party), than a New York City seven-year-old boy hit the news for an unwanted kiss. Although De'Andre Dearinge had been in trouble with two girls before (described by school officials as "in the realm of what second graders do"), this boy received a five-day suspension. Tearing a button from a girl's skirt—apparently because the bear in Dearinge's favorite book, *Corduroy,* was missing a button—warranted the additional days plus a letter explaining that the punishment was for **Sexual Harassment** in big, bold words.

These cases are balanced by a fourteen-year-old California girl's lawsuit against a school district that settled for $250,000. She had endured a nearly endless daily harassment by her sixth-grade classmates, including vulgar words, dirty jokes, and death threats, and a jury found that the school officials in charge had ignored her complaints.

The problem is that the one-size-fits-all approach, given the prevalent fear of lawsuits and threatening attorneys, sweeps in the Prevette and Dearinge cases, along with that of the fourteen-year-old girl. The harassment net captures innocent butterflies as well as stinging wasps, regardless of motives, situation, age, occupation, or philosophy. Situations with the best romantic intentions at times can be thrown into the gutter with the basest sexual harassment cases.

As one female defense attorney commented: "It's an unfortunate fact of life that numbers of sexual harassment claims aren't raised until the employee's demoted or threatened for some nonrelated reason. It's a frequent claim and knee-jerk reaction argued when a worker resists being terminated or is bringing a wrongful termination lawsuit. These types of legal attacks cheapen the real harassment claims. Sexual harassment is sexual harassment; what isn't should not be thrown about. You look at a complaint or some of the cases where the complainants failed to prove their position and just shake your head." For example, one court held that an employee had failed to prove his claims of quid pro quo sexual harassment, arguing that his refusal to engage in sex with his supervisor was not the reason another boss had disciplined him for absenteeism and tardiness. The court concluded that nine absences in nineteen days and eleven tardy reports in a seven-month period was an unacceptable level of dependability and warranted the discipline.

Matt, the experienced, ex-pharmaceutical executive, observed: "At my company, the harassment laws stopped the overt action, but the people went more and more underground. One gal in her early twenties wore tight, short skirts and tops. She wore tops with this thin fabric, so that when the sunlight hit it, you found it hard not to stare. One guy, let's call him Casey, was working a couple of levels down from me. The young gal made a sexual harassment complaint against Casey, saying that he had 'ogled' her and made a lewd remark.

"His new boss told me Casey was in trouble before the charges were even made. Under our policy in that situation, he would have been warned and given a second chance. If this type of problem didn't occur again, it wouldn't have been used against him. That boss then fired Casey on the unsupported charge made by that young woman. Why? He didn't have to go to the trouble of supporting and documenting bad work performance. Casey was going anyway, but it was just easier to use harassment grounds.

"This isn't what those laws were made for, and they shouldn't go into true relationship areas. You can meet someone at work, then leave or transfer and get back together with that person later. You can meet, break up, and get back together again later. Sexual harassment laws shouldn't be allowed in this pattern. The problem's that they're brought in when someone feels slighted or wants to get even. Then the company pays the price, if they don't act fast enough, or some poor employee takes it on the chin. We've had complaints in areas that no one intended by those laws."

The one-size mentality can affect basic human interactions, as well. "I'm not in favor of harassment—I wouldn't want it for my fiancée—but it allows for unconscionable, silly little games," said Jeff, an older manager with an insurance company. "There's a woman in my office who recently joined the firm, and she's about my age. Well, we talked and worked a little bit on a project. This woman is formal on the outside and always shakes your hand. She was dressed nicely one day, so I complimented her on her dress. She just responded dryly, 'And you're wearing a nice shirt and tie.' I didn't have a tie on, so she made her point. It was the first time I had that problem with a woman. So you don't forget it.

"I gave her a lot of room from then on, polite but staying out of her way. So we're talking in the hallway on business one day. I started to walk away, and she put her hands around my shoulders, like all of a sudden we're buddies. I didn't say anything, but I didn't like it because I knew I couldn't do the same thing with her. When we're in her office, she puts her hands on mine and actually massages them to make some point.

"I told my wife about it, who met this woman at the company Christmas party. Her conclusion: 'This one's into control and using the system the wrong way.' Pretty observant, I thought. A buddy of mine said he didn't trust her. Well, I don't either. It makes no difference whether you're man or a woman, that type of inconsistency is plain wrong."

The same person in the workplace can be sexually harassed by one person, either at the same company or somewhere else, and fall in love with another. In Chapter 2, we discussed the case of Roberta, who was harassed at one job and then fell in love with a worker at another company. Carrie, in Chapter 3, had the same problem, plus the same benefits of workplace romance. And there are numerous other examples. The point is that harassment is one thing, romance is another, and Title VII tries to cover all of them. This is not only impossible and impractical, it doesn't make any sense.

Persistence or Harassment?

The Jonathan Prevette "one-size-fits-all problem" is seen in many cases. Andy, thirty-two, worked for a large truck manufacturing company in its accounting department, and its employees were scattered over a number of buildings. He met twenty-eight-year-old Vicki at a company softball game, and it was love at first sight for Andy. He maneuvered in lunch on a business pretext, and they had an enjoyable time. Since Vicki worked in sales, their departments were in different buildings. They lunched a few more times during the next two weeks.

Vicki told Andy that she was having problems with her boyfriend, which really made Andy's day. He mustered up his courage and asked if she would like to talk about that over dinner some evening. Vicki said "fine," and they set a date for the following week. At that early dinner, Vicki talked to Andy about her problems, and he listened as best he could, because he really liked her. She invited him back to her apartment and they talked for an hour more. One hug later, Andy headed home.

He'd make excuses to stop by her office now and then, and they would chat pleasantly for fifteen or twenty minutes. Vicki gave Andy her home phone number, and they would chat at times during the evening. They had dinner the next week, but this time they ended up drunk and making love in her apartment.

It was tough getting up the next morning with his hangover, but Andy made it to work to find that Vicki was out on an appointment. He tried calling her that night, but her line was busy. Once back at work that next morning, he stopped by her office. Vicki looked up at him and said they shouldn't be meeting at work any more because someone might get suspicious. When he called her at home that night, Vicki became curt and said she would talk to him tomorrow at work.

Andy walked over to her office the next day. At that time, Vicki said she was back together again with her boyfriend. It had happened that night, and they had worked out their difficulties. Vicki wanted to continue being friends with Andy, but her news was a major blow to his ego. Andy quickly became upset and closed the door to her office. During the argument, he called her a "two-timing, two-faced bitch." Vicki asked him to leave her office. He refused, then apologized for his remarks. They talked tensely for ten more minutes before Vicki ordered him out of his office and he did as he was told.

That afternoon, he received a telephone call from Vicki's boyfriend saying that Andy had upset her and that he had better watch out for himself. Andy marched over to Vicki's office. She told Andy that her boyfriend had called after their argument and she told him about their fight, but not that they had slept together. At that time, her boss stuck his head in the door and asked if Andy was the one who had been "harassing her." Vicki apparently had talked to her boss during the interim.

There was an investigation, and Andy was given a written warning for sexual harassment. He was warned that one more episode like that would result in his immediate dismissal. Andy left the firm that next month, and he's now the accounting manager for a small company.

The point is that there are relationship issues that a company should not handle under its standard sexual harassment policies. They clearly involve different factors. These are personal relationship problems and not legal ones. Companies should strongly enforce reasonable sexual harassment policies, but also use a standard of reasonableness and understanding with relationship problems. The standard should be to manage these difficulties and stop any disturbances to the workplace, but it shouldn't be punitive or repressive.

Let's take a hypothetical situation. Tony used to be involved with his boss, April, but they eventually broke up. However, April acts as if they were still together. She gives him affectionate glances and touches, calls him for special meetings (but only she shows up), and talks to him about past personal matters. Most of us would conclude that April's conduct is not appropriate given that Tony tells April he doesn't like this behavior.

Whether these facts meet the legal tests for harassment depends on Tony's ability to prove that April's actions created a hostile working environment (provided she didn't give him an undeserved bad review or lower his salary or benefits because they broke up). The presence of this "hostile working environment" would depend on whether April's conduct is "sufficiently severe or pervasive" to alter the conditions of his employment and create an abusive work environment, along with whether his perceptions of this meet both the objective and subjective tests placed on a complainant as discussed in Chapter 4. The company's response will decide further whether this is actionable illegal harassment—remember that a business has a strong defense if it takes timely steps to stop the complained-of action (for example, if April's supervisor quickly warns her, and this action stops the conduct).

It can make a practical difference if Tony and April get back together again. All relationships have conflicts, even the best, and Tony certainly wouldn't be complaining then. However, this discussion doesn't mean that April's actions are condoned—certainly not. Her actions are adversely affecting the workplace and must stop. She should be warned, advised to see a therapist, have her responsibilities changed, or even use counseling so she and Tony could still work together (provided Tony agreed); however, she shouldn't be terminated or demoted. These extreme alternatives would be used if she didn't stop or take remedial action after the company interceded. Since Tony isn't contributing to this problem, of course, he wouldn't be held jointly responsible for its solution.

Other cases go further into the area of outright harassment where a suitor was clearly too persistent and past the point of no return. Whether opposite or same sex, these pursuits are unreasonable under any standard, and you question how there could have been any normal romantic intent at all.

For example, two IRS agents worked in an office. A man was assigned to work two rows behind a female coworker. They never became friends and didn't work closely together. We'll call the man, Brown, and the woman, Ala. Brown asked Ala to go to lunch with him one day and she accepted. Having forgotten to pick up his son's lunch, Brown stopped by his house and gave Ala a tour. It was after their lunch, Ala alleged in her federal district court case (it went to the U.S. Court of Appeals for the Ninth Circuit, which decided for her in 1991), that Brown began to pester her with unnecessary questions and hang around her desk. Brown asked her out for a drink and she declined. He asked her out for lunch and she once more declined.

He handed her a note saying he had cried over her. Brown followed her into the hallway and demanded she talk with him. She refused and went quickly to her supervisor. Ala told her boss he didn't need to intercede and that she would handle it by herself. She asked another coworker to tell Brown that she wanted to be left alone. After that happened, Brown reported sick the next day.

Ala left for a four-week training trip, receiving during that time a typed, single-spaced, three-page letter from Brown. After she had read it, Ala concluded that Brown was "nuts." She telephoned her supervisor, told him about the letter's contents, and discussed the problem. That same day, Ala's supervisor advised Brown to stop what he was doing, also informing him that he had the right for his union to represent him according to the union bargaining agreement (this representation was for discipline procedures).

The supervisor told Brown "many times over" that he couldn't contact Ala in any way, and Brown then transferred to another office. The IRS and union settled the grievances in Brown's favor, allowing him to transfer back to the same office, provided he spent four more months at the new office and promised not to bother Ala again.

Ala became upset when she learned about Brown's potential return. She filed a formal complaint with the EEOC alleging sexual harassment and obtained permission to transfer to another office. Brown meanwhile sought joint counseling for the two of them; he also wrote another letter to Ala suggesting that they had some type of a relationship going on.

The Treasury Department rejected Ala's complaint and decided that the facts didn't prove a pattern of harassment under the EEOC's then-standing regulations (the rules were changed later, and it's doubtful that the same decision would be reached today). When the EEOC turned down her complaint on procedural grounds, Ala brought a hostile working environment lawsuit. The district court agreed with the IRS's contention that this wasn't the case; however, the court of appeals reversed and held for her.

Although Brown's conduct clearly was outside the realm of acceptable limits, Ala needed to battle in the courts to prevail, owing to the presence of the union bargaining agreement and legal procedures. There must be a better way than relying solely on sexual harassment laws. Mandatory counseling and more balanced administrative procedures aimed at solving these problems practically would be better.

Unequal Power, Favoritism, or Just People in Love?

Suzanne and Jeffrey

Suzanne and Jeffrey worked for a large, West Coast computer manufacturer. Jeffrey, forty-six, was a respected product manager and Suzanne, thirty, worked for him as an assistant product manager. Although Jeffrey was married, they fell in love. Since their company frowned on chain-of-command romances (although it didn't have a written policy), they kept their relationship quiet and met clandestinely during the off-hours.

After being discreet for several months, Jeffrey and Suzanne decided to go public with the news of their romance. However, before they could do this, they had to change their reporting relationship under the company's informal policy in order to continue working there. They convinced another product manager to accept Suzanne as his assistant. Although the manager was puzzled and wondered why they "weren't getting along," he knew she was an excellent worker and allowed Suzanne to switch laterally to his department.

However, Jeffrey's wife had become suspicious and confirmed their affair. The wife, who also worked for this company, told a male friend in Jeffrey's department about the goings-on. He also complained bitterly to the human resources department, griping that Suzanne had only gained the move because she was sleeping with his boss.

After meeting with everyone, the HR manager decided Jeffrey and Suzanne should be punished. Jeffrey was given a written warning, and Suzanne demoted one level to report to a new boss. They left the company that year and married after his divorce was final.

What's sad is that the human resources manager didn't dig deeper into why the coworker complained. Further, Jeffrey and Suzanne already had split off their reporting relationship before going public, in accordance with the company's policy. The HR manager should have allowed Suzanne's new supervisor to make the decision on whether she could stay with him or not. If that had happened, the company would have retained two well-trained managers. What happened is that both left after a mechanical application of the firm's standard sexual harassment policy. We'll look more closely into the details of Suzanne's and Jeffrey's experiences in Chapter 11.

Attorney Golden and Anita

As in the case of the irate ex-girlfriend who brought charges against the female surgeon, sexual harassment complaints can arise when clients and professionals enter into personal relationships. It is ironic at best that this is considered to be sexual harassment by the professional if the couple breaks up, but just another story of romance if they stay together.

Attorney Golden was a married, respected divorce attorney in a large Midwest city. His client, Anita, was in the middle of a disastrous divorce. It was some months later that their working relationship became a personal one. They had drinks after late afternoon meetings, then those ended up in dinner, then that ended in a relationship. Neither knew how Anita's ex-husband discovered that fact, but it came up during a hearing on the case.

Attorney Golden was at a sidebar conference (a confidential meeting with the opposing lawyer and judge on the side of the bench) when the other attorney accused Golden of having an affair with his client's wife. Despite Golden's argument that the affair wasn't relevant, the judge cast a stern look at him. He lost that motion, as well as another crucial one before that judge. Although the arguments could have gone either way, the affair seemed to Golden to be causing problems with the court. He soon left his wife and moved to an apartment.

Eventually, the case was settled but on less advantageous terms than Anita had expected. She and Golden broke up in a bitter argument over his handling of the case. Anita then consulted a malpractice attorney who sent a threatening letter to Golden. There was a modest settlement, and both went their separate, upset ways. The moral of the story: get all of your work done before you begin celebrating or romancing.

The Extramarital Affair

If you're dedicated and perhaps even lucky, your marriage or relationship is working. The problem is that one-half of all marriages aren't. "People don't worry about closing out the old before they get on with the new these days," said one human resources vice president. "They don't miss a beat. We turn a blind eye to these happenings, unless someone makes a work-related complaint. Then we treat it as if the person was single, reviewing it under our standard policy on harassment, such as discouraging chain-of-command romances."

Businesses are caught in a bind, because they hear the moral arguments about extramarital affairs; however, what they see in the workplace are people who are searching for satisfying personal relationships. This includes the people at the top, as well. For example, Dana is an enterprising woman who owns her own business that brokers the loads for trucks to haul across the United States. One of her clients owns a transportation company with fleets of trucks. One day, his younger secretary called her up asking if she had any ideas for her boss's birthday. Dana had a hunch as she remembered that he always complimented his secretary, at least to her, and said she should send him a card inviting him to dinner that night. "We're both married," the secretary protested, "although I don't know if his marriage is as bad as mine. Besides, I couldn't afford the restaurants he eats at."

"He'll pick it up, and he likes you. Trust me," said Dana. The secretary did as she was advised. On the appointed evening, Dana arranged for a bottle of champagne to be delivered to their table as the two of them dined. The boss and his assistant married soon after their divorces were final and are still together.

Attitudes depend on the prevailing corporate climate, and this can differ dramatically among companies. See Chapter 6, "How Cold's the Climate?"

The Horror Stories

Anyone can dredge up the horror stories about the clinging suitor or stalking ex-lover. One such case involved the two IRS coworkers, Brown and Ala. There are the vulgar ones at best, such as the boss who continually propositioned a female worker, including rubbing himself against her back and bottom when she bent over. She sued and won. That's just plain despicable behavior and should never be tolerated. We are continually reminded of such situations by the lurid media accounts of automobile assembly lines and "Animal House" sales meetings. However, these situations thankfully do not occur nearly as often as inferred by these accounts.

Other horror stories deal with complainants who feel they've been sexually harassed but lose in an administrative hearing or in court—a much more common result. One court held that a coworker's three sexually suggestive comments over a three-month period didn't constitute sexual harassment. Although the words were offensive, these suggestions didn't rise to the legal standards of unreasonable interference with the plaintiff's working environment. When the complainant failed to show that her supervisor adversely affected a condition of her employment (after refusing his persistent sexual requests), then this was fatal to her claim. It's a horror story to sue over what's considered to be sexual harassment, expend significant time, money, and emotions, and then still lose the case.

None of this is about romance.

Flings and "Just Plain Sex"

There are people who just want a good time and not a commitment. Sometimes this can cause a whole lot of problems. The fifty-year-old artistic director for a nationally recognized theater was caught between the sheets with an eighteen-year-old page. He was forced to resign, after the parents screamed sexual harassment but settled for his job. The theater didn't even give the ex-director a going-away party, and frankly, it shouldn't have. He got off lucky. If this had happened a few months before, he could have been charged with statutory rape.

However, a forty-eight-year-old female art professor views affairs with her younger students as simply "grazing rights." She also believes that "aging, white males wouldn't have a prayer if they tried to live by my philosophy."

And there are the one-night stands. A lawyer hired a male paralegal for her one-woman office. After an especially gratifying court win, she bought him dinner as she had promised. That night they walked on the beach and made love for the first time, before both headed back to their homes. The following morning, she arrived a little later than he did. He said, "Nice night, last night." She nodded her head, and they went back to work. Both were involved with others, never mentioned the incident again, and worked together for two years without another replay. He then left to take a higher paying job that she couldn't match, and each has always highly recommended the other.

An attorney headed over to a client's office for a party celebrating the opening of their new offices; she ended up late that night drunk and making love with one of the owners on the new conference table.

A professor had sex with a younger graduate student on his office desk, which fronted the main grounds; at least this also happened at night. A hairdresser took time with her last customer to do a good job, drank several toasts during the styling, invited him over to her house, and ended up making love all night. A fast-tracking financial officer and his assistant went to dinner and wound up making love on her living room floor. The stories would fill up the rest of this chapter. For the record, one-nighters aren't romance. However, if they don't go any further, they can't be considered sexual harassment either.

Despite the Rules, It Still Depends on the Person

It makes no difference whether a romance is at its beginning or its end, it's why the players are acting as they are that decides if there's a legitimate harassment case. "The perception of the other person's motivation is an important ingredient," observes Professor Pierce. "If you have sincere or genuine motives for the relationship, not trying to get something out of it, then there's a better chance at its not ending in a controversy. If you perceive the other party as having good motives, even if he or she's persistent in their attempts to begin or keep a romance going, then you'll be more understanding." This is common sense.

Moreover, even the armed forces with all its rules still has more problems from consensual sex and this basic attraction ingrained in people which results in breaking the regulations. Although Tailhook, the U.S. Army Training Center, and military sexual harassment scandals grab the headlines, what's not widely reported are the romantic entanglements that involve many more military men and women. For example, the military discovered that more than half the men and three-quarters of the women troops in one unit during the Gulf War had as much or more sex in Saudi Arabia than when they were stationed back home. Thirty-six women sailed back home now pregnant after working on a repair ship during that conflict. This happened at a time when women made up only 13 percent of the nation's armed forces—just wait as that figure increases. Rules are made to be broken. Right?

And when harassment rears its ugly head, some people don't allow themselves to become victims, but handle the situation in a way that quickly solves the problem. For example, a commanding officer repeatedly pressured his young female sergeant to sleep with him. The woman finally agreed to go with him to a hotel. He took off his clothes quickly in anticipation of sex and disappeared into the bathroom. The enterprising, nonconsenting woman grabbed his clothes, left the hotel, and dropped them off with the military police. That ended the problem, once and for all.

The Minefield of Legal Rights

An ex-lover can be upset with both the company and the ex-partner. Noninvolved employees can complain about a relationship, whether they're truly affected by those actions or not. People can threaten or sue a company for sexual harassment, whether they're employed there or not. In fact, who's threatened or sued only depends on how creative the lawyer is when arguing his or her client's cause. Although the overwhelming majority of workplace romances don't end up in court, there are a number of areas to keep in mind.

The Lovers Against the Company

Controversies between lovers and their employers occur primarily over three areas of company policy. These are whether the business can (1) prohibit dating, (2) treat married couples differently, and (3) look into their employees' E-mail messages.

Right to Prohibit Dating

Court challenges to an employer's no-fraternization or "you're fired, if you date" policies historically haven't been successful, and an employer generally may legally prohibit dating among its employees in the work environment—but there are exceptions. Complainants have used right to privacy, breach of good faith, lack of equal protection, implied employment contract, intentional infliction of emotional distress, and other legal theories. Case decisions have held that a manager's right to privacy has not been infringed when he or she has been discharged under such a policy following complaints from coworkers about a personal relationship with a subordinate. A lower court has held that the employer's discharge of employees under a rule against romantic encounters on the job did not violate public policy. Signed contract disclaimers, where the employee agrees as a condition of employment to follow the reasonable rules of the employer, are usually upheld. The U.S. Supreme Court hasn't ruled directly on this broad issue and all its implications.

However, we have seen that the great majority of companies don't use these restrictive policies for sound reasons—including that court cases based on protecting a worker's right to privacy would multiply out of hand if they did. Practically, these rules make no sense, and companies might lose in today's legal environment (see the discussions later in this section on IBM's court cases).

As Professor Troyer points out:

> When a company employs a restrictive approach to what happens naturally, conflicts and employee turnover increase. First, subordinates in a work relationship are put at a disadvantage, because they can't report problems to higher-ups, since doing so would make it clear that they had violated the company's policy. Second, there is increased hostility by coworkers directed at the involved parties because they're perceived as doing something that has been defined as being "bad." Third, workers seem angry toward management for trying to "control" aspects of their lives that the workers perceive as being "none of their business."
>
> Companies with constraining rules force people to go underground, and these companies are shooting themselves in the foot. People basically can't live with unreasonable or unnatural rules; the employees react in different ways that lead to their perceptions of unfairness and unequal treatment.

Moreover, the court cases indicate that *how* a company learns about its employees' relationships is also important. If a business "snooped" on personal conversations, "bugged" telephones, or used surveillance techniques on what were the private activities of its employees, a court would most likely declare the company's conduct to be illegal, no matter what its policies provided.

More than twenty states have enacted statutes protecting an employee's right to privacy outside the workplace. Some states, such as Colorado, New York, and North Dakota, passed statutes with broad language protecting employees against discharge or discipline for off-duty, legal activities. Although these statutes usually aren't construed to apply to policies regulating a worker's conduct at work, they do show the strong legal commitment to the right to privacy.

Reasonable restrictions on dating (such as those centering on boss-subordinate relationships) usually will be upheld legally. Those regarding public sector employees have received a more mixed response in court due to the different standards of judicial scrutiny that are used. Moreover, an employer's ability to discipline a worker will be restricted if that employee is a union member (as we saw in the Brown and Ala case). The results depend on the negotiated labor contract grievance and penalty procedures that are in place.

A different matter is presented when a company attempts to regulate an employee who's dating someone outside the company. In *Rulon-Miller v. IBM*, the California State Court of Appeals held in 1984 that IBM couldn't fire a female employee who dated a man then working for a competitor. They had met previously at IBM, but he had since accepted a job outside the company. The court awarded a $300,000 judgment to the fired worker, concluding that IBM had created an express policy protecting its employees' privacy for off-duty conduct. The California court recognized an implied covenant of good faith and fair dealing that resided in the employment relationship by itself. The company's own internal policies in this case protected its employees, unless it discovered employees were passing trade secrets or engaging in other detrimental conduct.

Regulating Married Employees

Courts generally overturn no-spouse rules and discipline taken against married couples for extramarital affairs. As we have seen, there are numbers of state, county, and local statutes that protect the marriage relationship from discrimination. These prevent not only treating married couples differently from single employees as to promotions and responsibilities (although you can employ reasonable rules to prevent conflict-of-interest situations such as with financial capacities) but also penalizing only married workers for having affairs. Given the turnabout from prohibiting married couples from working together at the same firm just two decades ago to today's active recruiting of the same couples, these types of restrictions are becoming a nonissue.

For example, Wal-Mart once had a policy against dating and committing adultery with fellow employees. Its problems began when the company fired two employees for having an affair, one single and the other then separated from her husband but still legally married. The New York state's attorney successfully sued Wal-Mart on the ground that an employer was prohibited under New York law from interfering with its employees' private lives when what they were doing wasn't illegal (New York has a strong privacy law). Now, Wal-Mart's policies only prohibit direct reporting relationships.

However, reasonable work rules, even those affecting married workers, have been uniformly upheld. Let's take the example of a hospital nurse and pilot who married each other after working in the same unit during an emergency medical services airlift. The hospital's application of its antinepotism policy in requesting the *transfer* (but not the termination) of either spouse was not held to violate public policy favoring marriage. The court decided that nepotism policies would be valid when (1) the policy didn't directly or substantially interfere with the right to marry and (2) nothing in the applicable state or federal law indicated that the specific provisions violated public policy (there was a reasonable policy objective, such as combating favoritism or unequal treatment). Thus the application of reasonable conflict-of-interest prohibitions when married couples work together would be upheld.

Regulating E-Mail

E-mail leaves a trail and, unlike mere words, is preserved on the employer's computer system. Despite the recent striking advances in technology, E-mail is still in the Wild West when it comes to the law. There is little legal guidance or precedent as to when E-mail messages may be legally opened and read by employers, whether they're private messages or not.

Although there are no controlling Supreme Court decisions in this area presently, most firms take the position that they have this right. They argue that it's their system and they can do what's reasonably needed to police their workforce. They argue that if they're to be held responsible for controlling harassment, they should have the ability to monitor their workers' communications. The National Association of Working Women, however, is on record as saying that E-mail sexual harassment is so rare as to be a "nonissue."

Nevertheless, lovers who use E-mail to communicate should exercise discretion and caution. Coworkers might come across these communications and give them much wider circulation after discovering these private messages (despite the use of passwords). Employees with a political agenda would certainly have an adverse motive. The best advice is not to use E-mail; use the telephone instead.

An Ex-Lover Against the Company

Lawsuits against employers have been discussed in detail, whether the complaint concerns a romance, reporting relationships, or true sexual harassment. Remember that the company has available a strong defense if it took prompt, remedial action pursuant to its stated policies after learning about the alleged act. If the problem involves two warring ex-lovers in the same department, the company typically transfers one or both, or warns and tells both to solve the problem themselves. This situation rarely finds its way into the hands of either the EEOC or the lawyers.

Ex-Lovers Against Each Other

When a relationship is over, it's normal for an ex-lover to feel hurt and angry—especially the one that didn't call it off. People who are hurt can strike out in all directions against their ex-lovers.

Remember that everyone is responsible for his or her own misconduct. Employees who sexually harass others are personally liable, even when the company incurs its own separate liability. Although the corporation usually pays because it has the money, the employees who cause the problem are also at risk.

Companies take various responses, depending on whether the ex-lovers are in the same department or can be transferred (see Chapter 14, "When Good Things Come to an End"). If the company is small, the ex-partners either learn to work with one another or one has to leave. Given the number of jobs and careers an average worker experiences in a lifetime, some don't see this choice as a particular risk when they first enter into a relationship.

Coworkers Against the Company

The problems of favoritism (the general argument used by coworkers) due to reporting relationships have been discussed previously. A woman worked as an administrative assistant at a publishing company. After she and the president of the company met, they started up a two-year affair. Her working skills weren't particularly impressive during this period, but she was promoted five times and eventually became a vice president. This situation presents the classic case of "reverse" sexual discrimination for the coworkers. Every worker who was unfairly leaped over had a technical complaint of sexual harassment against the company. It's for this reason that relationships between bosses and subordinates (which include presidents of companies, who have supervising responsibility over all the workers) receive such scrutiny.

Given the rise of women managers in the workforce, it might be possible for a subordinate to harass his supervisor. For example, a male worker might make work miserable for his superior, and in a way that it becomes a hostile working environment. However, in reality this is going to happen rarely—who really wants to harass someone who can fire you? People try their darndest to get along with the boss.

Courts generally don't rule favorably on favoritism complaints brought by outside third parties. For example, one court held that even though a commanding officer was accepting sexual favors from a female applicant (who was eventually promoted to a civilian employee position within the U.S. Navy), the male applicant who was denied promotion was not the victim of sexual discrimination. There might be other grounds to argue, but this wasn't held to be a Title VII violation.

Surprisingly, the Supreme Court of Texas in 1994 actually was asked to decide if an employer was liable to the cuckolded plaintiff spouses of two married employees who had an office affair. The plaintiffs argued that the company owed a duty to prevent its employees from engaging in such extramarital affairs. The court, in reversing the lower court's ruling for the plaintiffs, held that it had never recognized a cause of action in that state for negligent interference with the family relationship. Who said attorneys weren't inventive?

Third-Party Relationships

A dinner party directed loud, sexually explicit jokes and comments at a waitress, and one customer in particular made obscene sexually suggestive gestures. Although the waitress complained to her boss who also was the owner, he failed to take any action against the harasser who was his friend. The employee told her boss that the same man had harassed her on other occasions, but her employer did nothing. A court held the owner liable for sexual harassment due to his not telling the customer to stop after being told about the unwelcome conduct.

The EEOC's guidelines explicitly state that an employer may be held responsible for the harassment of its workers by third parties when that employer knows or should have known of the conduct and fails to take prompt and corrective action. The fact that the EEOC guidelines take this position doesn't mean that it is the law. This is an administrative body position, not a federal statute, and the courts are generally split on an employer's liability in this area depending on the facts.

There is a trend toward finding an employer liable for nonemployee or third-party harassment when *clearly:* (1) the employer knew or should have known about the harassing conduct; (2) the employer didn't take immediate and appropriate corrective action; and (3) the employer had sufficient control and legal responsibility over the nonemployee harasser.

Although the wise course is for an employer to do all that it can to prevent harassment of its employees by a third party, there can be difficulties. For example, dealing with vendors is obviously different from dealing with customers. Vendors want your business, so it's easier to control any harassment; on the other hand, a business wants its customers and this makes the situation more delicate.

Romance, again, involves much different considerations. The problems of chain-of-command, domestic partner reporting, or coworker jealousy situations usually aren't present. The great majority of reported cases involving third parties don't involve romance or ex-lovers. Provided an employer isn't faced with a stalker or overly aggressive suitor, romantic relationships with customers might even be tacitly ignored (given no coworker complaints) just to keep the ongoing business.

One human resources executive said, "Third-party liability isn't a problem for us. We have a strong harassment policy and that includes our customers and vendors. If one of our sales reps is dating a customer discreetly, then we treat it the same way as any other workplace romance. However, if there's a continuing revolving door of affairs with our customers, we'll sit down and talk with that employee, because the image wouldn't be good for us. If the ending of the relationships affects our business, we will again sit down and talk seriously with our employee. However, the fact that there's a romance out there in itself isn't our concern and never will be." This is a common approach.

Professionals and Their Clients

In response to publicized abuses, states have been enacting legislation that deals with sexual harassment between professionals and their clients. Such laws recognize the fact that harassment can occur in independent contractor (third-party service provider) relationships, not just in the employment relationship between employers and employees. Situations can arise when a professional, such as a therapist, attorney, or physician, gains a position of trust and manipulates it for sexual and relationship ends.

These cases aren't about love; they're about control. An attorney tells his client that he won't represent her further in the trial unless she goes to bed with him. Or a therapist advises a patient that they should have a relationship because the patient would find this beneficial. The elements generally are a sleazy attitude, control, and circumstances such that the client can't easily extricate him or herself from the professional relationship without damage.

For example, California created a statutory cause of action when harassment occurs involving a professional. A professional relationship is defined very broadly as one involving a client, patient, beneficiary, student, or other party and a "marriage counselor, social worker, attorney, physician, therapist, dentist, real estate agent, appraiser, accountant, banker, trust officer, collection service, financial planner, teacher, landlord, property manager, or a relationship that is *substantially similar to any of the above*." The aggrieved party must prove that the harasser made sexual requests, demands, or advances; that this conduct was unwelcome and persistent; that these actions continued even after the aggrieved party requested that they stop; and that the victim was unable to terminate the professional relationship easily without suffering tangible harm. If the plaintiff (or aggrieved party) is able to prove these elements, then he or she is able to receive actual damages, punitive damages, and attorneys' fees.

The same considerations we have seen before apply. There's no question that unwanted sexual harassment is not to be tolerated, but the problem, again, is the one-size-fits-all approach. It's difficult to distinguish in every case between sexual advances that are invited, uninvited but welcome, offensive but tolerated, flatly rejected, and so intolerable that they adversely affect the professional relationship. It's hard to prove what happened between two people who usually acted in the privacy of the office or at home.

Again, the test is applied in hindsight by trying to evaluate what the real intentions of the actors were at the time: or Will the real truth stand up please? Ex-lovers can be angry and vindictive. Even if a relationship was solid for a time, ex-lovers can lash back and complain that there was professional misconduct. We saw this before with attorney Golden and Anita—the result is not justice, but which side is best able to prove its version of what happened.

A married woman had a very close and satisfying affair with her married rabbi for four years. When the relationship came to an end, she went about her life with purpose and didn't charge sexual harassment. A doctor met and married again after meeting his wife as a patient in his office. The real test under these laws seems to be whether the relationship works out or not.

For those considering a romance with someone covered, let's say, by the California law, the advice is clear and straightforward. First, complete your professional responsibilities before you ask for a date. Second, if you can't, then arrange for someone else to complete those duties, being sure that all of your professional responsibilities are met. Third, remember that honorable motives go much further in life than one-night stands and sexual gratification.

Educational Institutions

Although universities and colleges have fretted over harassment lawsuits, clamping down hard on student and faculty "excesses," people still are taking their chances. Students continually party, date, and get involved more often than colleges would like to admit. Professors still have close relationships with one another, and students and teachers still date—despite the restrictive codes that flatly ban these relationships without exception.

The educational world is admittedly different from business life. Young students at a vulnerable stage in their learning development should be protected from being overly swayed by older professors. High school teachers should not be dating their students, and college instructors shouldn't be involved with 18-year-olds. The difference is the age and experience of the participants.

However, you would think that a thirty-year-old working student would be mature enough to date, whether the opportunity arose at work or in the classroom. You would hope that teachers who become involved even with older students would exercise enough discretion that they don't unintentionally abuse their professional relationship. The problematic element, as with boss-subordinate affairs, is the built-in "control" in these romances due to the mentoring relationship between students and their instructors; some argue that the student can never give informed consent to a teacher, even if they're no longer in the same classroom.

When educational institutions enacted sexual harassment laws (a good idea), some also tried to define all unacceptable conduct, leaving by implication what was permissible (a bad idea). The problem of consent is particularly a problem, especially when deciding whether pursuit, an affair, or even later reconciliation efforts (between two students or professors, but not between a professor and a student) have been welcome or not.

As one college administrator admitted: "We know that there are many more times the number of consensual relationships out there [than sexual harassment claims], but we just want to be careful." A better idea is to rely on administrative hearings to flush out whether conduct's unwelcome or not by looking at each set of facts, not trying to legislate morality or acceptable conduct with a host of rules and regulations—the one-size approach simply doesn't fit romance very well.

Sexual harassment is not to be tolerated, but romance should be. Unfortunately, whether a student is with a student, or a student with a professor, people will have to continue taking their chances that a romance works out—even with someone of similar age and experience, given the broad sweep of these laws.

Where Do You Go?

The prime risks of any workplace romance occur, of course, at the beginning and the end. Whether the problem involves the persistent suitor, a boss-subordinate relationship, or an angry ex-lover, the first direction is within the company. This is the easiest, quickest, least expensive, and best way to handle these problems.

The Buck Stops Here

Trying to work the problem out confidentially with the other party, before the coworkers pick up on what's happening, is the best, first approach. If you aren't interested in someone who has approached you, then tell them nicely that you aren't available. Put yourself in their shoes before being too direct, irritable, or insensitive—remember how you would feel if you were in the same position and receiving that form of rejection.

An assistant told her manager on Secretary's Day that she had a "crush" on him; he didn't say "you're not my type" or "forget it, we're at work." He replied in a soft voice that he liked working with her, but that he couldn't handle anything further other than their working relationship. When she asked again to meet after work, he was still considerate but firm, telling her that he had very little time then for socializing. He never brought it up again and always treated her with respect. They worked well together for years, and both later happily married others.

Remember also that circumstances can change. For example, Anne and Wally (see Chapter 2) knew each other at an investment banking firm. When Wally first asked if Anne would go out to lunch with him, she said, "No, but thanks anyway." Wally's reaction was to smile and inquire, "And why wouldn't you head out with such a handsome fellow?" She told him she was seeing someone else at the time. Wally asked a friend out for lunch instead; later, when he heard Anne was free, he asked again. She accepted this time, and the rest is history.

This doesn't mean that anyone gets three or four bites from the same apple. Use your common sense, and if someone's requests for a date are persistent and bothersome or offensive, then complain to the company when your response isn't enough.

Inside and Outside the Company

When trying to work it out directly doesn't work, ask a friend to intercede. If that doesn't work or you don't want to, then bring the problem to the company's attention. Depending on the size of the business and its policies, this company person could be the owner, your supervisor, the human resources manager, or a designated person. Bounce this off of a friend, if you aren't sure, for the right approach. What you do and how you react can affect your career, whether it's unwanted pursuit or a difficult ex-lover.

Companies take different approaches, depending on their climates: do nothing, talk to both, mediate the differences, work up the discipline ladder (warning, transfer, suspension, termination), or just fire without an appeal. Businesses typically handle such problems in the beginning informally. The executive in charge meets with the complained-about employee and tells him or her what the company needs to have done pursuant to its policies. "Many situations are handled, right then and there," said one manager. "We work out quickly what needs to be done, depending on the facts and situation."

If you're not maneuvering within the company with your lover or partner (as Suzanne and Jeffrey were, for example), then you're handling this alone and are probably upset. When you're working through the company's procedures, remember that you need to exhaust your administrative remedies first before heading outside. Unless the business is stonewalling your complaints, or there's no one in the company you can talk to (including the president), the outlined procedures and policies should be followed. If you can make no headway—which can be the exception these days—talk to a lawyer before you quit your job. Consult Chapter 15, "Read This (Before You Hire a Lawyer)."

Men on the Other Side

Harassment is not exclusively a male problem. Although author Michael Crichton's book and the movie *Disclosure* (the story of a female boss's sexual harassment of her male subordinate) sensationalized this, it's true that women, as well as men, pursue and harass the opposite sex. Carrie said succinctly, "We're now equal to the guys, and I've been just as aggressive in getting someone into bed as they've been."

Although this can be a controversial area, the statistics are proving the case. In a 1995 survey by the U.S. Merit Systems Protection Board of over 20,000 federal workers, 15 percent of the men reported being sexually harassed, compared to about 40 percent of the women. Even the EEOC's own statistics indicate that men file 15 percent of all sexual harassment complaints, and the number of these complaints is increasing 10 percent each year. With greater numbers of women coming into managerial positions, this fact of life shouldn't be too surprising.

At one company, a woman in love refused to leave her coworker alone, continuing to send love notes and E-mail messages, even after she had received a severe warning. It wasn't until after she was suspended for two days without pay that she received the message. "Unfortunately, there can be a double standard, especially when the woman is more discreet," said one executive. "I don't really see many men complaining about unwelcome pursuit, because you'd think they'd want it. However, control is control, whether you're a guy or a gal."

The attorneys and courts are readily following men down this warpath. A federal judge ordered Domino's Pizza chain to pay a former employee more than $237,000 in the first case involving female sexual harassment brought by the federal government (a 1995 case). The man alleged that his female supervisor had squeezed his buttocks, commented about his body, and made inappropriate comments. The supervisor fired him six days after saying she loved him and he then refused to move in with her. The company didn't act on his complaints and lost the lawsuit.

In the case of the "Jenny Craig Eight," eight men sued the weight-loss treatment company, alleging that they were terminated, denied promotions, or given unfavorable assignments just because they were outside the female-dominated corporate culture. There's no question about it, either sex can harass and act badly—although men have been the prime culprits. On the more positive side, both sexes also find, nurture, and sustain close long-term relationships many more times than they harass one another.

When the Accused Fights Back

Companies can't automatically dock the men in favor of the women when sexual harassment claims are made: this is a violation of the Constitution's equal protection clause, among other legal arguments. Consequently, men have been hitting back hard when fired due to a sexual harassment complaint. Their legal weapon of choice has been the wrongful termination lawsuit, and this is being used more and more each year.

A jury recently awarded $26.6 million in damages to one Mr. MacKenzie, who had been dismissed by his employer, the Miller Brewing Company, for telling his secretary about a *Seinfeld* TV episode that had a racy twist (the "*Seinfeld* verdict"). IBM was sued four years ago by an ex-employee, Daniel Manicelli, who was fired when the firm discovered that he was dating a subordinate; Mr. Manicelli won a $375,000 jury verdict, which was upheld on appeal. This court decision contributed to the change in IBM's policy whereby bosses involved in an affair with a subordinate generally may continue the relationship, as long as the reporting aspect of that relationship is ended. This approach is an emerging trend being used by firms today to keep their valued employees when confronted with a boss-subordinate relationship (and it avoids wrongful termination litigation).

The weapons employed by those accused of harassment include bringing a counterclaim of defamation against the complainant. A Houston deputy sheriff, accused by a female subordinate of sexual harassment in her lawsuit (as well as in television and newspaper interviews), countersued for defamation and was awarded a $3,000,000 judgment against the woman. The chairman of the New Jersey Republican Party (and departing assembly speaker) filed a defamation action against the senior legislative assistant who accused him of sexual harassment in her lawsuit. A professor at the Chicago Theological Seminary filed suit against the seminary for defamation over their handling of a student's sexual harassment complaint; the university had issued a formal reprimand and put notices of the reprimand in the mailbox of every student and teacher at the school. From general counsels to airline pilots, lawsuits and countersuits are filed to answer claims of sexual harassment. It is a plaintiff lawyer's heaven and a company's worst nightmare.

Lawrence J. Ellison, the founder and CEO of Silicon Valley's Oracle Corporation, ended up in a widely publicized sexual harassment case. He had been dating various women, including an office assistant, Adelyn Lee. When she was dismissed from the company for poor performance, Ms. Lee filed a wrongful termination lawsuit alleging that she had been bullied into having the affair. Mr. Ellison testified that he had a relationship with Ms. Lee but said he had not ordered her fired. Oracle paid Ms. Lee $100,000 to settle the lawsuit, and she retracted her accusations. Later, she was convicted of perjury and falsifying documents for sending a phony E-mail message that helped her with her lawsuit. She was sentenced to one year in prison and ordered to return the $100,000. The criminal conviction has been appealed by Ms. Lee and is pending at this time.

Employees and companies alike must remember that motive is all important. Whether it's a boss-subordinate affair or unwanted attention, businesses must look into not only why the complained-of conduct occurred but also why the charges were brought in the first place. Harassment complaints have been made to get even with someone for a bad review or for breaking off a relationship. Unfortunately, these knee-jerk reactions trivialize the legitimate complaints—but people act for their own interests and sometimes not in the best of ways. The redeeming factor is that there are many more employees with "romance in their hearts" than "greed and dollars in their minds."

How Do the Sexes Differ?

"It depends," says one expert in the field. "Substantially," says another researcher. As you would expect, the sexes vary widely in their approach to sexual harassment, among other work-related areas.

Charles Pierce, Herman Aguinis, and Susan Adams conducted a study using 226 sheriff's department employees (Pierce, Aguinis, Adams, 1998). The results were based on these employees' reactions to reading a vignette that portrayed a dissolved workplace romance with a sexual harassment accusation, the accused being a man and the complainant a woman. Their findings were:

1. The blame for sexual harassment varied depending on the accused's and the complainant's motives for participating in the romance.
2. Males responded more favorably to the accused while females responded more favorably to the complainant.
3. Males and females responded less favorably toward the accused when a chain-of-command relationship was involved, as opposed to a relationship involving coworkers or peers.
4. Males and females with positive as opposed to negative attitudes toward romance and sexual intimacy at work responded more favorably toward the accused.

However, this research didn't indicate an attitudinal difference by sex toward romance and sexual intimacy at work. According to the authors, the lack of such a sexual attitude difference may have been due to the male and female employees in this research having received sexual harassment training and being aware of their organization's sexual harassment policy, among other factors.

There are numbers of surveys in the areas of sexual attitudinal differences at work and in relationships. The findings vary widely, depending on the size of the sample, targeted group, sample questions, research approach, and other built-in biases. Depending on the selected industry, individual company climate, and the types of workers approached, the research supports quite different conclusions. Books have been and will continue to be written on the different attitudes and approaches taken by the sexes at work and in their relationships. As one married woman said, "The difference are there; we just think differently . . . and hurrah for the difference. The little disagreements even make my day more interesting, as long as I win." Her husband said the same thing.

What About Cultural Differences?

In this age of global trade and workplace diversification, you would expect problems to arise from cultural differences between workers. A man culturally trained to arduously pursue the "beautiful and opposite" sex as an art and to never take no for an answer would create friction in a U.S. workplace—and this would be putting it mildly. For example, a Guatemalan businessman explained his pursuit of one complaining woman as being "not only part of my heritage but the way my father courted my mother."

Well, the corporations aren't buying it, at least for their operations in the United States. Randall was the senior vice president of human resources for a large financial services company of which some one-half worked overseas. He observed: "With my company in the United States, you might be called on the carpet for speaking too loudly to your secretary or thrown out for yelling at her to 'Get that coffee in here!' If you traveled to our operations in some Latin American countries, they got away with that and a lot more. That's just the way they do things down there. There's more flirtation, touching, suggestive remarks, and allowable continued pursuit.

"Our Paris office looked like a brothel with the way the women were allowed to dress. Back in the United States, it was all button down and prim and proper. It wasn't close between the two offices as to what was permitted in either clothes or actions. The question, however, is what happens when these cultures are mixed. Let's take, for example, the mega–telephone call centers where the employees are thrown together to service an entire continent. In England, you would have seven cultures together to serve Europe. In India, there were Pakistani and Indian employees, whose countries have feuded with each other for years, working side by side.

"Our policy was that no slack is allowed. There is sensitivity training and workshops, along with written policies and supervisors that enforce them. Our message to all our workers in the United States is: you can't behave here the way you do back home or the way your friends and relatives do. If you want to work here for us, then you do it our way, according to our rules—inappropriate behavior won't be tolerated, even if it would be in your country."

Meanwhile, Ted is the human resources vice president for a computer software company. He said: "We have numbers of fine employees from different backgrounds and cultures. Our message is very clear to everyone: if you work here, you can't use cultural differences as a defense. They won't be considered when there's a bona fide complaint about sexual harassment. You will work and act respectfully with everyone, just as you do with me.

"I flew to Hong Kong a few years ago. The manager was flaunting an affair that he had had with one of his employees. He allowed the working environment to deteriorate and morale was down. I asked around and discovered that the employees weren't clear in their own minds as to what was acceptable behavior and what wasn't. He was gone that day."

The message is clear that you go with the company line, and it makes a big difference whether your firm's policies are restrictive or not.

Chapter Six

How Cold's the Climate?

"Love endures. It persists in the most arid of places," said one manager. "Romance is romance, and it'll be there no matter what policies you put in place." In some corporations, it's encouraged; in others, romance and dating among coworkers is discouraged. All in all, romance happens, no matter what management does.

The question is how does the company view its workforce? Does its management look at employee interaction as a worrisome problem, potentially leading the company into dangerous sexual harassment charges and expensive lawsuits? Or do the officers feel comfortable with their workforce, trusting them to work on behalf of the company's goals, and, in turn, supporting their employees with progressive policies such as day care and recreational centers, flexible workweeks, ease of social interaction, and a "hands off" attitude? In both cases, strong sexual harassment policies are in place and followed. Which company would you prefer working for?

Well-run companies recognize that people attract each other and work within this basic fact as a cornerstone of their human resources policy. This translates into:

- Maintaining at least a neutral (if not positive) attitude toward employee dating;
- Supporting the inevitable marriages that occur;
- Becoming involved only when relationships end and cause workforce disturbances (but supervisors are trained on what to do);
- Being watchful for chain-of-command relationships, then taking steps to end potential favoritism charges, but retaining those employees; and

- Most important, supporting concepts of employee trust, gender equality, day care and elder care, family leave, and other "pro-interactive" policies.

Companies have always faced a competitive market in finding, attracting, and retaining the best workers. The old, "theory X" days of "father knows best; we'll tell you what to do—or else you're out" have been discarded. The more modern "theory Y" days of "we know our employees work better if we assume they're self-motivated and trustworthy" is being supplemented by pro-interactive theories.

As women stream into the workplace, they demand the right to work at the same company with their partners. If this condition isn't met, then both find a firm where it is. A company's strongest asset is its workforce, and the better the workforce, the better that business does in today's competitive global economy. It is a business's attitude toward its workers that is its most important policy.

The Corporate Climate

Corporate climate is a company's culture and philosophy. This climate is the summation of its attitudes, values, and approach to its workers. Those in power enforce their definition of the company's culture.

Industry environments alone can create the general climate of companies operating in that field. For example, the corporate culture of software development companies is quite different from that of more conservative manufacturing or banking companies. Culture can also be a function of how young the managers and employees are: a higher proportion of single, younger, socially more adventuresome employees will force a firm into a less conservative climate.

One executive said, "A no-brainer is that some fields encourage or discourage romance just by the industry. The entertainment, real estate, and software development industries tend to be more liberal and, as a whole, are more accepting of office romances. Investment banking, commercial banking, and the large accounting firms are viewed as being less tolerant and more restrictive—although there can be differing environments depending on individual companies."

The studies have shown that company cultures regarded as "conservative" or "traditional" are also neutral or discourage office romances. Businesses viewed as "creative" or "action oriented" are typically neutral or encourage these relationships. Gary is a Harvard

MBA in his early fifties who has worked for years in the theatrical and entertainment world. He observed: "The entertainment/theater world is incestuous, romantically and professionally. It's a project-based industry so relationships pop up and then disappear all the time. It's part of the creative process. I've dated a number of actresses over the years, married one, and had long-term relationships with three others. I've always been attracted to real talent and found it easier professionally if I'm with the best, most talented actress around. That way, no one involved with the production can gripe she got the role because she was sleeping with the producer.

"My fiancée is a very talented actress, and I run a theater. I had decided to take a new tack and try to keep my romantic life separate from my business life. She decided she wanted me, so we got together. We've been living together now for two years. If Karen all of a sudden becomes a star, which she is very capable of doing, our relationship may change. But we'll cross that bridge when we come to it."

We discussed Judy Kaiser in Chapter 1. To make ends meet while looking for a job (she had recently graduated from college), she worked as a waitress for a large, prestigious hotel. Her observations: "There was a lot of flirting going around, and it was a young crowd. It was fun. I was young, pretty, and a flirt. It was so much fun that when I found a corporate job, I kept that job for a few months more (the money was also good). There was no policy against dating at the hotel, and the employees took advantage of it—and I looked forward to going to work. Frankly, it made no difference whether they had a policy in effect or not, all of us would have ignored it any way."

Companies within industries, of course, can be either pro-interactive or restrictive. One HMO chain was particularly restrictive with its policies. The human resources executive in charge said pointedly: "The clear policy here is that what you do on your own time is your own business [a typical response]. However, it's understood that if you become involved with someone, then one of you, or both of you, will leave the company [not as typical]." Another executive with a large hospital said, "You're always going to have people coming together, and we don't try to track those things. However, if someone complains or there's a boss-subordinate relationship, then we will intervene and work something out [more typical]."

Harry, the ex–general counsel of a large Fortune 500 company, said: "It depends not only on whether the culture is conservative or liberal, but also on the type of job. Are you covered in soot from working in a coal mine or pounding nails, or are you in a yuppie advertising agency where people play racquetball after hours? Are they many women where you work or in that department? Practical things like that make a difference.

"Are you thirty or fifty years old? Are you in a fun group? Remember that there are also the Club Meds of work. For example, the parent company I worked for was conservative with wingtip shoes; however, one of our subsidiaries was a multilevel marketer of natural health foods. Their annual Christmas party was a free-for-all where everyone left with somebody else. There's also a big difference whether your job is selling outside or inside balancing the books, not to mention where you boss is at that time."

Depending on the firm, corporate "rituals" can develop that are pro-interactive in and by themselves. Regular social functions encourage more social interaction and a more liberal climate. Company climates can shift overnight, as management changes or reacts to a discrimination lawsuit or EEOC investigation.

Interesting enough, departments within the same companies can be either more liberal or more conservative, depending on the function and the people in charge. For example, the marketing department can be freewheeling, while the accountants aren't; this can be reversed, simply by changing the managers in charge. Look around your company and decide for yourself.

For example, Matt, the seasoned executive, disclosed: "I knew several couples who dated within the company. Most of those relationships were long term or ended in marriage. They would try their level best to keep it a secret but there always were the rumors. One of my assistants did pull it off. She had been dating another employee for several months, and although I heard the rumors, I discounted them because her office was so close to mine.

"They went public with their relationship when they sent out their wedding announcements. Some people were surprised, but some people had already figured it out before the news. This couple had no choice but to operate this way, because our company's informal but strong policy discouraged dating at the office. This all changed later.

"The marketing department, however, was just something else. We had some young women there who seduced anyone that came around. If one of them wanted some guy, then that was it for him. They dated customers and had one heck of a time. I have to admit that some of them were cute and they did get the sales. And get this, it made absolutely no difference as to their advancement or careers."

A particular department's climate can depend not just on the person in charge. A conservative, "hands on" executive ran a large company's financial department. However, his second-in-command, a younger single man, was the exact opposite. Although the single man outwardly espoused all of his superior's concepts, the coworkers would come to him with their private woes because he was more understanding.

Smaller companies have widely differing climates, ranging from the very conservative "you're gone if you do it" to the small real estate developer where Steve and Alice worked. Jack Erdlen, vice president of Romac International's human resources division, observed:

> It's interesting to see how small firms differ from the larger ones in this area. Smaller companies are more likely to put off having a written policy in place, saying they'll get to it later, when they should be doing this now. Although small firms can make decisions faster with more flexibility, their policies are more dependent on the one owner or person who's in control. It is this person's social philosophy that's key to how restrictive or progressive a small company's policies are. Small companies now are increasingly centering their attentions to having written policies in effect.

As a business becomes smaller in size, the options available to couples and ex-lovers also become smaller. As the ability to transfer to other parts of the company lessens, the ability of ex-lovers to work out their differences becomes more important. The owner's philosophy, not individual officers or managers, matters.

Ask about a particular business's climate *before* you accept a job offer—this caution can save giant headaches later. Or, as more and more employees are doing, if your present company isn't in tune with its workers, find one that is. Even in tough job markets, employees look for firms where the work is fun and interesting. You need to be comfortable in your running shoes before you can win any race.

A Few Cases

What's impressive is that many couples endure and stay together, regardless of the policies in place. Whether they stay at a particular company is another story.

Bill and Vicki

We were introduced to Bill and Vicki in Chapter 1. They worked for a management consulting company, and Bill was Vicki's supervisor. He was fast-tracking up the company's ladder. Bill was forty, recently separated, and Vicki was ten years younger. They worked for a company that took a dim view of employee dating, especially among those in boss-subordinate reporting relationships. Vicki commented: "I was attracted to Bill soon after I joined his department. He was easy-going on the outside, but I could feel his strength just by looking in his eyes. We worked closely together for a few months and hit it off. He was having some real problems with his marriage, but he didn't talk about that with me. At least, until after we got to know each other better. I really liked him.

"We flew together on a consulting project with a Southern automotive parts manufacturer. Our hotel rooms were on the same floor, but not beside each other, because our firm's informal policy prohibited any hint of impropriety. It was after a particularly grueling meeting that we ended up in an empty restaurant for a late dinner. Although we were tired, we really talked with one another that night.

"It was getting late, but afterward we walked next door to an indoor nightclub and ordered after-dinner drinks. As we sipped our drinks, the dance band started to play one of those haunting tunes. Bill asked me to dance, and I quickly accepted. As we whirled over the floor, my heart beat louder and louder. I was feeling nervous and loving it all at the same time.

"I turned toward him and invited a kiss. It was more passionate than I could ever have dreamed. We began carrying on like teenagers on the dance floor. Without a word we left for my room and made love until the early morning. Bill soon left for his room, just in case someone called. He called me soon afterward. He was nervous and said we should have breakfast together. That's all he said, and the line went dead.

"He apologized at breakfast, said he really cared for me, but that it would be the death for both of our careers if we continued. The company performed financial audits of publicly traded companies, as well, and there were strict rules to avoid any conflicts of interest. Married couples couldn't work on the same account or even work in the same office. It was so conservative that the policy manual stated there had to be a wall between every possible perceived problem, and our type of relationship was flatly prohibited. That's all it said, but we knew that at least one of us was gone if our relationship was discovered.

"I was tired from not having enough sleep. I felt so sad inside, and I guess my face showed it. I took a deep breath and instinctively reached over to his face. The next thing I knew was that Bill leaned over and kissed me. When I looked at him, I knew that he felt as I did. We completed our assignment that day and flew back to New York. On the trip back, we talked about everything, from what we didn't like at work to what we liked to eat. When the plane was landing, Bill said he wasn't sure how we'd do it, but he wanted us to stay together. That was exactly how I felt too.

"When we would be alone in his office, we wouldn't kiss or do anything. The reason was simple: we didn't want to start something that would end up on his conference table. We'd try our best not to make any romantic eye contact, but a few pet words and we knew when to meet over at his place. We would leave separately and take different subways or taxis. We would rendezvous in dark dinner places, late at night. On Thursdays and Fridays, I spent the night at his place. We'd take the same route to work, then split up a few blocks and come in to our offices separately. At times one of us would start feeling anxious, insecure, even guilty about our relationship and work, but we would talk about this together and work it all out.

"I don't know if it was bad luck or not, but one weekend we were enjoying an intimate dinner on the other side of town. I couldn't believe it, but someone who worked with me came up to us with her date. We chatted briefly, and then they took off. Bill and I were worried, and it turned out that we had a right to be.

"She apparently complained to a senior vice president buddy about favoritism. Bill was called the next week into that senior VP's office. He told Bill that becoming a vice president around there would be difficult, if he caught his drift, and ordered him to stop our affair. Bill and I talked about it later, and I decided that I should be the one who left. Bill told that to the senior VP. I was transferred to another department and it took me time to find another position.

"We continued seeing one another discreetly during this time. However, he received less favorable marks on a review than he had ever received before. We knew it was because of the politics in that conservative company. So the handwriting was on the wall. It took him a few months to find the same type of work at the same position and salary, but he did it. I joined that same firm, and we told them that we were engaged. We were by that time, and we married one year later. We're still at this company, both of us enjoying solid career advancements although in different areas."

Steve and Alice

A fax poll for *Inc. Magazine* in August 1992 indicated that 83 percent of large companies (those with one hundred or more employees) had sexual harassment policies in place. Only 25 percent of small companies (six to ten employees) had these policies. The corporate climate of smaller companies is many times dictated by the personal philosophies of the owner and not by concerns about harassment. These owners don't feel the public image pressures that larger businesses do; however, all companies, regardless of size, should have sexual harassment policies in place—for both ethical and practical reasons. The trend is in this direction, especially given the latest U.S. Supreme Court decisions and as lawyers continue to bring more lawsuits.

Steve and Alice were fortunate and admittedly so. The company they worked for didn't discourage office romances, although Alice worked directly for Steve as his assistant. Although the owner was absolutely committed to success, he was equally charismatic and motivated in "living the good life." The community viewed him as a happily married, family man. What it didn't know was that he loved women and pursued extramarital affairs with the same gusto that he did his business ventures. His companies didn't have nonfraternization rules because his life was dictated by the very opposite principle.

Companies can be conservative, as well. Another business in the same community was active in real estate development. A conservative man who adored his wife and actively discouraged his employees from dating clients or coworkers owned it. When one property manager, Jimmy, left the "rocking and rolling" real estate company to join the more conservative one, he became just as conservative. Although single at the time, Jimmy quickly settled in with one woman whom he had met at a chamber of commerce meeting. He didn't date anyone else the entire time he was there—a complete turnabout from his dating habits at the first company.

Alex and Samantha

Alex was a professor in his mid-fifties who taught English at a college in Colorado. He had been married for twenty years, but the relationship had fallen apart. Their kids had grown up and moved away, and he and his wife hadn't had sex for several years. While working on a research project involving an eighteenth-century poet, he met Samantha at the university library. She was working part time to make ends meet there while she completed her degree. Samantha was in her mid-twenties and living with her parents to save money.

Samantha helped Alex with his research. As they worked together, a fondness developed between them. They would "talk, talk, talk" all the time. One evening, Samantha stayed past her regular hours to help Alex. When it became late, they decided to call it quits. While talking in the hallway, Alex kept thinking about whether he should lean down and kiss her. It seemed the chemistry was there and that she wanted to kiss him, as well. When he leaned to kiss her, however, he spotted the large sign above them warning students and teachers about the dangers of sexual harassment. He kissed her anyway, trembling with worry about what would happen underneath the school's policy and what could happen if this didn't work out.

When Samantha recalled that first kiss much later, she chuckled at the thought of gentle Alex, nervous as he spotted the university's rules on sexual harassment. It would have been his head—but she kissed him back. Their romantic involvement now was under way.

One night in a secluded park, they made love for the first time. They kept their relationship a secret. First, Samantha's parents would "shoot Alex" if they ever found out since he was nearly thirty years older. Next in line, Alex's wife was a problem; she, as Alex said, was "certifiably crazy." Third and not the least, the university would take a dim view of their romance. Although people had their suspicions, Alex and Samantha were able to keep it quiet.

When Alex told his wife that he wanted a divorce to marry Samantha, she went "absolutely nuts," threatening him, Samantha, and his career. Later, she called the chairman of the English department, telling him about everything that was going on. The administration did disapprove strongly due to its legal worries and severely warned Alex, but Alex was tenured and Samantha loved him. Everyone held their breath that the relationship would stick, and there wouldn't be a harassment problem.

In fact, the relationship prospered. Alex divorced his wife, and he and Samantha married. However, the reaction of the administration and a few coworkers soured both of them toward the college. They just had a beautiful little girl, and Alex recently gave notice of his retirement after twenty years of service.

Terry and Marlene

Terry and Marlene were managers for the same business conglomerate but hadn't met before, owing to the size and diversity of its operations. They played against each other in a volleyball match in their company league. After this, they became acquainted and signed up to play together on the same teams, including the company's softball league. They were dating within a few days. Several months later, they married. They're still with the company, and they wouldn't have met, or started dating, had it not been for the company's pro-interactive policies.

Two of the organizations described above either lost valued employees or created an enduring dislike—and they didn't have to. If the corporate climate had been more progressive, there would have been none of this friction and discomfort. Further, they would have kept productive and happy employees. There is a lesson here to be learned.

Climates Vary

We've discussed a few individuals and how their working and personal relationships were affected by company culture. Let's hear more from Randall, the ex–senior vice president of a large financial services firm, then about Autodesk, a large software development company based in San Francisco.

Randall

"At this company, you work so hard that there's no possibility of having any social life outside it—and relationships at work are so incredibly frowned upon there. Although we had a very strong diversity program in effect, strong written sexual harassment policy, diversity workshops, and training, the atmosphere was stifling. Harassment is taken very seriously at this company, and the accuser wins in a tie. One executive apparently made an unwelcome touch, although no one else was around, and he was gone in two days. The company told the executive that if you fight this, you risk your severance package. He chose the money.

"We don't have a policy on dating or socialization. However, the unwritten but well-known rule is that you don't socialize—you just don't, no matter who you are, because of the potential for rumors. Although this company is so strict, it takes a 'wait and see' approach. They wait until someone complains or there was something concrete that the company could rely on. Then the heavy hitters come down. As you are promoted higher into the company's hierarchy, such as a vice president, then you are expected to keep your hands off the merchandise. It makes no difference what your intentions are, how much in love, the type of relationship, or that you are even single.

"When something comes to the company's attention, a superior calls the couple into their office and gives a simple but direct ultimatum: 'The relationship has to stop, or one of you leaves. It's up to you to choose which one is out of here.' That's it: either the romance goes or you do. And we've lost good managers over this. Contributing further to this environment was that the head of one of our divisions made some poor decisions a few years ago.

"He tried to streamline the organization and laid off a number of people. Unfortunately, they fought back legally, won based on discrimination grounds, and cost the company millions of dollars in the ensuing settlement and legal fees. As a result of this, the attorneys made a presentation to the board, saying in essence 'institute a zero tolerance rule to prevent this from happening again.' This company tipped too far in implementing those recommendations.

"It is now allowing more married couples to work here, but it's also taking real care to guard against favoritism or spouses' working for one another. They've had to make this change, although there was resistance at first, because good, solid husband-and-wife teams were simply leaving to work for companies that were more flexible. The company is going to have to change more. It has a worsening management reputation at this time."

Autodesk

An officer of the company commented: "We have over 2,600 people in thirty-six countries with 60 percent of our employees located overseas. We're headquartered in the San Francisco Bay area with 1,000 workers, and our sales presently are over $600 million dollars annually. Most of our employees are in their thirties and forties, and they're good people. Although I'm in my fifties, I'm one of the oldest people on staff.

"We don't have a policy on dating. Our philosophy is that you don't legislate morality, and that such a policy would create an environment that we simply don't want. We have an open policy on sexual preference; in fact, 10 to 15 percent of our workers are gay. It's okay to come out with your preference, if you want, as we're quite respectful of diversity. Whether it's same-sex or opposite-sex relationships, our company is comfortable with work relationships.

"We're family friendly. In fact, we have several generations of workers here right now, such as a grandmother, mother, and granddaughter. Children are welcome at our social events, and our employees can even bring their dogs to work. We have many engineers here who work long hours, so if your dog would be left alone at home, then you can bring it in with you. We do have a manual of 'Dog Behavior' and a rule of 'Three poops and you're out.'

"We take any hint of sexual harassment very seriously and don't tolerate it even in our offices overseas where local culture might have a different attitude. We won't fire a worker for a dirty joke, but we'll let him or her know that these acts won't be tolerated.

"Very few of our policies are written down, because we trust our employees. All of our managers attend a one-day seminar on topics including harassment. If someone comes to them with a complaint, then we promptly investigate and take the appropriate steps to ensure that the conduct doesn't happen again. Although we have had many romantic attachments at work, we haven't had one sexual harassment complaint here for over two years, even with the size of our workforce.

"Our philosophy dates back to the company's founders, and a lot of our employees' social life derives from work, although now we also have married couples with children here. Everyone joins in our firm's activities. For example, we have a 'Friday beer night' tradition that dates back to our very beginnings. It's a once a month tradition, and as there are twelve of us on the executive staff, each one takes a particular month. We go all out on our assigned nights; for example, I hosted a Saint Patrick's Day celebration in March. We have a fun place to work, and we do get a lot done."

Pro-Interactive Companies

There's no question where people would rather work. Pro-interactive companies want their employees to interact positively with one another and to work in a mutually supportive environment. These firms trust their employees and make a two-way bargain: we'll treat you with mutual respect and support, just as you in turn support our goals and objectives.

S. C. Johnson Wax

Johnson Wax is a privately held company. It is one of the leading manufacturers of products in household cleaning (Pledge, Windex, Glade, Vanish, and more), personal care (Edge Shaving Gel and Aveeno Bath Products), and insect control (including Raid and Off!). It is also a leading supplier of products and services for retail, commercial, industrial, and institutional facilities. It employs more than 15,000 people worldwide with 4,500 located in the United States and 3,000 of those in Wisconsin. Despite its visibility and financial success, Johnson Wax is a leader among pro-interactive businesses.

The company is continually ranked in *Working Mother's* "100 Best Companies for Working Mothers" (now ten years running), as well as *Fortune's* "100 Best Companies to Work for in America." It opened a child care center in 1985 for its workers; this became a 20,600 square foot complex for 250 children that provides full-day kindergarten, summer camp, and before- and after-school care. It provides parental leave, job sharing, flextime, work at home, compressed workweeks, phase-back time for new mothers, alternative work scheduling, casual dress days, scholarships for employee children, profit sharing, and many other benefits—you name it, and they've probably done it.

Johnson Wax's statement of values is indicative of its corporate climate: "We believe the fundamental vitality and strength of our world-wide company lies in our people, and we commit ourselves to maintain good relations about all employees around the world based on a sense of participation, mutual respect, and an understanding of common objectives."

It owns a 146-acre park located midway between its two prime business centers in Wisconsin. Open to all employees and their families, this center includes an aquatic center with a children's pool, whirlpool, fitness room, and an aerobics facility; a stocked fishing pond; picnic sites, softball fields, and outdoor tennis courts; a miniature golf and driving range; and volleyball courts, playground areas, archery range, and horseshoe pits. The Lighthouse Resort in northern Wisconsin is a seventeen-cottage lake resort. There are daily commuter buses to Chicago, a company theater, and travel clubs. Facilities around the world are available to their international workforce with benefits similar to those in the United States.

According to JoAnne Brandes, senior vice president–general counsel:

> Our philosophy is that your greatest resource is your employees. Women came into the workforce in expanding numbers during the eighties and into management, and parents wanted child care and other family-friendly services and policies. We responded to these changing employee needs in order to retain the best employees.
>
> We know that numbers of our married people have met at work, and we don't have a written policy on dating. We don't need it. Just look at the activities the company backs. We do have a policy that prohibits chain-of-command reporting relationships. We have a strong, extensive policy on sexual harassment, although we don't have many problems in this regard, as you would expect.
>
> Dating hasn't been a big issue in this company either, and we don't get too involved in our employees' personal lives. We trust our employees, and they, in turn, trust us. Companies need to be progressive to keep the best employees—that is the way of today's business climate.

Delta Air Lines

Bill Berry, Delta's director of corporate communications, says:

> We don't have any rules against dating. Our expectations are simple: you need to maintain a professional and businesslike approach at work, and this guideline applies to all work-related relationships at our company. If this dating leads to marriage, then that's fine. Our only guideline in that case is that we don't allow one lover or spouse to supervise the other. Other than that, as long as people continue to maintain the same proper business conduct, then they can date, marry, and work in the same office—even in the same department.

Johnson and Johnson

Chris Kjeldsen, vice president of the Community & Workplace Program for Johnson and Johnson, says:

> In the early eighties, we knew numbers of women were and would continue to enter our workforce, including taking over quite responsible managerial and executive positions. We realized that we

needed to accommodate this trend, including working mothers, elder care, and other quality-of-life issues. Hence we adopted various programs which were picked up as one of *Working Mother*'s best one hundred companies. Some fifteen years ago, if you met someone at work and married, then one of them had to leave. We would try to arrange a transfer, but if one wasn't available, then they would have to pick which one left. That was the dark ages.

We then said that this approach was crazy. We had more and more workers meeting and marrying, including workers that were living together. Now, we say that you can continue your relationship, married or not, but you can't supervise one another; you can work in the same department—but if one party has access to personal, personnel, or medical records, then you can't. We've had continuing high morale and less sexual harassment problems than most companies in our industries.

It does come down to a company's philosophy. Ours goes back to our credo which was that our responsibility was to our customers, employees, community, and stockholders. We added later in writing to this that we must be mindful of the ways needed to help our employees help their families.

And All the Others

An entire book could be devoted to pro-interactive companies. Like Johnson Wax and Johnson and Johnson, these firms believe in and trust their employees. They encourage their workers with corporate amenities and accept social interaction in the workforce. They expect that their workers will work long hours, be rewarded in return, and even fall in love with fellow employees at the same time.

For starters, there's Bankers Trust located in New York City; Odwalla, a bottler of fruit juices and water, headquartered in Half Moon Bay, California; Borland Computers, a software company in Scotts Valley, California; Ben & Jerry's, the manufacturer of premium ice cream, located in Waterbury, Vermont; Apple Computers, the computer manufacturer in Cupertino, California; Bain & Company, a management consultant company, located in Boston; Quad/Graphics, a printing company located in Sussex, Wisconsin; and Tom's of Maine, a natural personal care products company in Kennebunk, Maine. There's AT&T, Corning, IBM, Ford, Autodesk—and the list goes on and on.

Further, it seems evident that the more "pro" a company is toward women and their careers, the more flexible that firm is with romance. Firms on *Working Mother*'s survey of the "100 Best Companies for Working Mothers," compiled by Milton Moskowitz for years, share not only top benefits for women and working mothers, but also a tendency toward a flexible approach with office romances. In fact, 30 percent of the companies on that list (see Appendix 2 for the complete 1998 listing) made it onto *Fortune*'s "100 Best Companies to Work for in America," by Robert Levering and again Milton Moskowitz. This indicates again that well-managed companies are just that, including their approach toward how men and women relate together at work. This doesn't mean that every firm on these lists will have a pro-interactive approach—but it does mean that many lean that way.

My apologies to those pro-interactive firms that aren't mentioned. There's only so much space—and the list of large and small ones would take up volumes. However, please keep in mind that being mentioned on these lists or in this book doesn't necessarily mean that a specific office romance and its circumstances will be sanctioned there. It depends on all the facts, as well as that CEOs can change and managers in the same firm can have different philosophies.

It's an Attitude

Springfield Remanufacturing, a company that rebuilds over 50,000 truck, refrigerator, and heavy-duty engines each year, is located in Springfield, Missouri. It employs presently nearly 1000 employees and has sales approaching $150 million per year. The company's sales have enjoyed a near tenfold increase, all since its spin-off from International Harvester in 1983, and its employees own it.

This is a pro-interactive company that heavily endorses employee socializing and interaction. For example, the firm finances twenty-two "activity committees" that support functions ranging from picnics and softball games to employees who are starting up company-related enterprises. But it isn't the employee-friendly concepts that stand out, as much as it is Springfield's basic philosophy and its climate.

John P. Stack, Springfield's chief executive, said:

> There's so much in life that needs to be shared, and we need to wipe out the perceptions of differences and inequality—what the Harvard Business School doesn't teach you is heart and soul. I rose up from the ranks and looked in the eyes of my friends. I saw what happened when you went from hourly to salary and became a manager: you lost some of your humanity along the way.

We teach around here to "open up the books," that you can make a difference. We want you [the employee] to build up your esteem and to learn that you can win. We're all people and companies need to reduce the barriers between their people. We want our people to see that they can take risks and fail—and that's okay.

I worked for a Fortune 500 company once before and saw the barriers that were raised as people "rose up" inside the company. The rule was "you don't socialize" and that was crazy. We've had a 15 percent growth each year for the last fifteen years, and we run the numbers and concepts. However, we methodically measure attitude just as strong: you gave your word to someone, and we will measure you against your word.

We respect our people. . . . There's a lot of profit in trust, and trust is an organization's culture. You don't measure this by any quarter-to-quarter fluctuations, but it's there in a company's earnings expectations and as that increases over the years.

How Does Pro-Interaction Develop?

Professor Lisa Troyer advises, "The reasons for an individual company's approach to this area vary widely. It can be based on the chief executive office and upper management's decision, come up from lower ranking workers, even occur when the company later doesn't have a clear reason for why that policy evolved."

Burke Stinson of AT&T stated:

Our pro-interactive policies dated from two important events in our history. The first was when the U.S. Government broke us up in 1984, whereby we decided not to weight ourselves down with a lot of written policies and regulations—hence the policy of benign neglect on personal relationships. Second, in 1989 we signed a labor contract with the Communications Workers Association, International Brotherhood of Electrical Workers, in which we agreed to flexible workplace programs and child care, elder care, and other workplace benefits run mutually by us and the unions.

What's important is that our philosophy is one based on openness, honesty, and a mutual respect between our workers and ourselves. It's a philosophy of reasonableness and that people know that they will get a fair shake if they come forward with the same fairness."

We previously commented about the Manicelli case involving IBM's liability for the discharge of a twenty-three-year-veteran manager who had been dating a subordinate. This led to a change in IBM's policy whereby bosses involved in an affair with a subordinate may continue the relationship as long as they stop supervising them. This requirement means that the manager must transfer or arrange for another position that doesn't involve that reporting relationship (or some other "stripping" of that supervision)—it also means that IBM doesn't lose well-trained employees due to their work relationships.

Robert DeMallie is the director of external communications for Corning Incorporated. He commented, "Companies which have an underlying respect for their workers have better workforce morale and productivity than those who don't. James R. Houghton, the chairman of the board of directors and who retired three years ago from Corning, was the prime guiding force for the positive changes in the workforce that occurred here."

But, as we have seen, both large and small companies have clearly been turning away from the repressive policies of before to the more pro-interactive policies now growing in force.

Where Would You Work?

"To work in an uptight one?" questioned one executive. "You must be kidding. I did that in my first job and vowed never to do that again." Evaluate how a company is in this area before you accept a job offer. It can make a world of difference.

The lack of a policy can be a policy. For example, if a firm's policy isn't formal and the unwritten rule is that subordinates and bosses can't date, then they may very well be leaving romance alone as a formal policy. However, you will want to check out what the informal policy is between particular managers, the company president, and anyone else who may have authority over your activities.

Working for a progressive company doesn't means that you can be "hyperactive." An Autodesk spokesperson said, "We expect our employees, whether they're dating or not, to perform their responsibilities and not let their personal lives interfere with their jobs." This applies to all companies, no matter how pro-interactive.

Ask Before Drinking at the Well

"I wish I had gotten an idea of what was okay or not okay," said Katherine (whom we discussed in Chapter 1). "Although it probably wouldn't have made a difference as to my problems, at least I would have thought about what I was doing. The breakup was tough, but I made it worse trying to get back together, not thinking about what the company's response would be."

You need to continue monitoring your company's official and informal positions, because they can change as executives and company fortunes do. As Randall reflected, the environment at his company changed overnight to a restrictive one when the company lost a very expensive lawsuit and overreacted. The climate can change to a less intense one just as easily (as we'll see below).

The Trend

Companies are nurturing social relationships more and more because of the satisfaction this brings to their employees and work. The experiences and studies indicate that the more open a company's culture, the less problems it has with sexual harassment charges—not to mention enjoying a more satisfied and committed workforce.

Company policies continue to change, generally to more employee-sensitive ones. Two editors met seven years ago while working for a New York City business publisher. They fell in love, but before they could marry, the woman left to work for another company because their employer had an antinepotism policy in effect. The two married and have been together ever since. If they met today at that same publisher they could come together, marry, and stay there, although one might be reassigned to a different department.

Matt put this into perspective: "When I first came to the firm twenty-five years ago, it discouraged dating and prohibited married couples from working here. Then people who were married could work here, but they couldn't work in the same department or report to one another. Ten years ago, a new human resources manager came in and said that's ridiculous. He changed the rules so employees could date and marry, even work in the same department, but not for one another. The one place married couples couldn't work together was in finance—which made sense due to the 'collusion with checks' problem."

Smaller companies have more of a laissez-faire attitude, because they generally aren't as worried about these considerations as larger firms are. This doesn't mean that they shouldn't be, and their policies understandably depend on the owner's attitudes.

Which Is Best?

As we've seen, two approaches are taken (although there are "middle grounds"). Some authors write: "Although there are possible difficulties with 'no fraternization' policies, they can prevent more problems than they cause if carried out properly." This strict approach forgets that trying to regulate love in the office creates greater problems—unequal policy enforcement, the difficulty of distinguishing unacceptable "dating" from friendships that aren't romantic, and the threat to privacy rights of workers—and it just doesn't work. More important, the overwhelming majority of firms don't attempt to police their workforce this way.

The argument for not having a repressive policy can also be observed in the experiences of Staples, a Boston-based discount office supplies retailer. Martin Hanaka, the president of Staples, was having an extramarital affair in late 1997 with a member of the support staff, Cheryl Gordon. Following Hanaka's arrest on assault charges (alleging that he had grabbed her arm at her apartment and spun her around), which were subsequently dropped by Ms. Gordon, Staples conducted an internal investigation. It concluded that Hanaka had violated the company's antifraternization policy, which prohibited a manager from having a romantic relationship with a subordinate. The company said that Martin Hanaka had left voluntarily, and Cheryl Gordon is no longer with the company. Had Staples used a more flexible approach, it arguably wouldn't have been forced into a "no win" situation. A respected board member could have interceded, even mediated the quiet termination of that relationship—or some fair handling for both participants—and avoided all the negative, continuing publicity after the first disclosures. You can't affect people's conduct by written prohibitions. These rules simply make difficult situations worse.

It's reasonable for businesses, however, to restrict boss-subordinate relationships, and many companies have taken this position. The question is what guidelines should be in place and how should they be enforced? In turn, *employees should be evaluating their current and prospective employers on how restrictive or pro-interactive their work policies are.*

A Written Dating Policy or Not?

Whether a business should have a formally written, an informal, or even no policy in place depends on the particular company. Some businesses do just fine with nothing other than the culture of the organization, a strong president, or a clear understanding of what's okay. Other companies need and should have written formal but fair guidelines in place. Attorneys, on the other hand, argue for the enactment of formal policies so that if a lawsuit is filed, the company can argue in its defense that it followed those understood, reasonable guidelines in a timely and consistent manner.

Businesses can have differing approaches to handling office romances, even among the largest in any given industry. For example, Chase Manhattan Bank presently has no formal policies in place; BankAmerica prohibits its managers from dating subordinates, but Chase doesn't do so formally. Citicorp has a detailed policy mandating that an employee who becomes involved with a coworker must disclose this, and Banc One Corporation strongly suggests that managers not date their subordinates. However, other banks such as First of American Bank Corp, Comerica, and Norwest Corporation don't prohibit these situations (although all banks take steps to prevent conflict-of-interest situations).

It also depends on the industry itself. For example, highly technological companies usually don't have as many formalized rules as banking or financial institutions with a history of "formalization." Companies with an acquisition bent may have this flexible orientation—or the need for it, if there are several different organizational concepts in place from previous acquisitions.

Professor Lisa Troyer comments:

> Some companies have a culture of informality and autonomy [very few operating rules and a tendency to allow workers to make many decisions about their work]. In these companies, the imposition of formal policies on workplace relationships will more likely be met with resistance. That is, the workers will feel it is an unreasonable imposition—"it's none of their business" and "they don't think I can manage my own life, do they?" There is evidence on the tendency of firms in the high-tech industry to be characterized by greater informality and employee autonomy than firms in the fi-

nance industry. Also, I have evidence from my research on social interaction in teams that the imposition of other types of formal rules and procedures [like operating procedures, strict scheduling of employee work time, use of decision hierarchies] in a firm characterized by a culture of informality and autonomy generates dissatisfaction among the workers.

Some researchers argue that the professionalization of workers in different types of careers also makes them more or less resistant to the imposition of formal rules. For instance, doctors and lawyers are trained to carefully collect and critically analyze information, then use their "own" analysis to make decisions. It seems that we are similarly professionalizing engineers and computer programmers [who are common figures in the high-tech industry] to develop skills in autonomous decision making.

This line of reasoning should not be taken as a prescription that organizations do nothing if their culture is one of autonomy and informality. Rather it seems that providing employees with information and education, then allowing them to use that information to make their own decisions may be the optimal strategy. It would be consistent with the norms for how work is usually conducted in such organizations. At the same time, if and when personal relationships become problematic in the workplace, an "education" does not prevent employees from openly seeking help to resolve the situation.

For some companies it may not make that much difference whether their positive dating policy is written down or not (provided the one on sexual harassment is)—although some attorneys may disagree on this. There are numbers of firms though that don't see the need to cover in writing all of the possible situations that may arise in their work relationships.

What's important, however, is the company's approach to its employees. Is it pro-interactive or not? Do the employees feel comfortable in their working environment, pushing toward corporate goals, or is the climate restrictive, punitive, and unyielding? Companies should ensure in any event that their policies, including those on boss-subordinate relationships, are communicated to all employees so that everyone knows ahead of time where they stand.

Don't Confuse Harassment With Love

As we've seen at Chapters 4 and 5, a major problem occurs when sexual harassment policies are used to regulate office romances. Separate policies about romance should be in effect and apart from the harassment guidelines.

"There's a chill in the air," said an officer at one restrictive firm: "I read about the doormen in New York City who now can't greet the tenants with hugs, as they did for years. Some tenants who didn't get hugs apparently complained, or maybe the lawyers were worrying about harassment charges. This company is no different, as to expressions of feelings, having relationships, or even close, nonsexual friendships. That's nuts." A study in the *Personnel Journal* indicated that 90 percent of the respondents didn't clearly understand what was a common definition of sexual harassment. That's not surprising. See also Chapter 16, "Companies Are People, Too."

Don't Police the Workforce

A court won't allow an employer generally to snoop around just to see what can be found—there has to be a specific, business objective such as investigating bribery or the passing of trade secrets. As Liz, an experienced trial lawyer, observed, "You just can't legislate love. It's the same problem as trying to tell people whom they should fall in love with or marry. People are going to have affairs, married or not, and they're going to break whatever rules you put in their way. Taking a tough, rigid approach just drives the people underground. They'll do it anyway."

Interestingly enough, two-thirds of all companies ignore the fact that unmarried employees are living together (according to a recent study in *Personnel Administrator*). A married employee dating someone else would be ignored by one-third of the respondents and prohibited by only 2 percent of the firms in this study.

Maintain an Open Door Policy

Companies want their employees to come to them when they have problems, regardless of the type or form. If workers feel free to discuss what's bothering them, there's less chance that the lawyers will get into the picture and muddy the waters. The company and its employees are able to solve problems that are getting in the way of their business goals.

Randall, the ex–human resources officer, said that increased travel is becoming a source of conflict in employee relations. "A married man worries about traveling with another woman. What will his wife think? What about office gossip, especially when senior people are traveling more with junior level ones. The men (and sometimes women) say to themselves, 'I don't want a rumor, so I won't travel with X.' The women are becoming miffed because the man's saying he doesn't want to travel with her. These types of policies are also clearly getting in the way of women's career plans."

The problem is that restrictive, closed-door policies simply make this situation worse. If employees are able to talk about their concerns with superiors without fear, potential problems can be solved before they become worse. As Liz said, "A restrictive policy can force a result that's exactly opposite from what you want. People don't talk and react positively when they're chafing against tight policies. A company doesn't want a climate of fear, but that's exactly what some have created. What they need to do is to let the positive interactions grow, knowing full well that they'll find effective solutions to their problems."

Emphasize Solving Problems, Rather Than Punishing

Companies should work with their people. It can simply be the difference between mediating employee problems and using a witch-hunt to find and fire the "guilty" one with loudly beating drums.

Toni is a long-time human resources executive who said: "The HR person for a competitor told me their philosophy the other day. Basically, the policy states that it's the employees' business whether they date or not. It becomes the firm's business if that conduct begins to interfere with the workplace. When this happens, then one of them will have to go and it's going to be the lesser valued worker. I was happy to hear that. This company will be a good source of valued employees for us.

"We use mediation for even the knotty problems. If there are claims of favoritism, or harassment has occurred, we follow a strict harassment policy—investigate, make a decision, and discipline by the policy. However, not every problem requires firing someone. Our workplace romances usually are affairs between decent, valued employees. When problems occur, we use a mediator to help them sort out their problems.

"What I couldn't understand was using punishment on conduct that was basically human behavioral in nature. Twenty-five years ago, divorces were granted only after a trial proving legally which side violated the law. Then matrimonial law became enlightened. The legislators and lawyers said divorce was simply a relationship problem. You didn't have to prove fault; all you had to show was that there were irreconcilable differences.

"The same approach could be used in the office romance area. Of course, where there's clear-cut harassment, there should be prompt and effective discipline. The problem's that this can be one person's word against another—and people do lie at times. That's why we try to work out these problems through mediation, many times on a non-fault basis." See Chapter 16, "Companies Are People, Too."

Chapter Seven

Getting to Know You

A collection manager for a publishing company walked past the desk of a newly hired woman on his way to his office each morning. She had joined the company as one of two public relations managers and reported to the vice president in charge. They would smile and say good morning to each other every day. Both were single, although Lyle was a few years younger than Vi who was thirty-five at the time.

One morning, Lyle wasn't looking forward to arguing collection matters all day again, but his attitude picked up when he thought about Vi. He stopped by her desk and asked if she'd like to join him over a cup of coffee. They talked for fifteen minutes in the coffee room, and then she had to leave for a meeting. Vi smiled back at him as she left, saying that she had enjoyed the coffee.

Lyle found himself coming by her desk earlier, so they'd have the time for what became a fairly regular fifteen-minute cup of coffee. A week later, he stopped by her desk at the usual time, but she wasn't there. Lyle located her telephone number in the office directory, then called her at home. She had a touch of the flu, so they talked a while about sports—which they both enjoyed.

When Vi was back at work, Lyle asked if she would like to join him for the Knicks basketball game that weekend. They had an early dinner, saw the game, had some coffee later, and he dropped her off at her apartment. They started dating, found themselves in a romance, but always tried to have their cup of coffee together in the morning at work.

Vi later told Lyle that she had grown to like him over their cups of coffee, finding him to be polite and friendly—not the usual "collection man interested in just the dollars and cents." He, in turn, liked her quick mind and laugh. They were discreet and did their best to keep their relationship a secret. Both wanted time to be sure the relationship was solid, and they didn't think it was anyone else's business, even if their company's policy only centered on reporting relationships.

The first casualty was their morning cup of coffee, which seemed to be an obvious tip-off. Lyle and Vi began spending the weekends and a couple of nights together each week, and they felt comfortable that their fellow workers hadn't figured anything out yet. Their relationship was off to a good start, and we'll come back to their story later.

A woman hired a contractor to reroof and remodel her house in Atlanta. In her early forties then, Elizabeth was single, a career manager, and living alone. Kenny was married and had a solid business with a reputation for doing quality work. He quoted a reasonable bid, his references checked out, and she quickly hired him.

Elizabeth said: "Kenny started working immediately on the house. My job called for me to leave early in the morning to be at work by 7:30 A.M., but this also meant I could beat the bad traffic, leave earlier than the others did, and be home by 4:30 P.M. This schedule allowed me to help Kenny out when he was short-handed, even working late into the night. We worked together side by side on the roof, nailing down tar paper and roof shingles. After a day's work was completed, we would chat, sometimes drink a glass of wine, and Kenny headed home.

"We did this for several months, and nothing happened between us. We liked each other's company and that was good enough. After the work was done and Kenny paid, he'd still come by to fix something we had missed or just help out. One night, we ended up in a hot tub with a second glass of wine. He stayed the night and never went back again to his wife. We've been together for fourteen years now, and Kenny and I still haven't completed all the work that needs to be done on the house and grounds. We keep figuring out new projects to do."

A female sportscaster interviewed a semipro male basketball player for the local newspaper. He called her up for a date, she accepted, and they ended up living together. A successful small business entrepreneur met his wife at a business seminar, and they married after a long-distance courtship. The head chef at a four-star hotel met his fiancée, the head of its marketing department, at a company promotion she had put on. The situations change, but the concept stays the same—people are meeting each other at or due to their work, taking their chances, and becoming involved.

There are also the breakups. A legal secretary dated her boss but they broke up after two months. The tension was too great in that one-man office, so she left soon for another job with the memories and a good job reference. Two police officers had an affair that lasted several months; the relationship ended when they quarreled over whether she would leave her spouse. Because they were in different departments in a large police force, neither the relationship nor its ending affected their positions.

Two real estate salespersons became involved at an office in Southern California. The man followed his lover when she left the company to form her own real estate firm. They split up two years later, he complaining about her long hours and she upset over what she thought was his insensitivity. He left the office and moved to Northern California to heal after their breakup. Several years later, and after other relationships, he moved back to the area, rejoining his ex-lover's firm. Although they aren't romantically attached, they are now good friends.

Katherine and Eric, whom we met in Chapter 1, began their relationship when he asked her out for drinks after work. They shared common interests from enjoying classical music to hiking. Their problems after breaking up were compounded by the close proximity of their offices. These were made worse when she tried to get back together by sending him long E-mail messages—she should have contacted Eric instead on their off-hours. However, she didn't feel she could talk directly with him at the time. Her banishment to a faraway office probably wouldn't have happened if she had worked for a less conservative company, or one that didn't handle relationship problems by applying their standard sexual harassment policy. She should have been given a written warning, even undergone counselling, but still allowed time to see how she performed afterward.

What's Great at Work

With men and women spending extensive time together at work, regardless of the industry or career, it's natural that these long hours result in relationships—a January 1998 survey by the Society for Human Resource Management of its human resources professionals reported 60 percent said that the number of workplace romances at their organizations had stayed the same or increased over the past five years (and 55 percent said romances at their companies resulted in marriage). People of similar interests and expectations are always around. It's possible to get to know someone without the risks of the bar scene, singles clubs, newspaper ads, cruises, or the infamous "blind date." Married people can shed bad relationships without having to battle over where she or he had been that night.

Who doesn't have a war story about their worst date? Carl was an insurance agent in Boston. Recently separated from his wife, a client had set him up with a blind date. The two couples sat down at a table in a good seafood restaurant. Before they could even talk about the weather, his date ordered an expensive bottle of wine, then the most expensive lobster dinner on the menu. She didn't bat an eyelash at the prices, although Carl gulped inside.

His date spent the whole time talking with his client's wife. No one said a word when the bill came, and he gallantly (although somewhat naively) ponied up the bill for both of them and all the drinks. He could have paid for four dates on what she had ordered for herself. After she gave him a sisterly hug at her front door, the evening mercifully came to an end. As she closed the door, she thanked him for a good time and said she was leaving the area to take another job.

An attorney in her thirties said that a date, met the previous night at a bar, called her twice to reset the time when he was due to arrive. Over two hours later, he called for the third time and canceled out. Her prospective date sounded the last time as if he was drunk and calling from the same bar.

Of course, you can have bad experiences on dates whether they're from work or not. However, you have more time to get to know someone at work before taking the plunge. You can discuss the little things like where you like to eat, inexpensive or grand places, and even the types of wines, before you ask someone out for a date.

One man in his early twenties joined a local newspaper as its photographer. He met an older woman there who was working in classified advertising. They became a "twosome," although the other coworkers didn't support their romance. He "cared less" about either the workers' problems or their "beefs." She left after a few months to go back to school in another state and complete her college education. They kept in touch, and when she came back after graduation, they started seeing each other again. She took a job then with another newspaper in the city, and they'll be married in a few months. As he said, "It was inevitable that we would marry. We're in love."

Lia and Rick

Lia and Rick met through Lia's work as a private banker. He at the time was an investment banker with a New York City firm and met her at her office. "He was referred to me by a mutual friend who was a good referral to me of business leads," she reflected. "However, I knew that Rick wasn't really interested in business when he kept calling to ask me out. However, I kept saying no because I wanted to keep business and work separate from my personal life. Eventually, I said I would go out with him to discuss potential business, as a favor to our mutual friend.

"I agreed to meet him on a Sunday so we wouldn't run into any of my friends. It was a blinding snowstorm, and throughout the entire time, I was frosty and gave Rick no encouragement. However, he wasn't deterred. After dinner, I was ready to call it quits, but he prevailed and we ended up much later at his house for coffee. It was then that we talked about personal and spiritual things—and I found myself becoming quite interested in him. We've been married for several years now and have two wonderful babies."

Rick is a testimonial to the advantages of low-key, positive persistence. "I first saw her when I came in looking for a bank to handle some of my business needs. Or let's say, a small part of it. When I first saw her, I became very interested, to say the least. When I saw her talking to a mutual friend (who also banked there), I called him up and asked who was that great-looking lady. With that in hand, I called Lia up and asked if she wanted to meet over coffee—and set up a second checking account. She wasn't overly encouraging or friendly that time. In fact, she turned me down a half-dozen times, and it took two months before she finally agreed to meet me on that wintry, Sunday early evening."

Some of the Stories

You can meet a person anywhere. We hear about people meeting clandestinely behind the broccoli at the supermarket, chatting in line after a church service, and even when out walking the dog. The problem is what do you do when the boss just called and you're too busy to buy the food (you order in), pray in church (that's a problem), or walk the dog (hire someone else). As everyone knows: it requires sacrifice, very limited personal time off, and a commitment to your work to earn a decent living today. Work and its connections then provide the most convenient and likely way to meet your social needs as well.

A police lieutenant was second-in-command for a small force in a rural California city. His seven-year relationship with a woman had ended, and it was a hard time for him. The dispatcher for the department took him out for coffee when he was having a particularly bad day. She was a good listener and a kind woman. They began dating and married later. Although they divorced after several years, they're still friends because, as he said, "We had been friends when we started, and we decided we'd remain friends at the end."

Whether it's a large company or small one, coworkers and supervisors fall in love every day. An assistant to the president of a small company said she had a problem that they needed to talk about. She wouldn't tell him what it was about at work. They had been working together for some months and both were married. At lunch, he asked her what was wrong. She said, "I love you." They had a long-term affair that lasted until he left the company for a larger one, and she decided not to join him and stay with her family.

A manager and her assistant product manager worked closely together. He said one night that he couldn't work any more for the company. When she asked why, he answered that he was in love with her. They married three months later and are still together eight years later. It is great when it works out, as the hopes are with any potential relationship.

A physician, worn out from the medical emergency caused by a severe earthquake, fell exhausted into the arms of a nurse. They slept together for a few hours on a hospital couch, entwined in each other's arms. They married shortly afterward. When paramedics, police, firefighters, or the medical profession work together, those "heart-thumping" times can create special bonds.

Third-party dating is another prevalent type of romance. There's limited risk from jealous coworkers, and if you're on the road, opportunities abound. Jake is the head bartender for a prominent restaurant that overlooks the ocean in beautiful Santa Barbara, California. He has been the bartender there for several years. The restaurant chain owning that location decided to purchase an expensive computerized bill-ing and inventory system for it. Maureen worked for the software company and flew in from New York City to oversee the work.

Over the next two weeks, Jake and Maureen became good friends. Jake, a twenty-nine-year-old fun-loving guy, thought she was "an absolute riot and a cool person." Although she headed back east after the system was in working order, Maureen returned three months later on her vacation to spend time with Jake and brought along a friend to party with them. Although she and Jake are "just friends," 3,000 miles doesn't seem to be too long a distance for her.

A forty-five-year-old man owned a civil engineering firm with his brother. One of his employees had been dating a cute, smart woman who was twenty years younger than he was. When they broke up, he asked his employee friend if it was okay for him to date the ex-girlfriend. "No problems" came the answer, so the owner called the woman for a date. She accepted and "things worked out." They lived together for three years, then married, and have been together now for ten years.

A businessman attended a local chamber of commerce social. He met a cute, young TV reporter. They ended up in his hot tub and dated for a few months before going their separate way. She went back to the next chamber of commerce get-together and ended up becoming engaged to the man she met that time.

And Some of the Ways

At Work

The ways to meet range from the business lunch and after-work drink to the "order in pizza late" approach. As Judy Kaiser observed, "A 'work-date' is the best way to see if they like you the same way. Make up some excuse related to work, whether it's to chat about a policy change or actually related to what you're doing. If they say they're too busy or suggest a meeting in their office, then you know—what a painless way to be turned down. Who wants the bars or singles' ads when you have this in front of you every day?"

One female software programmer pointed out, "Employer-sponsored events are the easiest way to get to know someone, and you don't need to ask for a phone number if you're interested, like in the off-work scene. Simply ask the easy question: what department are you in? After the softball game or company party, ask casually if they would like to get together later. How much easier can it be?"

A gay couple, both in their fifties, had been together for twenty years and built up a chain of exquisite garden boutique shops located throughout California. They constructed a house in the Napa Valley worth easily over a million dollars. A younger gay man was hired to work at one of their shops. The couple broke up shortly afterward, with the ex-lover who had worked closely with that younger man now in a close relationship with him.

Even the remote locations and limited social opportunities of the park service create on-the-job romance. For example, two park rangers met when they worked together at a national park in Alaska. The wife said, "We had a couple of years of long, dark winters—lots of time to get to know one another."

Don't forget the fields where men and women work together constantly in unstructured ways, ranging from entertainment to real estate. As one real estate broker said, "You're on call seven days a week, twenty-four hours a day. You're not working inside some office in a zoot suit and tie—you're out showing houses and working with lots of people. You're dealing each day with people, brokers, and agents, and you're always moving around." Remember the stories of Steve and Alice, then of Gary (the Harvard MBA who loves the theater—and it's easy to see why).

The Commute

If you're working for a firm that frowns on its coworkers getting involved with one another, don't worry because there are even better ways to meet people—and one of the best is the commute. Tanya is an energetic, Irish woman who said: "I used to drive to work from across San Francisco Bay to Oakland. My codriver was one of the managers who also worked for the same glass company. We would talk and talk. . . . You know how those long commutes are. We started getting interested in each other, as what else are you going to do to kill two hours each day in a car. We just fell for one another. I think it was all that time driving and talking together that did it. He was a nice guy, but not my cup of tea, if you know what I mean. We broke up a few months later, but it sure was fun while it lasted. We'd get up in the morning and drive into work, then act like we didn't know one another at all. I loved it."

Judy Kaiser became involved with someone when "he provided

the transportation" to one of her jobs. "It was inevitable," she said. "He was good looking, we were together, and I had the time." Two elderly passengers took the same bus regularly to different parts of the city where one did volunteer work and the other worked part time. They began chatting one day, swapped schedules, then worked out their times so that they always could share the same bus ride back.

The Business Trip

Harry is the ex–general counsel of a Fortune 500 company. He spent nearly twenty years in the corporate wars before accepting a tidy, severance package. He observed: "The traveling road shows are made to order. You head out to a trade show, far away from home and all those corporate power players who'd love to get the goods on you. You're in adjoining hotel rooms, there's booze in the cabinets, and you have the ability to sneak out when you want. It's a big temptation; in fact, it's made to order. When you're teaching at the local high school, then you don't have this opportunity. You have many more opportunities in the high-tech workforce, as just one example of an industry where you can really swing."

Carrie said, "Conventions are usually good for me. I got involved once with my teacher at a convention."

And Tanya told this story: "A friend of mine has been married for fifty-one years, but he's been carrying on this affair for the past sixteen. I met him when he and his buddies left me a $350 tip at the restaurant I managed. He met this gal that I'll call Natalie on one of his trips. Well, Natalie is a kind of single 'homeless mutt,' and he's on the executive committee for this big company that flies them all over the world.

"Well, Natalie goes with him, whether it's to Puerto Rico, Chicago, or New York City. The company knows about the affair, but everyone keeps it a big secret. Natalie just shows up with him and the committee. What I love is that the local newspaper does this big thing about him being so happily married for all those years. And then I think about Natalie."

Customer, Client, or Candlestick Maker

A frequent alternative is found in third parties: those individuals who are the firm's clients, customers, or vendors. The person can be your computer repairperson, marketing representative, patient, or client, and it makes no difference whether it's a physician's office, fire department, or large corporation—these types of relationships occur all the time.

For example, an attorney invited his client to attend a seminar he was holding for the public in his legal specialty. She owned her own software computer business. They had drinks after the seminar, then they began a long, satisfying affair. A doctor married an ex-patient, several months after meeting her later unexpectedly at a party. A computer repairman looked forward to when one particular client had problems with his company's products: that department was a training area, and the women trainees rotated every three months through there to another department. A Xerox saleswoman happily called on businesses in her assigned area, knowing she would never have any problems in getting a date. Then there was the woman who attended a "living as a happy single" seminar just to get a date with the "cute" lecturer.

A friend of mine was a raucous, fun-loving man in his late thirties who died recently. Tucker was an accountant and had relayed this story: "I was hammered at a bar after a long, hard day. This real attractive lady looked down at me and asked what I was drinking. I said it was tequila, so she makes this face and says 'Ugh.' Well, I asked what her problem was, and we started arguing. At that time, we didn't even know each other. She got mad and threw a drink at me. Can you believe that? We both stomped away mad, thinking that the other one was a putz.

"Three months later, a friend of mine said that he knew someone who needed some tax help. So I talked to her on the phone, we laughed, and got along great. I quoted her a decent fee, so we set up a time to meet at my office. When she showed up, I couldn't believe it. It's the one, the one who threw the drink in my face. She looked at me so strangely, but I'm playing it cool and didn't say a word. She asked, 'Do you remember me?' But I'm not a dummy and I answered, 'No, should I?'

"We sat down, talked, and laughed like we were meeting each other for the first time. I asked her out that night, and we drank a bottle of wine, ending up over at her house. We spent the weekend together and began dating. After we had dated for two months, I asked her to join me at the same restaurant where she had thrown the drink at me. Once we were there, I told the waiter to bring over a shot of tequila. He brought it over, and she stared at me with that same strange look again. 'You SOB,' she said. 'You knew it all the time.' We eventually broke up, but she was a real sweetheart. . . . Had a bit of a temper, though." Tucker laughed heartily again, and his many friends miss him.

Friends of Friends

Staying friends with fellow workers also pays dividends. Judy Kaiser met her latest boyfriend through her roommate. She had known her male roommate when both had worked for a large law firm on the West Coast as paralegals. Her roommate had invited a friend of his, whom he also had met at work, over for Sunday breakfast. His friend and Judy hit it off, and the two have been together for the past two years.

A manager of a city recreation department set up a coworker with her newly separated brother-in-law. A real estate developer introduced a friend to his secretary. A professor introduced his wife's sister to a colleague. A secretary introduced her boss to a friend when having a drink after work. And the beat goes on and on.

The Fears of Men and Women

With women working alongside men, some competing fiercely for positions of power with strong male competitors, the whole question of social relationships can take on different twists. Role reversals are not uncommon. Although competition between the sexes has increased in the workforce, that doesn't mean that romance has been thrown out the window, as we've seen so strikingly so far. However, the players have to be smarter in today's climate.

As Mack (who had been with Kim) said: "For men, there's no question that the climate has changed from what it was only ten, even five years ago. There's not only the fear of rejection, but also of a harassment charge if things don't work out. It's as if there's a double penalty." This is on top of the normal "will she, or won't she like me" concerns in the very beginning. The problem is that people can be so different on the inside.

Mack continued: "Conduct or an approach that's acceptable to one person, may very well not be to another. One woman likes that you flirt, then another goes out of her way to tell you that it's unwelcome and won't be tolerated. You used to deal with this by saying 'that's how the cookie crumbles.' Now these days, someone might complain about what's a totally innocent thing.

"Then it depends upon your supervisor and how he or she feels about this. It's become a totally subjective deal, and managers have different feelings about the same complaint based only upon their personalities. Even if they're duty bound to investigate, they might be thinking, 'What a waste of time this is. That person [the one complaining] must have something better to do with their time. Another might be thinking, this one [the one complained against] has a real problem. Companies should set up consistent policies on this and train their supervisors accordingly, so that you don't have these inconsistencies."

Mabel makes a different point. "Women want to be taken seriously in their job efforts and dedication to their careers. It's been a struggle to get to where we are now and the struggle isn't over. I don't want to be judged on how I look in a miniskirt, just on how I work and get things done. It's okay to ask me for lunch, but I'm into work, and that's what our discussions should be about. I have no quarrel with romance outside the job, but it doesn't belong in the workplace." Another woman said, "I'm at a stage in my life where I'm happily married. I'm not interested in relationships. I look around and see younger women having fun times at work. That's okay, as long as they keep their feelings to themselves."

Judy Kaiser said: "I'm into my career now and don't fool around on my job. There once was a time when I did, but as I think about it, I'm not going to rule out an office romance yet. In fact, a few months ago I was asked out to lunch by a colleague, and he tactfully asked if I was interested in going out. I said no, because I wasn't interested in dating then. I'm into enjoying myself, like drinks with my buddies after work. I'd also have to break up with my current boyfriend. Then, it would take a great guy for me to have an affair at work. It would depend also on where I was with my life—but I do want the freedom to decide for myself, even if it is at work."

Writers, authors, and political commentators see different sides of the political coin. One side argues that today's climate in many companies is one of no or limited toleration, that there's a chill in the air, and that the relationship between the sexes is being adversely affected. The other side says that's fine, we're balancing out past inequities, and the old ways were worse.

For the rest of us who are caught in the middle, the war between the sexes is doing just fine. People meet each other, fall in love, and marry at work. Some relationships work out, others don't. When romances fall apart, people try again—and whether this is at work or not, doesn't seem to make a difference. It depends more on where a person is with his or her life, and how appealing the other person is. All we need to do is to look again at the statistics.

To Flirt or Not to Flirt

People shouldn't say demeaning, sexually oriented words to anyone, whether it's at work or not. This conduct doesn't have a place in our society. However, this doesn't mean people can't flirt discreetly in a fun way with people they know.

The question is how do you define a "flirt." Is it something you can pick up, identify, and categorize like birds and decide if one's appropriate or not? What's apparent these days is that the flirting skills haven't disappeared, it's that the sexual and social roles have become confused.

Whether flirting is received well or not depends on the person, the place, and the time. People's reactions can vary for the slightest reasons. It can make a difference whether you're walking through the company's gardens on a beautiful spring day, or you're cooped up in a fluorescent-lighted cubicle. There's a difference between a made-up compliment after a heated argument over some marketing decision and genuine approval coming from a friend.

Remember that we're not talking about sexual harassment when someone flirts, compliments, or greets another affectionately (we understand that there are limits). If someone takes this conduct the wrong way, then just don't do it again with that person. Persistence isn't a virtue if the other person is on a different wavelength. My brother, Jimmy, says succinctly, "You can't argue with a drunk." Provided it's not you or your approach, look for someone else who would like to be your valentine.

You must use discretion and remember that not everyone will appreciate your advances, no matter how subtle. For example, a post office employee had met his wife at work. She even left her first husband to have an affair with this man, then divorced that unlucky spouse to marry the new one a few years ago. This man's in his forties and considers himself to be "pretty hot stuff," according to one co-worker. He winks at the women; some ignore it while a few others think that it's "funny." An attractive woman then joined the office. She was in her late twenties, and the "winker" did his number on her. The only problem was that she didn't like it and told him to cut it out. He went straight to his supervisor, complained about her reaction, and said, "I don't want anything to come about this, such as sexual harassment. She's the uptight one." They aren't getting off to a good start, are they?

Flirting should be selective—light, not serious. It should be fun and complimentary, not a leering or a long look. It is easier and less risky to do with someone you know than with someone you don't. It can be a genuine compliment on someone's dress (less risky) or a wink (more risky even if you know the person). It can be fun with the right person, and both sexes should hold onto the right to flirt and use it in the proper circumstances.

But What's Permissible?

We've discussed the differences between legal harassment, "unwelcome" behavior, and borderline situations previously, and these differences should be kept in mind—especially since two people can react differently to the same act, even the same person later can respond differently depending on the time and their mood. The U.S. Department of Education Office for Civil Rights in 1997 released their sexual harassment guidelines, and these can give general guidance.

There are no hard-and-fast rules saying what's right or wrong, because even this agency recognizes that the area involves conduct that's situational and circumstantial in nature. The problem of precise definitions lies in the constant clash between the First Amendment freedoms of expression, speech, and association against individual statutory civil rights and liberties. However, the guidelines do give examples.

First, it's not harassment for a coach to hug a winning athlete or a teacher to hug a small child who has fallen to the ground. However, repeated hugging where there's no outward reason (such as being congratulatory or consoling in nature) could wind up as harassment. A single casual incident of unwelcome behavior isn't necessarily harassment either. A professor can assign literary excerpts containing explicit sexual descriptions in a college creative writing class. The guidelines stress that good judgment and common sense are to be used, stating that: "Sexual harassment must be sufficiently severe, persistent or pervasive that it adversely affects a student's education [or a worker's job] or creates a hostile or abusive educational [or work] environment."

Remember that the existence of harassment isn't to be equated with the fact someone else is convinced that the conduct is unwelcome. This doesn't mean workers shouldn't respect the feelings of a coworker and not do it again with him or her—but it means that people should be free to act *reasonably* even if someone else might become offended by that action. There is an objective test (Does the reasonable woman or person look at this act the same way?) that is an equal part of the test on whether behavior is truly welcome or not.

The problem is that organizations, whether they are the police, a university, or a Fortune 500 company, want to prevent any behavior that could possibly wind up as a complaint or sexual harassment lawsuit. The phrase "taking preventive action," unfortunately, can mean ruling out anything that someone else finds or just says is unwelcome. The nature of its response indicates whether an organization is an "uptight" company or a "pro-interactive" one.

What needs to be remembered is that any person, unreasonably or not, can complain and sue in this country. Organizations should work toward zero tolerance on unreasonable behavior that evidences legal sexual harassment, not zero tolerance for any behavior that one person complains about. That is allowing plain and simple tyranny to be created by one against the majority.

At times, behavior is culturally driven. Let's take the example of a Mexican American (or an Italian American, or some American) who has been raised to believe that greeting family and friends with affection is part of their cultural heritage—and it doesn't even have to be culturally oriented, because this can be just the way you were raised. Then that person is informed by a superior that "so and so has just complained about your unwelcome touching." The complainant might have come from a family where there were no outward displays of affection, or perhaps for some other reason they'll always feel uncomfortable. Does this mean that this complaint should be elevated to a sexual harassment grievance? No, unless the unwanted behavior persists and affects some term or condition of the employment.

Hopefully, a simply apology by one or *both* parties can iron out the difficulties. If the behavior is reasonable (if most people wouldn't be offended), the complainant must understand that he or she is part of the problem. There must be some element of fairness to avoid the implicit injustice when the "one who screams the loudest, is the one who's heard."

"Companies should show more courage in this area, but they cave in for what's easiest, rather than hold to the principal of what's right for the entire workforce," said one human resources executive. "They should take on the unreasonable complaint that could freeze normal working conditions, even if that means taking on another attorney. Unfortunately, the sexual harassment and political correctness area can disintegrate in companies into primarily fights over control."

Clearly, this discussion doesn't mean employees should feel free to act however they want: everyone should treat others as they would like to be treated and with *mutual* respect. Having good relationships with people means taking into account the feelings of others in a positive way. This comes down to using plain, old-fashioned etiquette, and this is what romance is about.

Dating Etiquette

There is nothing new in this area. What worked years ago between men and women romantically is just as appropriate today. It is simply a matter of common sense to avoid many of the problems. This is a very simple rule: *Be respectful and polite.* Some minirules should also be observed:

- Try to know the person better, before making a compliment.
- Compliment performance or attire, not physical qualities ("that's a nice color on you" rather than "great bod").
- Receive permission to be freer in your conduct and comments, as the relationship grows over time.
- Watch how coworkers relate to one another to see what's okay or not.
- Keep eye contact light and happy, leaving your "bedroom" eyes at home.
- Ask first when you aren't sure how someone might react to an approach.
- You can't please everyone all the time. Don't take offense if a person says they're uncomfortable with something you've done—accept it graciously, apologize (if and when appropriate), and move on.
- Keep your cool if someone acts like a jerk; you might be there one day.

- Touch between elbow and fingertips, until you know the other better.
- Do what's natural and easy for you, but follow the "Golden Rule."

Some women have become more aggressive, and this is taking some of the pressure off the guys. Carrie laughed heartily when she was asked if women were more aggressive now. She responded: "Sure, and honey, I'm one of them. Tell the men to walk their talk. They're always saying they want a woman to be the aggressor. They say why do we have to do all the work? But the minute a woman does that, most men can't cope. The trick is to open the door for men, but then to let them walk in. Men become interested with a woman who doesn't hang onto their every word. A less attractive woman can win over a knockout lady if she's a bit of a challenge. You asked about my favorite type of guy: very smart, able to pay his own way, and can fix a faucet or a car. Not a wimp or one that looks like he'd break if I was on top of him in bed."

Roberta, whose Vic in Chapter 2 was stolen away by his female manager, emphasized her feelings that "women today are just plain more aggressive." It depends on the person, of course, but the conditions are quite different in today's workforce.

Men can accept the strengths of these trends. It's easier to work in a relationship where the partner is on an equal footing. Decisions are easier, living standards are higher for both, and your worlds are more complementary. As Frank said, "My life turned around when I met Karen. She was my light."

But Be Aware of Miscommunications

People can misunderstand, misinterpret, and misconstrue nearly anything, even when it involves the same sex. When we add in sexual differences, it seems amazing that people and couples communicate with each other as well as they do. Just think about the miscommunications you've had in your relationships. Suzanne and Jeffrey (and the studies) point out that the differences in sex can not only create the basic attraction, but also some miscommunications.

Suzanne explained, "From the second I met Jeffrey, I was in love with him. He was smart and I liked him from the start. Jeffrey offered a lot to me. He, on the other hand, took more time to get to the same place, and it was more sexually oriented when it did. . . . But the first or second meeting after starting to work for him, he started coming down on me. We hadn't talked much, but he started asking me pointed questions.

He said, 'Why are you here?'

'To work,' I answered.

'How many people did you talk to today?'

'None,' I said. He was coming down on me, and I knew it. I started crying, then said, 'I want to be intimate.'

He continued on with me, 'They don't want you to be intimate. What is it that you aren't saying or telling me?'

'That I love you,' I said. And that really surprised him.

He then said, 'I love you, too.' But he wasn't being romantic or intimate, although I was when I said that to him. Jeffrey said it like he would say it to someone he knew well at the office, not intimately as I did."

It depends on who's involved. Common misconceptions occur when another person is naturally friendly. This can be misinterpreted as particular interest in the other, when in fact it's the way he or she is with everyone. Differences owing to sex clearly show up in the communication area.

For example, a common misconception among men is that when a woman winks or flirts with them, she's interested in a relationship or has a sexual interest. Not all men are this way, but a man can have a different response than a woman would expect to her remarks or conduct. Suzanne said, "Jeffrey said he was interested in me sexually when he became interested. I was more mind oriented at the time, then I became romantically interested."

The miscommunications between the sexes at work and play, owing simply to gender differences, are well documented, closely studied, and widely written about. The academics and scholars study what we all know is common sense: the sexes are different and these differences show up in the way they communicate, miscommunicate, and understand one another. Men can say one thing, women can hear a different message, and vice versa. Such mistranslations are due to varying assumptions, upbringing, and sexuality. There's no question that gender differences shape office behavior and communication between the sexes.

Let's just take one of the no-no's: when a man relates to a woman the way he does with the guys. Even if innocently intended, men get into understandable trouble when they engage in "locker room" talk with women. Some men don't know any better, especially if they weren't raised with sisters. Women who've never had brothers can have similar inexperience.

An element of common sense should be used. Most men know instinctively that you talk to men one way, and you talk to women in another. And women do the same thing. Larger companies crack down hard on the offending men, but smaller firms look at times the other way. This isn't to say that men should get off because "they don't know any better," but only to point out that there are commonsense reasons why men and women act differently and always will with each other.

Mabel argues passionately, "We want to be treated as equals, but be recognized as women. I'm not interested in being treated as a guy. I will be treated as a woman with respect and dignity and honor. Do you understand?" All of us, men and women alike, couldn't agree more. However, if a man treats Mabel like "one of the guys," even if done innocently, that act will start a nuclear war.

It's also true that women usually have a better chance of getting away with flirting, and men are reacting adversely to this fact of life. As one executive commented: "Women shouldn't feel that they can flirt and men can't. Over the years, I've seen men who were experts in this. They just knew which women would like a compliment, or a discreet, acknowledging look . . . not a stare or sexual message, but a complimentary, affectionate glance. There are women who could manage this equally well, with style and grace. What seems to be happening today is some men are becoming uncomfortable with flirting, not only with themselves but also as to a woman's reaction. . . . Pity. They won't say this to the women, but the thought is that 'if I can't do it, then you better as hell not do it either.'

"There are women who don't want any compliments in the workplace, although this can depend on the industry, company, and coworkers. While many women don't have this reaction, it does depend clearly on how well you know the person, what's said, and whether it's an honest statement. If a man compliments a woman on her dress, but the clothing's average, then a woman knows this; but if it's a nice-looking outfit, and she knows the man, then that can be different."

He laughed to himself, then said, "There's an old adage: if the interest comes from a young, handsome, well-dressed *GQ* man, then it's a compliment and welcome. However, if it comes from an older, balding, middle-aged man, then that's harassment. There could be some truth there."

A woman's innocent flirting or even advances can turn off some men, especially if they don't think that they have the same right. Although this can depend on the person, the best approach seems to be one of using common sense and being sure there's a sense of mutuality between the two. It's also better not to make assumptions about what someone likes or doesn't like—ask first.

This is primarily for the guys (but it applies to all): if you want to tell a joke but aren't sure about the reaction, ask if the woman would be offended. Ask, "I heard a joke involving two lovers and it goes into (don't be too specific). . . . Do you want to hear it? If you don't like it, then I'll know it should be buried." Break down the ice, before you drive through like a Mack truck.

As Judy Kaiser observed, "Just be natural and yourself—that should be easy enough. If you're anything but that, then people will see through you. Check things out with the other person, too. Communication means asking what they like, or don't like, at first. If you want to take someone out for, let's say a pizza, wouldn't you ask first to see if they liked it? You wouldn't just order it."

What People Do

What amazes even the executives of an uptight company are the chances that people take for love. "It's like watching *One Flew Over the Cuckoo's Nest,*" said one older female executive.

A female student wrote her home telephone number on an exam given by her professor with a note to please call. She got mad at him when he didn't follow up on it, but during the summer, they had the opportunity to meet over coffee. They started dating, were married, and have two children they love dearly.

One enterprising female E-mailed a message to a man she liked, asking if he wanted to play tennis. She not only won, but also asked him out for a date, and they started a long-term relationship.

A man asked a woman out, but she said no. He thought about how she had said it, then asked her out a second time a few days later, at the same time handing her a beautiful bouquet of wildflowers— she then said yes. And remember the quiet persistence of Rick with Lia in this chapter.

One enterprising employee dropped a rose each day for a week on a woman's desk, then sent her a cryptic card with directions at noon to a nearby park. She was curious and walked over at twelve o'clock. Her grinning coworker stood by a tree and motioned her to a nearby table. A wonderful array of bread, sliced meat, cheeses, and a floral display were spread over a silk tablecloth, complete with silver-ware and goblets. This couple stayed together for several years.

People get together after the company picnic, for dinner after closing an important deal, or for drinks after work. Meeting someone is the operative word, not whether it's viewed at the time as being a date. This happens all the time at work.

When you've met someone you think is Mr. or Ms. Right, then the real challenges begin. You ask yourself whether this should be taken further—a difficult consideration. On the one hand, there are the risks such as the company's climate and reaction, whether the ro-mance works out, the potential career damage, and other penalties if the two of you don't make it. On the other hand, there's love, compan-ionship, and a partner. Guess which one wins out?

Chapter Eight

The New Rules of Romance

The continuing march of women into the workforce, management, and inevitably positions of power has spurred powerful changes in business. We've seen how this trend has brought about the rise of pro-interactive companies, as well as the accommodation of married couples at the same firm and recent easing of dating taboos.

It has also brought about new rules of romance. No longer does a female secretary or lower scale clerical worker have to hitch her career to a male supervisor's evaluation or his ability to climb higher in the organization. Women set their own independent career tracks, make their own decisions and marks, and plain just "do their thing, their way." New rules for relationships have accompanied these changes.

In today's midnight-oil-burning, teamwork-playing, gender-mixing furnace, men and women are thrown together for long periods of time with the obvious result: business is better and romance is flowering. It's no longer one partner who determines these relationships—they're now decided by both. As the two lovers today can enjoy separate career paths, so have their relationships become joint affairs. Here are the rules.

Know What You Want

At the very beginning, figure out what's most important with a potential relationship: life without the person or the tricky problem of having Mr. or Ms. Right working in the same company. You need a good feeling that this romance will last, especially with the potential pitfalls ahead.

Some surveys indicate that up to one-third of all work romances are extramarital. Although people in vast numbers enter into affairs when they're still married to someone else, companies and their executives may not be so understanding. Despite the obstacles, these relationships can and do end in endearing, long-term situations.

The U.S. military (and especially the U.S. Air Force) is not very understanding, as contrasted with various businesses, when it unearths relationships. The U.S. Air Force drew a controversial line with B-52 bomber pilot, First Lieutenant Kelly Flinn, in charging her with (among other things) committing adultery with a married man before granting her a general discharge. Then the U.S. Air Force later threatened the court-martial of Second Lieutenant William R. Kite, Jr., who became involved with an airman he later married, before granting him a general discharge also (which forces the loss of most benefits). However, the military in other nations (as with their civilian counterparts) generally tend to take a more pragmatic view on adultery and affairs than the United States. French, British, and other European armed forces simply aren't as concerned with "fraternization" problems as are the U.S. armed forces.

If your boss (male or female) asks you out, or a subordinate makes an approach, boss-subordinate involvement rears its head with all its attendant difficulties. A relationship with a coworker in the same department also has risks, but not as many as a chain-of-command situation. Harry, the ex–general counsel, observed: "Be careful of becoming involved with someone in your department versus another who works in another department. You won't see the one in that other division everyday, if the relationship doesn't work out. There's less of an impact on the workforce and your coworkers if it does end, and, consequently less stress on you. However, the people continue to become involved, regardless of where they work."

Usually, people don't have the luxury of making an intellectual decision on these matters. If they did, things would be easy. The problem is that you work closely together, with so much being on the line, then you wake up in love, or he or she's now lying beside you in bed. Or you're from the same department and head off for drinks after work. "It was a very spontaneous thing and just happened," said one manager. Affairs of the heart are this way.

The line between work and social life can be so quickly erased these days, if you aren't careful. The other person is attractive, funny, and witty, and it's easy not to give the negative factors a second thought. You're at a company picnic, having been alone for months after your last relationship fell apart, then you're playing volleyball with someone who's your "other half from another lifetime." Who thinks about the complications then?

Donna worked for the airport authority of a large city on the East Coast in an administrative position. She liked her job, which provided support to several departments, but wanted to do more with her life. She volunteered to work on promotional projects in her off-hours, which involved working with George, the newly hired manager of marketing and promotion. George was new to the area and didn't know anyone; Donna had been in the area for some years and was well acquainted with the people and places. They worked closely together for several weeks planning several after-hours public relations events.

One evening, they were on a dinner cruise aimed toward promoting the authority with the media. As Donna recalled, "George had been showing some interest in me, and this was quite appealing. The activities had ended, and the ferry was returning to its dock. He was standing close to me, and it was a beautiful summer's evening. It was a romantic setting, and the sun was setting. The boat ride gave a striking view of the towering buildings and the city's magnificent skyline; we both sipped chablis from thin-stemmed wineglasses and toasted one another.

"George looked into my eyes and said he was very interested in me. I told him softly that I had the same feelings. He asked me, 'What about our working together?' I said I could handle that, and that I wouldn't let other people stop me from doing what I wanted to do. We launched into our relationship that night." We'll come back to her story.

Start Out as Friends

Start out as friends, whenever possible, although that can be a challenge if you suddenly wind up in bed after a cocktail party. Steve and Alice worked together for nine months before they became romantically involved. Their early time together seasoned the relationship when it turned serious. Steve said: "We worked closely together to lease up an office building that our company was building. This meant working together on lease agreements, meeting with prospective tenants, even walking the site to see how work was coming along. We would duck out and grab a hamburger or sandwich at a nearby restaurant and eat outdoors, choosing places that had views of the ocean, the beach, and even the mountains. We would eat different foods, such as tacos on a Tuesday or wontons on a Wednesday.

"Occasionally, but usually on a Friday evening, we'd zip over to a nearby bar with others from work and enjoy a drink or two. We both would then head home. One evening, Alice told me she had to leave early to meet her mother at seven. When that time came, I leaned over and told her that her mother was waiting. She looked at me in a funny way, then said, 'Are you telling me it's time to go?' I smiled and shrugged my shoulders. She said, 'I think I'll stay here a little longer, if you don't mind.' A few weeks later, we stayed longer afterward and ended up necking in the parking lot. That started our eleven-year romance, but it was set well in motion by working together for nine months and first becoming friends."

Work romances do that. You have the time to become better acquainted, not having to rush anything or even have a romantic intent. Karen and Frank took their time. They had the ability to work together before he was reassigned. They started seeing each other socially after they had established a working relationship of respect. Joanne (also from Chapter 1) had the time to work out what she thought were Tom's sexist feelings. It seemed to her that he didn't want to work with women, when in fact he was just shy.

Whether you're meeting one another at company-sponsored activities or continually working together, you are establishing a common bond of mutual experiences and respect. That's what friendship is all about, and the more solid the foundation, the better your chances at love.

Date Because You Like Each Other—Not for Power

It's a matter of common sense (supported by the research): friendship is a better foundation for a long-term relationship than an affair entered into because someone sees they can gain something. The danger of opportunism is greater with boss-subordinate situations than with peer or coworker associations. However, it can exist in any relationship, depending on whether the lovers are truly "in like" or one feels that the romance can help his or her career along.

It's important to become involved for the right reason. No matter how hard we try to be egalitarian and democratic in organizations, rank does matter and power plays its part. If a lower level worker tries to romance a higher-up for more power or prestige, coworkers pick up on this. They will be not only nonsupportive but even downright hostile. Charges of favoritism will become more than an academic concept. Think how you would feel if someone at your level became involved with your boss and you saw them holding hands? This is also why lovers keep their relationship to themselves, despite the organization's policies.

Anyone can have an impure motive, even outside work—this is what movies are made out of. If someone's working under you and you're interested, be sure to ask the age-old question "Do they want me for my money (status, power, new car, or whatever) or for myself." Harry observed, "People aren't stupid; they figure out what's going on. It just takes some people longer than others."

Obviously, if you think someone's not interested in you for yourself but for some work-related reason, then this has to spell trouble. For example, a woman dates a man to get a promotion. If the man figures this out later, he's not going to be very happy about it. Neither will the woman be happy if she doesn't get what she wants; this kind of situation can end up as a sexual harassment complaint.

Let's assume that the conspiring lover does get what's wanted— the sought-after raise, the good job evaluation, or more time off. Coworkers will go ballistic over this. It's one thing to suspect that there's favoritism, it's another to actually see it take place.

Even the appearance of an unfair advantage can trigger both coworkers and management to complain loudly. Professor Pierce observes, "The role of an insincere motive creates enormous complications, whether the romance ends or not. Even the perception of favoritism can cause big problems, affecting not only the participants, but also as to how their coworkers react." If you are going to "go for the gold," it's better to have good motives in mind. Fewer recriminations and problems will exist down the road.

Professors Charles Pierce, Donn Byrne, and Herman Aguinis analyzed studies in this area and concluded that female employees who entered a relationship with job-related motives (such as raises or promotions) stimulated negative gossip, whereas male employees who initiated an involvement with a sincere love motive fostered positive rumors. Thus workers who were perceived as participating in a workplace romance for the purposes of advancing their careers, gaining power, or reducing workloads were more apt to receive a negative reaction. These results shouldn't be too surprising; and, of course, all people (regardless of their sex) can have good, varying, or impure reasons for an affair and not just limited to the workplace.

The impure motive works in other ways. If a worker enters a relationship because he or she's afraid to say no to a supervisor's advances for fear of some work penalty for noncooperation, then this is prima facie evidence of quid pro quo sexual harassment. This clearly isn't romance.

Ask yourself: Are we dating because we like each other? Or is either one of us involved because he or she's afraid to say no? Is either one of us using this relationship to gain some influence, power, or work-related benefit?

The rules are simple: *Don't date because you're afraid to say no. Don't trade sex for power or any other advantage.* This isn't romance, it's sexual harassment. The only question is whether it is reverse harassment (the coworkers legitimately complain) or quid pro quo (an ex-lover does).

The good news is that most of us have better morals, ethics, and judgment. "The great majority of romances aren't this way. The people have more sense," said one HR executive. "Just look at the vast number of romances, long term or not, versus the much smaller numbers of harassment complaints."

Check Out the Corporate Climate

"Relationships happen because they just do. You can be interested in someone, but it takes two to tangle," said Roberta. Some of us, like Carrie, are able to coolly decide whether a potential relationship makes sense in the current company environment. She generally decided not to become involved with reporting situations, although she started relationships with men on training or travel junkets away from the office, including one short-term affair with a supervisor.

It makes sense to check out the corporate climate first, because you need to know what's ahead. We've seen that although most companies don't forbid their employees from dating, the courts have upheld their right to fire you if you violate a known and uniformly applied informal policy, such as prohibiting boss-subordinate relationships. You'll want to assess first the written and unwritten rules, followed by the possible reaction of your coworkers and whether there's a political hyena lurking about.

Let's say you've met an attractive person from the marketing department (you're in finance) after the company's annual picnic. You've "hung out" with some friends, had dinner twice, and a feeling of mutual interest has developed between you. Things could become romantic and that sounds fine. You're enjoying a drink after work, talking about company politics. He then mentions that his single boss is a fun person and they have a good working relationship. That's a good sign about his department and now you can think about yours.

Or you've already become romantically involved, and the two of you are discussing how certain players in the company would react to your relationship if they found out (and eventually they will). How the company and your coworkers will react are important considerations. Laurel, the bank manager who knew her employees well, stated, "Couples might talk about how others in the company will respond when they find out what's going on. Usually, the couple tries instead to keep it a secret from everyone, because that's easier and they don't need to deal with how anyone would respond. However, the coworkers put two and two together eventually, and then the couple has to deal with it."

The office hyena, busybody, or hatchet person exists in any office. It is an unfortunate fact of life when you're working for someone else. A manager became enamored with her assistant, and they worked closely together. She was single and her prime competitor for the next position up was a hard-charging, married man. There was no question that this involvement would cause her some serious political pain. She thought about it, because she also figured out that her assistant had a similar interest in her. At a "working dinner," she laid her cards out on the table. She said that she "liked him a lot," but that there wasn't much they could do about it at this company. He knew what she was talking about, including that the "hard-charger" would make the situation more difficult. They maintained a close, platonic working relationship—that is, until he accepted a job outside the company that had better advancement potential. Soon afterward, they began an intense affair. It turned out later that living together was more difficult than working together, and they eventually split up. In retrospect, both handled their relationship with common sense.

Evaluate the Career Pros and Cons

Evaluate the pros and cons for your career, both assuming the romance works out and assuming it doesn't. If you're in a lower entry position, there may be fewer political considerations and more "is this job really worth it?" factors. If you're at the executive level, it's more likely there's a company edict to "keep your hands off the merchandise" as Randall relayed. It's also true that there will be more impact on a career as a person's position moves higher up the corporate ladder. This doesn't mean that executives don't have romances, and it does help if you control the company, as Bill Gates does. When you don't, you need to be sure that this person is your soulmate before you make a decision that affects your present job or career.

Decide if there are alternative career paths within your company. If you can transfer to another department and maintain your career visibility, then well and good. If not, then it depends on how important your romance is. Frank decided that Karen was more important than any job. As Vicki said, "I wouldn't have entered into the romance, unless I really felt deep in my heart that Bill and I would one day be married." Jacqueline, the human resources director for a HMO, said that her upper level people were choosing their mates over their jobs because "they felt they could always find another one." Whatever your decision, just think this over so you're not surprised or hurt by what happens later.

The widely publicized relationship between William Agee, then the CEO of Bendix Corporation, and Mary Cunningham, a recent Harvard Business School graduate, is still written about—nearly twenty years later. She moved from being his executive assistant for a short time to becoming a Bendix vice president and in top management with stunning speed. Bendix employees, as well as Agee's wife, were quite upset over the long time the two spent together designing company strategies. In the end, Cunningham was forced out of the company and Agee left soon afterward. They married and are still together, embarking on career paths that kept them together. After running their own venture capital firm, Agee left to become the CEO of Morrison Knudsen in 1988, a huge engineering and construction firm. While he was the CEO, Cunningham oversaw Morrison's charitable foundation. They both left when he resigned in 1995. Their romance has met the test of time, and you have to admire this.

If you decide your career is more important, be respectful of the other person's feelings. Explain nicely that the current political climate means that a work relationship is all you can handle now. If their interest continues at your next business contact, you need to say firmly that there's only time for business. Don't drink wine at any subsequent after-work meetings—coffee makes more sense. Make an excuse for a coworker to attend so that later harassment allegations can't be made. In problem "they won't take no for an answer" situations, keep an up-to-date diary of all that's said, including dates, times, and who was present—just in case.

Most situations don't end up with Hollywood's problems of a *Disclosure* or *Fatal Attraction* (movies where an affair ends in one ex-lover's deadly obsession with the other). You can decide positively to pour your energies into work. Give some space and see later if the other wants to be friends. As Laurel said, "Channel your energies into getting raises and advancing within the company. Working toward a platonic, work-committed relationship can be better than having a hostile one or no involvement at all. Sell the other party on the advantages of this to both your careers."

Create a Mutual Partnership

Joint Partnering

One of the most satisfying developments in today's work environment is that couples are "joint partnering"—they have to, given the obstacles that various organizations and coworkers put in their way. For romance to win out, the couple has to bond and strive to make their work relationship a success. This means that equal decision making and joint responsibility are always in play.

Business consultant Tom Davidow said: "Whether they're supervisory or not, employees who become 'in like' should talk to each other. They should understand that this will change the nature of their work relationship. The couple needs to discuss what if it doesn't work out, what if the relationship does, and when should they tell their boss and coworkers."

Laurel relayed, "This is what causes the bonding in the first place. There always will be someone who's upset when they find out about your romance or some obstacle that's put in your path—that's life. You'll never please everyone, even if you stayed celibate, donated all your money to charity, and volunteered all your spare time for charities. Someone would complain that you weren't spending enough time on the company's business. When coworkers complain or companies discourage a relationship, then the couples are forced to pull together and overcome those problems as equal partners, even if one or both head off to another firm." See Chapter 10, "Partnering the Relationship."

Decide on the Rules in the Beginning

Partners need to discuss the inner workings of their relationship and their plan. How do you keep your relationship quiet and discreet? When do you tell the boss? If you're the boss and the other the subordinate, then who stays, goes, or transfers? Can responsibilities be realigned, such as performance and compensation evaluations, and keep the present working relationship? Whose career is to be protected, or does this even make a difference? "The process brings you closer. It's as if the two of you are alone in a fort trying to hold off the rest of the world," said Suzanne, echoing Laurel's point.

There are even more considerations. You'll need to decide whether to keep the same routine at work or not. Some couples decide to continue drinking coffee together, eating lunch as a couple, or participating with after-work committees, while others decide it's better to shed these tip-offs. The couple needs to decide the amount of work each will bring home from the office; how to leave personal arguments at home, including the times when you're really upset; approaching differences of opinion on work-related issues, so your coworkers don't think it's an argument brought over from home; and on (see Chapter 10 further).

Keep It Quiet and Discreet

The great majority of couples decide to keep their romance to themselves (one *HR Management* study reported that two-thirds of all workers try to keep it a secret). There are a few reasons: it isn't anyone's business; it's safer that way, because no one can get upset; and some people instinctively keep their private thoughts and affairs to themselves. "The best romance is one that no one at the company knows about," said Jacqueline, echoing a common theme. "How can employees get upset if they don't know what's going on; and companies don't act on suspicions, only complaints with some sort of proof."

People will go to great lengths to ensure this. They'll take different cabs from and to work, or one lover will drop off the other before driving into the parking lot. They try to act as professional as possible during the day, then leave separately from work to meet up at the appointed place. Or as Harry pointed out: "They play this game of 'you can't see me,' by coming to work separately. They split after work in different directions, walk a few blocks away, then meet and head off together. I saw that happen once from my top-floor office, and I'm still laughing about that couple. They might take different routes to end up at the same restaurant and other discreet meeting places. They'll head off on vacations, but one makes up an alibi that he or she was somewhere else—which I did one time. The point is: they'll fool some people, maybe most, but usually someone figures out what's going on. It's only a question of time."

However, some couples can become quite successful at this. An office manager and an architect at an architectural firm kept their romance a secret for two years, although it was a small office with only nine people. A lawyer and his paralegal met away from where they thought their coworkers would be; whether it was luck or not, they weren't discovered for eighteen months. It makes a difference, as you would expect, whether your town is small with 15,000 people or a large city with 2 million to hide in, and whether your company has 5 employees or 15,000.

Use discretion and keep the romance under wraps until the time is best to disclose it, but understand that someone might have already figured everything out (and see further Chapter 11, "Dealing With Those Around You"). Sometimes you're just discovered. When Alex and Samantha decided to elope and marry, they traveled by jet into Chicago to catch a later flight to the Bahamas. Once they sat down on their Chicago flight, they discovered a silent fellow professor staring at them from the back. He turned away and never mentioned it to them, even after they returned with the news that they were now married—it was to that professor's credit. Not all of your coworkers will be this way.

Keep Your Confidences to Yourself

Don't be too gushy or revealing with your E-mails, memos, or other communications to your partner. Remember what happened to Katherine and her E-mail messages: there's too much potential for trouble if the wrong people get their hands on them. One office hyena came across a lover's message and put copies in the in-box of everyone at the office; you wouldn't want your Valentine's Day love message E-mailed to every company employee.

This advice may be hard to follow, but try to avoid telling even your best friend about your affair. It's too easy for the information to be inadvertently leaked out. For example, Donna's romance had been humming along for a month. Then, as she recalled, "I told my best friend, at least at that time I thought she was, about what was going on between George and me. This news went through that organization in twenty-four hours like a wildfire."

Unless you're friends with an uncommonly understanding spouse or ex-lover, don't automatically tell them or "spill the beans" about your new love. If they're the jealous type, you could be opening yourself up to a sexual harassment complaint. We've already seen that with the ex-lover who lodged the complaint against the surgeon and her new love. When Alex told his wife that he wanted a divorce to marry Samantha, his wife ended up calling the chairman of his department and complaining bitterly about what was going on (and that truly didn't help matters). When Jeffrey's wife suspected his involvement with Suzanne, she hired a private investigator, then complained to the human resources manager of their company. The studies indicate that most relationships are discovered either by observant coworkers or because one of the lovers tells a friend. If you try your best to keep everything to yourself until the right time, your coworkers should respect your efforts.

Don't Hold Hands by the Fax Machine

The overwhelming advice from everyone who's had an office romance is to keep your affections to yourself. As one postal worker said, "People feel uncomfortable when others make 'public displays of affection.' Being involved is one thing, rubbing that relationship in your coworkers' faces is another. This just adds fuel to the fire." When Alex was asked whether he and Samantha held hands in the department hallway, even after they were married, he answered in a bemused way: "Are you crazy? We had enough problems with some faculty and administrators over our age difference, the prior student-professor relationship, and that I was still teaching all those other students."

A postal employee, who's married to the postmaster of a small office, said: "People should keep their affections to themselves. When we were seeing each other, we would go to office parties and stay at opposite ends of the room. We would meet people as individuals, not as a couple. We do that now, even though we're married." Although married couples can work together at the same post office, these two transferred to different post offices in the same Washington county, he as the postmaster of one, she working for a larger but nearby one.

A partner in a small law firm said, "Even though my secretary and I are married, we always maintain a professional image for all our clients." You must maintain a professional image for your company, clients, suppliers, and employees. Keep your feelings to yourself.

However, there's no question about the advantages of work romances, once the word is out. "If I was having a bad day," said Vicki, "I could head to Bill's office and talk." Suzanne said, "If I was bored, or had an off-time, Jeffrey and I always could take a walk together outside." Another couple agreed they liked being able to see other during the day. This gave them something in common to discuss every day.

As Donna said, "It's easier to respect someone for their own self and work, especially when that complements what you're doing or helps you understand what's going on. There's a comfort level in knowing that a close friend is just down the hall or in the next building." But keep this to a minimum, whether the word's out or not.

Exit Routes

Last, but certainly not least, couples should discuss the "exit routes" they'll use if the romance doesn't last—and in the beginning, not at the end. What will you do if the affair doesn't work out?

Even when flush with the excitement of a new romance, talk with your partner about how you'll handle working together afterward. This isn't being negative, it's just that there could be job or career implications should your romance end prematurely, not to mention the corporate climate.

If your affair is with someone you don't see often, there are limited problems in this regard. On the other hand, if you're working in the same department, you could be seeing each other every day—as long as both of you stay there. Ask yourself what you'll do if Mr. or Ms. Ex-Lover is working next to you and yells, "Your new lover's on the line, what do I say now?"

You'll need to maintain a professional image even when you meet your ex-lover, and that may not be easy to do. Let's say that you've met the "right one." If he or she works in your department, or for you, consider how important your job is to you, who can transfer (or stay), and what you can do to stay where you are, should your involvement end. Regardless of what actually happens later, it makes sense to discuss this with your partner before any problems could occur that would keep you from talking constructively with one another. See Chapter 14, "When Good Things Come to an End."

Chapter Nine

Running From the Blocks

It's an exciting time when you've met someone new, definitely like that person, and know the feeling's mutual. There are few things in life that match this high. The problem is when the feelings aren't mutual, and you've heard or told the person "no, thank you."

If after you've declined, the other person continues to make advances and not accept your responses, you still have alternatives: state more firmly that it's just not in the cards; ask a coworker to talk to the person on your behalf, then follow up with a written refusal; if the suitor continues, make a complaint to a superior; if all else fails and the conduct persists, make a sexual harassment charge. If the overtones were sexual in nature and not welcome, you have a harassment complaint at the very start.

But if you really like the other, and he or she seems to feel the same way, then it's time to smile. You've thought about the boss, business climate, and possible risks to your career. Right? . . . Probably not.

Although you should spend some time and thought making an objective decision, most of us really don't. We're eager and ready to spend some time with that person and get things going. Our heart usually takes over—love and the basic attraction between the sexes does this.

Starting Off

Work provides such wonderful ways to meet people and stay in touch. June worked at a post office in one part of the state, then transferred north to a smaller location. A clerk from the old branch, Tex, came later to that town on a vacation. Tex had always liked June, but she was married at the time to another postal worker—whom she had met at work. He stopped by the new post office just to say "hi" to her. When June said she was going through a divorce, Tex quickly asked her out for dinner. They've been in a long-term relationship for two years, and he's trying to transfer up to her location. Now, if that isn't a switch from when employees ask or are asked to transfer away when they become involved. It simply depends on the organization.

People communicate their romantic interest in a variety of ways. Jim was a program director for a radio station, and he worked closely with his secretary, Robin, for some months. They had never spent any time together socially or after work. Robin then told Jim she was quitting. When he asked why, Robin hesitated, then said she was in love with him. Jim blushed at first. When he answered, he said that he felt the same way. They started dating and married soon afterward.

Working at an office doesn't mean that your alternatives are limited to coworkers, vendors, or strict business relationships. Laura was a young woman who worked as an accountant for a department store in a small Oregon town. Lanny was enduring a divorce at the time, and a friend told him to look up Laura at the department store. This wasn't a problem for him because he usually shopped there to buy his fishing tackle. Not the bashful type, Lanny walked up to Laura's office and introduced himself. They talked and he discovered she also loved to fish. A few days later, Laura looked up and spotted a fishing rod leaning against her window. A rose had been attached to it with a note from Lanny inviting her on a fishing trip. They've been together ever since and have been happily married for over ten years.

An intern and a nurse worked together at a hospital. When a terminally ill patient in their care died tragically, they left the hospital to get away from it all. They bared their souls to one another over cups of coffee, and later that day he called to invite her out for dinner. They married one year later. However, they grew apart as people can and divorced after six years. The ex-wife remarried another doctor. The ex-husband married again, this time to a woman he met while walking his dog in a nearby park. That marriage didn't last, so he married a third time to a gynecologist he had met at the hospital, and this relationship has lasted. All of these relationships were work related—except, of course, for the dog.

A dispatcher met her husband when she was leaving the fire department to take another job, and he was coming there to accept one. Two reporters met in the newsroom of a major metropolitan newspaper; they've been married now for fifteen years and still work in the same office.

One worker became interested in the firm's receptionist but held off asking her out, worried about being turned down and about the company's policies. The firm had a turn for the worse and went out of business. He asked her out on the last day the doors were to be open, and she accepted. They married a few months later.

Toni was a marketing manager for a large company. She had briefly met a guy she immediately liked at a joint production-marketing meeting. Wanting to know him better, she called a friend in the production department and asked if he was single and available. Her friend said he didn't know but would check it out and get back to her. Toni received an E-mail the next day from the guy, saying that there were a few work details left over from their meeting that ought to be discussed, perhaps, over lunch. She learned later that her friend had gone directly to the source. There are so many ways to communicate.

E-Mail and Romance

There aren't meaningful statistics on how many people have discovered each other through computers and E-mail chat rooms. One thirty-year-old woman, divorced with two children, discovered her new husband through a computer service's chat room. After sending messages in front of others at one gathering, he invited her to meet in a "private chat room." An intense E-mail relationship developed between them, supplemented by long telephone calls, letters, and exchanges of photographs. He invited her and her children to visit him. After a long-distance relationship, they're now living together. As their relationship was developing, she was living 3,000 miles away in Southern California and he was living in New York City. As my wife Judy said, "It used to be that a 'geographically undesirable' relationship was when you had to drive a few hours to see your lover."

E-mail has changed the look of the future in many ways, including romance. A college instructor is dating a lady in another department; it started when she sent an E-mail message with "how about lunch today?" mixed in with the work details. A manager in his thirties with a small company would E-mail one of her customers back and forth on business details; she invited him to see her when he was next in town. He asked her out for dinner, and they've been together now for several years.

Another couple first met at a company dinner for its managers.

They corresponded by E-mail with brief, fun messages, as they worked in different buildings. The woman a week later E-mailed a light "do you like tennis?" He did, she did, and they started dating.

For the shy and sensitive, E-mail can be the ideal way to meet. It is easier to handle rejections, and some people seem wittier and come off better with their messages. Unfortunately, E-mails leave permanent trails. You should simply use discretion with your words. Don't send gushy messages if you don't know the person—be subtle. Or tell them in person, if you're already in a relationship. Show any message first to a friend before you send it, if you have any doubts.

There are the stories of prospective suitors who jammed a message box full of "love" notes with hundreds of E-mail messages. That's not love and indicates a basic lack of common sense at best—the great majority of us aren't this way. Be sure that your communications are romantic in nature, not blatant sexual requests or too "sappy." Courts in a few cases have held that coworkers have a harassment case simply by becoming offended when reading sexually explicit messages over another worker's shoulders. Although being issued a password to receive and send your E-mail messages offers some protection, you're always better off not using a medium at work that creates its own easily discovered trail.

Instead of sending personal messages over the company's electronic network, use the private chat room of an independent Internet provider with different passwords. Most couples simply pick up the telephone and use their own code to be sure that everything's kept quiet. The best rule is to keep the business to the office and personal communications at home.

Problem Situations

There are pitfalls, especially in today's politically correct world. Your advances can be turned down, and you can run into later problems, even if somebody accepts the invitation. The risks are there because nothing in life is free.

Rejections

The experts don't have to tell us that the sexes are different—all of us know that. For example, women tend to think a relationship at first will continue to be nonsexual, while men are inclined to believe that if it keeps going well, it will develop sooner into a sexual relationship. Women can be as sexually oriented as men, as we've seen with Carrie, but it depends on the person, place, time, and where their mind is at the time.

The problem is that either sex can misinterpret when someone else's interested in them. Communication is a two-way street, and problems occur when the man thinks there's sexual interest (and there isn't) or the woman's flirting (and that's all there is). Men tell stories of women leading them on, then refusing to go further into a more intense relationship. Women talk about having a fun time, then all of a sudden the man's making sexual advances. This in turn leads us into the treacherous waters of sexual harassment.

The one-size-fits-all approach in use today creates the emotionally charged "thrust and counterthrust" charges of sexual harassment, regardless of any true harassment intent being present. For example, a salesman struck up a conversation with a female sales rep at a branch office. They had dinner and both admittedly enjoyed each other's company. They stayed out drinking until late at night. When he tried to kiss her at the end of their date, she not only refused but also turned around and filed a sexual harassment charge against him. Apparently she felt duty bound under the company's policy to make this charge. The facts indicated that the attempted kiss was all there was to the salesman's conduct; the sales rep's charges were hardly more justified than those brought against little Jonathan Prevette for kissing a playmate on the cheek. The salesman countercharged that the sales rep had led him on and how could one attempt be harassment. He was warned—but both lost. This by all accounts is showing too much "sensitivity."

The good news is that cases like this are in the definite small minority. Keep also in mind that meeting someone at work, dating, and then breaking up can't by itself mean that a harassment case is present. Conduct must be primarily sexual in nature (although there's a technical gender discrimination argument) and adversely affect a term or condition of employment. What's unfortunate is that when the parties are being discreet, have a falling out, and the injured party (usually the woman) charges harassment—both lose in this situation unless this meets the legal tests (see Chapter 15 further). Fortunately, this doesn't occur nearly as frequently as most businesses fear.

Jacqueline, the human resources executive, said, "It's not the fact that someone asked someone out and was refused; or even that there was further pursuit. What I looked for was whether there was *retaliation* for that refusal, or whether there was such an effort made to get together, or back together, that the work environment was adversely affected."

An important rule of romance is that *you can ask a person out for a date and be rejected, even at work, and this isn't legal sexual harassment, or actionable as improper conduct.* You can ask again, and you're still okay (provided that you act graciously both in asking and in accepting the response).

For example, a businessman invited a coworker to a lunch to discuss some minor work details. While talking about personal matters, he asked if she'd like to go to dinner the following week. When she said no, he asked if another time would be better. She said she had too much to do at work. He moved on to another subject. Several weeks later, he asked her again and she said "no, thank you" again. That was the last time he asked. This approach could never be harassment in any sense of the word. In this case, the businessman wound up in a long-term relationship with someone in a different department.

As Laurel said, "Why waste your time on anyone or anything that's uninterested, negative, or surly? Learn to pass on the problems. Also, you should keep your follow-ups at work to an absolute minimum—call at home but use finesse."

However, part of any company's climate is what some would call "office protocol." There isn't one general standard for "proper" conduct, just as sexual harassment law relies on vague words and hard-to-apply concepts. It depends after all on the circumstances, the particular industry, the company, the people in control, and whether management makes managing its "image" more important than holding to what's fair for all.

Let's assume that a worker hands his coworker a valentine, asks her out for a date, but she refuses. He asks again politely a week later, but makes it clear that it's the last time when he's refused. The woman complains to her supervisor. In one company, this might become grounds for a written warning; in another, the supervisor might talk to both and let the matter drop. The whole episode might be ignored in the entertainment or real estate industry, and in most cases, this situation is not going to be taken further.

However, rejection in our current working environment carries with it more than just being turned down. Before you ask someone out for the first or even second time, ask yourself what their reaction might be.

Office Hyenas, Office Wolves, and Black Widows

A number of animals lurk inside offices. The office hyena waits for any scrap of meat that can get somebody else into trouble; we will discuss this species later in the book. Office wolves and black widows also frequent the working environment. Whether they're inside the office or outside at the gym, people can be on different wavelengths when they search for partners. Most of us can commit and are honest in our efforts. We also know there are people who only look to carve another notch on their bedroom posts—and both sexes are guilty of this practice.

The office wolf isn't the same animal he was in the old days. As Harry observed, "Men who have a reputation as the office predator with women are becoming toast. What was winked at fifteen years ago simply isn't the case these days. The sexual harassment laws and their enforcement have drastically changed everything."

Office wolves are becoming extinct in other ways. Carl, another business owner, told this story: "One of my employees was trying very hard to get something going with a married woman. She tried to handle it herself, but the guy kept coming on, and he thought he was pretty cool with the ladies. So the woman and I talked about what we could do, since all she wanted was for this guy to stop. I didn't want to fire the man either, because he would be hard to replace, but we didn't know what to do. I told her to tell her husband to come in— but not to tell anyone about the visit. If that didn't work, then I'd have to step in and hard. Anyway, her husband came in, and he's a husky man. He just stood in front of the guy, wordlessly, silently, and very menacing. When he left ten minutes later, our guy apologized profusely to the wife. He got the message, because he never asked her out again and became a very polite guy from then on. It was a very effective solution."

Another boyfriend walked into an office wolf's cubicle, smiled, chatted amicably, and left saying with a Hannibal Lecter look that he'd "shoot anyone who fooled around with my girlfriend." However, this species isn't extinct, nor is its female counterpart the "black widow." Be sure that you know whom you're becoming involved with in the beginning. Or if you want the adventure, at least you know you've been warned in advance.

Mike

There is something about law firms, *L.A. Law,* and the people in the practice when it comes to this area. It must be due to the daily stress of court deadlines, men and women working closely together, and the conflicts inherent in the profession.

Mike is a thirty-year-old manager who works for a huge Los Angeles mega–law firm with four hundred attorneys and offices located throughout the world; the firm is also highly rated for its legal defense of corporate sexual harassment cases. Mike is one of two managing paralegals, and he supervises many of the paralegals who work with the attorneys on their cases. He is attractive, personable, and energetic.

Mike found a job for his wife as a legal assistant with his law firm. His wife, who was "drop-dead gorgeous," and a lead partner became romantically involved, even though the partner was her boss, twenty years older, married, and the father of three grown children. The partner left to start his own boutique law firm, taking along other attorneys, employees, and Mike's wife. At the same time, Mike's wife and the partner left their spouses to live together.

Mike, of course, was heartbroken as another jilted spouse. He started "dating up a storm" in response. Mike was honest and up front with the women he saw, starting with the first paralegal he dated. He said that he couldn't relate to women due to "what his ex-wife had done," but that he wanted to become involved and know them. And that's exactly what happened. He treated everyone the same way on case assignments, work hours, and reviews. As one woman who dated him observed, "Some women got mad when he broke off from them, but no one complained because he was honest, up front, and didn't show any favoritism."

When his first affair died, the woman was angry and "didn't give him the time of day" because she had wanted to keep it going. However, there weren't any repercussions because she worked under the second managing paralegal. The word went out that he was available, didn't want a commitment, and was only out for fun. Mike had affairs with employees that year, all of them paralegals or legal assistants (some worked for him and others didn't). He treated all of the women he dated with charm and respect, although he couldn't commit, and Mike told that to everyone he dated. He stayed friends afterward with most, but two didn't like the breaking up—but no complaints were made.

Mike transferred on his own from L.A. to the firm's New York City office because working in Los Angeles reminded him of his ex-wife. He "cocooned" in New York for less than a year, then transferred back to the L.A. office after he became bored. Mike knew the people there, and it was easier to have a social life. He quickly entered into a relationship with another paralegal on his return. This one also recently ended, as had all the others.

Debbie

Debbie and Rex worked for a post office branch in Chicago. They worked the graveyard shift, where there weren't many others working that shift. Debbie was an attractive, middle-aged woman who wore nice clothes, even when they would get dirty from all the mail she handled. Rex, at the end of one shift, asked her out for lunch the next day, and Debbie accepted. They quickly fell into an affair, and Debbie just as quickly started to work on improving Rex's manners, clothes, and image. He loved it and started wearing more stylish clothes as Debbie wanted.

One day, he took home a box of candied fruit that had been returned and ate all of them. Post office's regulations are clear that workers must dispose of all dated material after a certain date. As one manager explained, "If the package is marked 'don't return,' then you don't return it; you throw the package away and don't use it in any way for personal use. This procedure saves the sending company from having to pay return postage."

Debbie turned Rex into his supervisor for eating the box of candied fruit. Although he hadn't made a practice of taking returned packages, Rex lost his job due to this violation. Shortly afterward, Debbie broke up with him. A coworker of Debbie explained: "This was a problem involving a hate relationship with men. She's an attractive woman and has outwardly good tastes. But Debbie's done this before with other men, either turning them in over some infraction and then breaking up, or just breaking their hearts when she thinks they're hopelessly in love with her. Around here we've named her the 'black widow.'"

The Ferrari

David is a dashing, entertainment mogul in his mid-forties. He built up his large, independent movie production company through hard work, good contacts, and a smooth manner. David also has a sweet tooth for fast cars and beautiful women. He's considered one of the most eligible bachelors around Hollywood. Mindy worked in David's executive offices in marketing and liked what she saw.

A young, beautiful woman in her thirties, she told a friend at work that she would "land" the boss. Mindy soon "accidentally" paraded through David's office wearing a wide black-brimmed hat, a halter top, and black leggings. A few days later, she waited for him by his car, a beautiful fireball-red Ferrari. She was dressed provocatively again, this time in a form-fitting red bodysuit with high heels. David asked if she liked the car, whereupon Mindy described in detail all of the features of that particular model, in comparison with other models and automobiles. Impressed by her knowledge, David asked if she would like to take a ride sometime in his Ferrari.

She replied, "How about next Tuesday after work?" He said fine, got into the car, and sped away. The following Monday, Mindy sent him an E-mail message, reminding him about their upcoming ride. He called her back that day saying now that wouldn't be a good time. They then set next Friday as the time. When he didn't answer her Thursday reminder message, she stopped him in the parking lot that Friday afternoon as he unlocked his car door. Mindy asked if this still was a good time to take a spin. It was. They also ended up spending the night together at David's house.

During the next few weeks, they spent a half-dozen nights together. David was also seeing an ex-girlfriend at the time, as well as other women. One Friday, Mindy sent him an E-mail, asking "How do you deal with a tension that's about ready to split your mind in half and send you screaming through your office plateglass window." He answered back, "SEX." The morning after another steaming lovemaking session together, she sent him an E-mail message asking to borrow $50,000 from him personally to invest in one of their movie productions. From then on, she asked David about this loan every time they met and had sex.

At the same time, Mindy's colleagues were grumbling about her work performance—the movie she was responsible for promoting wasn't doing well. The box office receipts weren't at expected levels. Senior executives became upset when she wouldn't return their phone calls asking for details. Her superior said she wasn't a team player, but Mindy shrugged the criticism off, saying that her boss was more worried about Mindy taking over her job.

After David turned down her last effort to get $50,000 from him, Mindy decided that she might be in trouble after all. When she was fired for poor performance, Mindy filed a sexual harassment lawsuit against David and his company, demanding a substantial amount of money. She alleged that David had raped her, charging that she had been fired because she had refused to continue their sexual relationship.

However, witnesses would testify that Mindy went out with David the next day after the alleged incident to see a matinee movie. Her case against David quickly evaporated, as witness after witness came forward to say that Mindy's bad motives were the reason for the entire situation and ensuing lawsuit. The settlement, according to the attorneys, was "next to nothing" and motivated to stop any further bad publicity, management downtime, and large attorney fees being expended on this matter.

Motive is all important to whether a particular romance will last—and should it end, then job- or money-related reasons coupled with the wrong person will lead to bitter confrontations. The good news is that vast numbers of romances are nothing like what we've seen above—but be sure that your lover is the soul mate you've been searching for all your life, especially when your job might be on the line.

People Are People

Love happens in strange places and ways. A man and woman traveled with other executives to Japan, returning without showing any apparent interest in the other. It had been an exhausting two-week trip. When they stepped out of the taxi in front of their corporate office, the man turned and said to her without thinking, "I love you." She replied, in front of her stunned companions, "I do, too." The movies couldn't be any stranger than what is seen in real life.

After another long, hard workweek, the company's golf tournament was about to start that weekend. Two vice presidents were paired off, although they had argued strenuously that week on opposite sides of a particular acquisition decision. Although it wasn't known what part the company president had played in the assignment, you would probably win betting on the side of Cupid. They played eighteen holes of golf respectably that day; in fact, they won their division.

Their names were etched on a permanent trophy, and the president toasted them at the awards dinner. As the two sat together, they discovered they had similar interests, which included ballroom dancing. It wasn't long before they started dating and romance took over from there. They married shortly thereafter and stayed with the company, working for a quite bemused president. The three of them worked together very well, up to the time when the company was sold and all three retired.

Other companies are not as progressive as this one and its president. And it takes passion and courage to continue a relationship in the face of the obstacles—which even include you and your partner. "At first," said one involved manager, "I had the guilts. It was as if I was doing something wrong, and I was single at the time." There can be the "what if?" worries. What if the boss finds out and disapproves? What if we don't make it? People are human and they can have insecurities, despite a newfound love. However, the good news is that you have someone now with whom you can share your feelings, whether warm and supportive or cold and insecure at the time. There are two of you.

It takes joint partnering these days to overcome the obstacles, especially at the less progressive firms. You will need to work together from the start.

Chapter Ten

Partnering the Relationship

If ever there was a "male prerogative" in romance, it's long gone now. The workforce is not made up of male managers with female secretaries as a rule. Men and women work together as equals today in many companies, and women are securing more positions of power over time.

When working as equals in the workforce, couples will work together more as partners to handle difficulties. Good communication from the beginning sets the stage for a solid relationship—or at least minimizes the problems. Whether the relationship works out or not, everything works better if the couple pulls together at the start. This is also why these romances have the better odds in staying together.

When people become romantically involved through work, they must decide on some rules—whether what's done is assumed and instinctive, or more considered and discussed in depth. As the organization and job responsibilities become more structured and formalized, couples are forced to consider more job-related factors, such as Lyle and Vi (then Tommy and Nicki) in this chapter.

Jill, then a waitress in her mid-twenties, told about one situation: "It was a young person's dream at this hotel, as everyone here was about the same age, some attending or already having graduated from college. It was a beach resort community. Although each of us was assigned a number of tables to work, you talked with other waiters and waitresses when working together. One guy worked close to me, and he asked me one day if he could take me out to dinner. I agreed and we started dating after that. We didn't tell anyone at work at first about what we were doing, even when we knew that other waiters, waitresses, and busboys were also dating. We didn't want this to cause us problems at work. It was our own personal business, and we didn't want people to talk about us. We broke up a few months later, and this had little influence on our jobs. We were discreet, didn't tell any-one, and focused on our work."

It Starts in the Beginning

When managers and executives become romantically involved, they're typically older and have already "sowed their oats." They are more serious and very career oriented. "These relationships tend to be more serious because there's more on the line," said Jacqueline, the seasoned human resources executive. "If you've spent some years building up your career, you're less likely to do what you did when you were young. You're not as likely to try out different relationships as you would shoes to find the one that wears best."

Whether they're young or old, lovers want a serious relationship to succeed. The key to having a successful one is "joint partnering," which translates to discussing and deciding together the important areas that will affect your relationship over time. Since both careers are affected by a couple's choices, today's partners are making these decisions together.

Start at the very beginning with these considerations. The discussion of your joint concerns shouldn't be treated like a negotiation between two attorneys trying to hammer out a deal under a rapidly approaching deadline—after all this isn't a business transaction, but a romance. Talk about what concerns your work, career, and cowork-ers away from the office, and choose a relaxed setting—walking through a park, eating dinner out, or sitting at home on a comfortable sofa. It starts with considering certain basic factors, including the work-related ones, that are involved in the relationship.

What Each Receives

What each expects to receive from the relationship needs to be dis-cussed. Is it just about fun and games, as Mike was clear to mention, or is this relationship more serious with job advancements on the line? Is one of you more motivated for job-related benefits or material goals? Are your feelings for each other mutual?

A relationship that meets the test of time is one in which both people receive and give so that the relationship survives. It obviously can't be a one-sided effort, as where one person receives much more than the other. For example, if one lover isn't around a lot because of a heavy travel schedule, this factor may very well become a problem. If one partner doesn't fully commit to the relationship, then it isn't going very far.

Judy Kaiser said, "I met someone at work and we started dating. We kept it quiet at first, then we decided to go public, at least when we told a close friend. We had a lot of fun together, good sex, and nice times, but he wouldn't commit to me. We broke up a few months later, because I wanted more from the relationship than he did."

What Each Gives

As part of this discussion, each lover must know what the other is prepared to give up for both the romance and the partner. If there's a problem with the company's climate or a reporting relationship, who will stay, realign responsibilities, transfer, or leave? You don't have to decide exactly who's going to sacrifice what for the common good, just what you might do if there are problems. If you can't agree, at least you know the potential pitfalls that lie ahead.

These are basic considerations that go to the heart of any romance. For example, if someone is married, the obvious question is whether he or she will leave their spouse for the other. As Laurel said, "Each party has to know that there's a mutual give-and-take attitude; if not, then this relationship is heading into trouble."

Both partners in a chain-of-command relationship must know that their intentions are serious and long term. As we've seen, a lot is on the line in such romances. Today's involvements are more complicated because each party will have a career path independent but joined by the relationship with the other. If one's a manager and the other is an assistant manager in another department, then each has a different career route. However, when their romance is discovered, the two will be viewed more as one.

When to Go Public

As one manager who had an office romance said, "Although you give this a lot of effort, keeping everything quiet for a length of time is difficult. At some point in the affair, you're going to have to deal with the fact that the word is out."

We were introduced to Lyle and Vi in Chapter 7. They began an intense association and decided to keep it quiet (a quite typical response). Then Vi became sick one Friday and spent the time at Lyle's apartment. A coworker called Lyle before he got home that night about a collection matter, and Vi picked up the phone without thinking. Each recognized the other's voice and the cat was out of the bag. Vi said that Lyle wasn't there, but that he would call back when he got home. When Lyle called back, he didn't mention how he received the information about the phone call—but people knew.

Vi and Lyle talked over the weekend about what they should do. That Monday they put their plan into action. They decided not to say anything further to the caller about their relationship. In fact, Vi didn't respond when she approached him on a work matter, even when she recognized a certain smug smile on his face.

They continued to maintain distance from each other at work, having decided to preserve a separate but professional image at the company. That day, Lyle and Vi each told their closest friend at work what was happening, asking for advice in turn. One friend was surprised, the other was not. Both agreed that Lyle's boss would be the trickier of the two because she was a stickler for office decorum. Lyle could only agree when he thought about it.

Lyle and Vi talked far into the night. They decided each would tell their supervisor about the relationship. This step would be important for both of them. When you tell a higher-up about your romance, you've decided that it has some lasting power (or it better have). When people break up outside the work arena, there isn't the embarrassment of having to confront people every day about the breakup. This isn't the case at work. Although Lyle's boss was hesitant in her endorsement of the relationship, Vi's supervisor was more understanding. The word was definitely out. We'll catch up with them later.

This Doesn't Mean You Stay Together

Joint partnering doesn't mean you'll stay together forever and ever. One-half of all first-time marriages end in divorce today, no matter where you meet. Nothing lasts forever—and people can decide to end involvements just as easily as they can decide to continue them.

Two managers at a small computer peripherals manufacturer began dating. They didn't report to one another, although they did work together on the job evaluations of workers whose responsibilities cut into both of their areas. They had just become a twosome, when a company executive spotted them together at dinner. He chatted nicely enough with them, but both could see that he hadn't bought their "working dinner" routine. Their company's approach to the relationship situation would be to transfer one of them to another department.

When they talked this over, they decided that their firm didn't have any openings where either could duck for protection. They talked about the problem for several days, before deciding to see the senior vice president. He was surprised and counseled them against continuing their affair. He confirmed that there weren't any openings (the bad news) but also that he hadn't heard anyone complain yet (the good news). The couple argued later at lunch and decided that the stress was causing both of them to feel uneasy.

It was a momentous decision when one lover said that they'd be better off if none of this had started. The other admitted to having second thoughts also. They talked into the night, then headed back to their own homes and beds. They agreed the following morning that their relationship wouldn't make it, and that their jobs were more important. They told the senior vice president they had decided to end their relationship.

What if the Romance Dies?

Yes, it's hard to think about, even discuss. When it's the best of times, who wants to talk about the worst? However, it's when everything's going right, that you should talk about the "exit routes" if you don't make it. You sure won't be communicating well when times turn bad.

It may seem antiromantic to discuss "bail out" strategies now, but the topic should be on the table. If your affair with a friend of the family ends, you'll only have to deal with that person on holidays. If it involves a coworker, however, you could be seeing each other every day—and being told by coworkers about their new lover, that trip to the Bahamas, or what a great day they've been having. Your exit strategy can be anything, ranging from specific career paths to a resolution to be distant but mutually supportive of each other.

As to the two managers, the decision they made while still friends (but already arguing) would have been much more difficult if they had waited. As Jacqueline commented, "If a couple can't make up their minds on who should leave, then we'll make that decision for them, and especially quick when there's a reporting situation. It's when the two people can't help us or each other out, that we as a company have to make that decision."

A good part of the discussion will depend on how often you actually see one another or work together. If it's not much, consider yourself lucky. If it is, you must decide on how you can stick to business if your personal relationship fails. One idea is to bring a third party to your meetings to keep all discussions on a strictly business plane. Even when you've agreed to "keep all contacts to a bare minimum," if you're still uncomfortable with each other afterward, then transferring and even leaving the company will be potential alternatives. You can also work with your supervisor and within your company's procedures, including the use of mediation (see Chapter 16, "Companies Are People, Too"), when you can't resolve the situation by yourselves. However, this path will be easier if you at least discuss the possibilities *before* any problems occur.

Bob and Betty

We talked about this couple in Chapter 3. The two of them originally worked for different companies (an initial advantage), but they decided to work together in their own company as a joint dream. Bob's story is interesting from both how he and Betty met to his son and grandchildren. Bob related: "My last relationship had ended a few years ago. My development company had run into financial problems, so I was starting all over again. I had to spend a lot of time developing my real estate brokerage business, so there wasn't much left over to socialize. One of my children, Tommy, went through a bitter divorce in Northern California. His wife took off and left him with two young children to raise. It was so upsetting to Tommy that he quit his job to leave the area with his kids and live with me in Southern California.

"I lived in a three-bedroom condominium, so there was room for him and the boys, but it was a tight fit. I watched the kids in between my setting up my real estate practice, while Tommy looked for a job. He located one at a local bank in town. What was ironic to me was that I had raised Tommy and my other children by myself for a few years, when my first wife and I split up, now I found myself doing the same thing with my grandchildren.

"We settled into a routine. I would watch the grandchildren when they came back from school, or a babysitter came when I was showing property or doing my deals. It took a lot of planning and cooperation to get this all done. After some months, we both met women who became the focal points of our lives. Tommy met his at work, and I was introduced to mine by a friend who was playing matchmaker.

"I have a friend who was an escrow officer, and she kept saying that she knew someone that I should meet. I kept saying 'Don't set me up, I'm too busy.' And she would say 'But you just need to meet someone.' And, on the other side, my now-partner was saying the same thing. The matchmaker simply answered, 'Look, let's go out and play some golf. Now how bad can that be?'

"I'm not the greatest golfer, but I can get by with some practice. It was soon evident that my friend hadn't been around a course. When she took a few 'rusty' practice swings as we were teeing off, she admitted she had never played golf before. The jig was up and we all laughed about it. Betty and I played at golf that day and totally enjoyed each other's company, as our matchmaker tagged along with us. We began dating seriously a few months after that first meeting and fell in love.

"Meanwhile, Tommy's girlfriend would come over and spend time with us. Nicki got along great with the grandkids, but it was getting to be real tight with the space. I thought about moving in with Betty, but eventually Tommy and the kids moved out, and Betty moved in. After being alone as long as we both had been, Betty and I are really enjoying our time together. We're happy as we could be." (Note: we'll hear more about Tommy and Nicki's story at the end of the chapter.)

Work Considerations

Even if you feel you can always find another job, the choice of most is to try staying where you are. It's easy to say that you'll willingly transfer or leave if you have to, but actually doing it is another thing. There are commonsense rules to follow at work, and companies assume that you'll be following them even if not written down (they're also included in the sample office romance guidelines in Appendix 1).

Maintain a Professional Image

Work as professionally as you always have. Coworkers complain about people who indulge in public displays of affection at the office because "work is for working," as one employee explained. This doesn't mean that friends (regardless of sex) can't put a hand on a shoulder or pat someone on the back. However, couples shouldn't walk down hallways holding hands or be caught necking behind the water cooler. This kind of behavior isn't within an office's tolerance zone. Nor are suggestive winks, sly looks, or sexual body language that's passed on to another—be discreet and sensitive to those working around you.

Make sure that your work performance remains top-notch. If people are jealous, worried, or angered by your relationship, don't give them any further cause for complaint. Your coworkers will pick up the slightest slippage in your work results. This is another reason why so many couples go to such lengths to hide or deny that there's anything between them.

Each partner should leave the personal relationship at home. Employees are graded on how they perform, not on why they had problems meeting their goals and objectives. Your personal relationship, whether it originated at work or not, isn't a factor you want included in your job evaluations. "Work is work, and home is home. You must keep them apart," said Elizabeth.

Create Safe Communication Channels

Until they've gone public with the news and it's fairly well received by coworkers, each couple must set up their own rules for communication. Some lovers keep in touch by E-mail, others by telephone or talking in person. We've seen that E-mail might not be secure enough or telephones confidential enough (if you work too close to others). You can't always steal away to talk with each other privately. So what can you do?

Your Own Code

"It was like making up our own magic decoder," said one woman who created her own code with her partner. Many couples, even if married, create their own private code or system. One couple used a simple formula: a lover would pick up the phone and dial the other's extension. When that partner picked up the telephone, the dialogue would be:

"How late are you open?" she said.

"Six o'clock," he answered.

"I'll be by later, maybe in an hour and a half to pick up my order."

He was saying by their code that he would be off work at six, and she was saying she would come by his place an hour and a half later. This system relied on each knowing the other's voice, but identification can also be handled by using a nickname.

Another enterprising couple created a table of their own words and symbols. If the first sentence had the word "crater" anywhere, then the caller was the other partner. For example:

"Is this Crater Automotive?" she asked.

"Yes," he said.

"How late are you open?"

The lovers change the key word, depending on how long it had been used, the people who were around, and so on. You can be as creative as you need to be. One couple set up a personal code of "two rings, then get ready." If the phone rang twice, then stopped, the other lover would be calling in a minute or so. This gave the listener time to end whatever was going on at the time, close the office door, and ensure confidentiality.

I know this sounds funny; but company policies sometimes force grown-ups to play these games. If you're at a progressive firm, normal conversations can be used; but you still must be professional and keep the relationship at a distance from your work obligations.

Act the Same as Before

Acting "uptight" or self-conscious is as much to be avoided as not being professional enough. Also, keep your romance under control when at work. For example, don't take long lunches or "nooners" with your partner. One couple decided to take a few long lunches, complete with "romps in the hay." Their boss noticed that they came in late after lunch and their clothing was disheveled. They were fortunate that they only received a warning and weren't fired.

Even if the word's out, you're now married, or the boss says your romance is "peachy keen," every involved employee needs to act professionally at the office. Your coworkers will complain if they perceive that you've changed your habits due to a romance. Enough complaints can force management to intervene, whether you're a lawyer, teacher, executive, fireman, or sales rep. Keep the relationship as unassuming as you can.

Keep Love Separate From Work

Don't confuse your love life with your work life; keep your private life out of your work life, and your job out of your private life. This applies whether you're married or not. Steve said, "There was only one time when I was so upset with Alice that I could have spit nails, but I decided to walk it off before I walked into my office. You have to leave your personal problems at home, or else you're going to feed the rumor mill that you're breaking up. Worse, your quality of work will be affected, and you know what that means."

Joanne said, "Work isn't the place to air out your problems, as that only gets you into even more trouble. We didn't experience this; our problem was keeping the peace when one had to work that night at home, and the other wanted to see a movie. 'Get the work done that needs to be done' is a good rule; however, you also need separate fun time together that's away from work."

Neither person should speak for the other—act like the independent entities you are. One worker pointed out, "My rule is simple: if a question is work related and involves my lover, I'll tell them to take it up with her. It's no different than if it concerned a friend I wasn't involved with; I just don't get caught in the middle of business dialogues. If it's a personal matter involving both of us, then I'll say I'll get back to them after talking about it with my other half."

Consult Frequently With a Work Buddy

Talk with a trusted colleague about what's going on. Although this usually will be after your secret's out, you need to know how your coworkers and the boss perceive your relationship. Is it affecting the work in your group? Are people uncomfortable with what's going on? It isn't as important what you think, it's how others might be looking at you. The information you don't know, as always, is what ends up hurting you.

Lyle and Vi relied on their close friends to keep them up on how others were viewing their relationship. As we saw with Donna, however, you must be able to trust those people.

Think Ahead

You must plan for the contingencies. What will you do when the secret's out? If you're in a reporting relationship, what are you going to do when the big boss calls? If you have problems with your relationship, are your exit routes still available?

Joanne said and Tom agreed: "We needed to stay on top of what was happening within the company, and then, how that would affect us. Everyone needs to know as soon as possible how the organization's problems and strengths will affect him or her personally. The same rule applies when you're involved in an office romance. People leave all the time, and new opportunities are created. Or a friendly ally leaves for a better opportunity, and someone you don't get along with moves into that position. You have to ask yourself if 'X' leaves and 'Y' moves in, then what will this do to us? For example, if there's a job shuffle, you might find yourself switched into your lover's department, creating conflict-of-interest problems. You have to know what happens if your boss leaves, or both of you are affected by an organizational change. It's easier to get your résumé out before there are problems than after they've already occurred."

This preparation includes deciding who's the highest person in the organization you can count on when you do go public. This may even be the person whose blessings you'll need to keep both your present job responsibilities and your relationship—the one who says "yes or no." The higher up this person is, the better the chances you will be supported despite a coworker's complaints about your relationship.

But Enjoy the Romance

As Donna relayed, "We had a real enjoyable time at the start. Dinners out, great romantic times, walks by the beach . . . I still remember them." It's at the beginning of a romance when the chemistry is highest and the emotions are bubbling so positively. Especially if you've taken some risk at work for your romance, be sure to start enjoying it outside the office. This is why you're together in the first place.

A friend of mine who's been married for years tells this vignette about he and his wife: "When we first started going out with one another, Susan would be the first to say 'let's go down to the beach and watch the sunset.' We'd pack a picnic dinner, chill a bottle of wine, and make our way down a narrow path to a secluded cove. By the time we finished eating, the sun would be setting and the views would be quite gorgeous and romantic. We'd always hold each other as the sun set, then make wild and passionate love. We married soon afterwards, had our first child, and settled in. Now, when I ask Susan if she'd like to go to the beach and have dinner, she says, 'Stevie, you know what that does to my hair. I can never get all that sand out, and she starts shaking imaginary sand out of her hair.'" And with that, he started laughing. They're still happily married.

Just think of a past romance you've had, how high it was in the beginning, and how you tried to keep the "high" going. Life's truly to be lived, and enjoying it fully with a partner you love is one of the greatest pleasures of life—but do it outside and after work hours. See Chapter 12, "When Love's in Full Bloom," for more on this.

Working Together

The extent to which you can continue working together, of course, will depend on your company's and supervisor's "climate." These policies, both formal and informal, can change over time—especially if they are restrictive. For example, two auditors in the same office began to date discreetly. The company's policy was to discourage these office relationships, concerned by what the officers had heard about potential conflict of interest and workforce disruptions. Couples at this firm simply went underground and didn't tell anyone what was going on.

One couple "low-keyed" it at work as best they could, maintaining a cordial but distant work relationship. When they decided to marry, they agreed that the man would look for the better job. When he found one at another accounting company, he put the word out that he was leaving. On his final day at that firm, the couple sent their wedding invitations to their dumbfounded coworkers. She stayed on there, and both enjoyed mutually satisfying careers. The policy at this firm was eventually changed to one under which a couple can meet, marry, and still continue working in their same areas for the company (but not on the same account or conflict-of-interest situations).

Tommy and Nicki

Tommy met Nicki at the bank, and both are still working with that firm. Tommy said: "I had to move in with my dad temporarily, because I was broke after the divorce and had nowhere else to go. Although I was twenty-seven years old, I was really lucky that the kids and I had a place to stay. It took time, but I finally located a job with a local bank. While there, I met Nicki. Although we worked in the same department, our supervisors were different. We thought that having two different bosses would make a difference.

"We went out once. But even though we liked each other, Nicki called back and canceled our second date. She was worried about mixing work and romance. I waited one week and talked to her about it after work. We went out on that second date, and we became committed to each other in a few weeks.

"At first, we didn't tell anyone about our affair. We kept it to ourselves, thinking that only we knew about it. One day, I dropped her off at work, right in front of the executive vice president's office. I kept saying to myself, 'Is this such a good idea?' But he didn't see us.

"After a few months we told our closest friends. Yeah, it was true that some of them had figured it out already. There was just something we were giving off that we didn't think about, although we did our best to be totally professional in front of everyone.

"It was hard to talk to each other on the telephone. Nicki has her own office, and I'm located in a cubicle. So when we talk, I have to hold my telephone tight against one ear and cup my hand over the mouthpiece. We decided not to use E-mail because we weren't too sure how secure that system was.

"What was great when we went public was that it was so much easier on the little things. I was carpooling with somebody else, and now I could be freer about what I talked about. I could say, 'I'm going to a movie tonight, can you get a ride home?' Also, then we had to talk in code, but now we can talk more directly and openly.

"The bank has rules that prohibit romances between people in supervisor-subordinate relationships or cash-handling situations. It makes sense that they wouldn't want people who are personally involved to be able to authorize cash withdrawals just by their two signatures.

"My fiancée is an assistant product manager in new products and sales. I'm now a technical salesperson on the sales side, having started from a computer/technical position. The problem now is that I received a promotion to where we're at the same level and I'm now reporting to Nicki's boss, as well. It helps that we're all fairly good friends.

"Nicki's boss met with the executive vice president of the bank and told her what was going on—including the news that by then we were getting married and taking our honeymoon in Greece. What's good is that the executive vice president likes both of us. Both bosses gave their approval for us to get married and stay at our present positions. We were lucky in this, because both of them agreed there wasn't a conflict of interest. It also helps that we still stay discreet, don't hold hands, and stay totally professionally oriented when we're on the job.

"Now we're trying to decide other questions. Will my wife and I wear our wedding rings to work? Will there be a formal announcement to all the employees, or just the ones that know us? There are still some people who probably don't know we're together, so should we tell them after we've returned? We don't want to offend someone by not telling them personally. The question is: How do we accommodate everyone at work when we get married?"

Tommy, his children, and Nicki located their own apartment before the wedding. They sent wedding announcements to everyone, but only the immediate family was invited to the wedding and the reception. They're still telling the stories about their honeymoon in Greece.

Chapter Eleven

Dealing With
Those Around You

What two lovers need to do with their bosses and coworkers depends on how much is already known. Human resources executives are nearly unanimously in saying that they don't police the workforce. "We don't check up on rumors, only concrete complaints," said one, echoing the common approach. The great majority of couples do take extreme measures to keep their relationships private— quite different from what they'd do if their romances weren't connected to work. A professor observed: "There were two graduate students in their mid-twenties sitting in the front when I lectured. They were clean-cut adults, one from Alaska and the other from California. They sat next to each other on opposite rows, participated separately, had different reactions to class discussions; the only common denominator was that they shared a textbook—a common enough occasion. I didn't think anything about this for some months, although this class required hours of classroom discussion each week. Then one day, as he bent over to pass the text back to her, she unconsciously caressed him affectionately on the side of his head. The gesture took only two or three seconds, but that act struck me. They must be a couple, I thought. They approached me after class on another matter, and I asked if they were together. 'Yes,' she said. 'We've been a couple for three years, and we're planning to get married. We've been keeping this from our parents. We decided to do the same with our professors, because it might make a difference.' One little move, I thought, and for all those months their secret had been safe."

The Signs of Love

People at work become used to their coworkers' habits and routines. "One always takes her coffee break at three o'clock," said Nancy, the long-time Ford manager. "Another eats a candy bar at his desk. Lucy, in the far office down the hallway, takes a walk around the building. There she is now . . . but who's that with her? Is that the new manager who transferred in from Texas?" Or "Have you seen Jimmy?" and the answer is "No, he said he'd be with Annie in the X-ray room . . . now I wonder why?" It's just that simple.

Changes in routine, doors closed when employees are talking, and affectionate comments about appearances are tip-offs. A tender gesture, like a loving caress on the head, or a long sexy look can be all that's needed to get a coworker's attention. As Tommy said about himself and Nicki, "There was just something that we gave off."

An obvious sign is more contact that isn't work related. Donna spent more time with George, both at dinner and working after hours on public relations. Although a friend gave it away, the time spent together was another giveaway. Vi and Lyle gave up their morning coffee together because they wanted to decrease the attention—but that could have been a tip-off anyway.

"More time together when there's less work reasons is a real sign," said Jacqueline, the HR executive. And, of course, there's being caught in the act as Lyle and Vi were. Or the couple that always disappeared about the same time every other day or so. A few workers trailed them to the man's van. They waited for twenty minutes, and the two reappeared with the man tucking his shirt into his pants and the woman putting on her makeup.

Restrain Yourself

The commonsense rules are self-evident. You must be totally dedicated to work when at work, keep your love separate, and act the same as before. Coworkers will pick up on any changes in your routine, sooner or later.

Of course, it makes a difference whether you work closely together every day or not. As Suzanne said, "I learned to become a good actor, as did Jeffrey. We would pretend to act outwardly as we should for the outside world, even though inside we were thinking romantic thoughts."

Maintaining your professional image is more than a series of words—you must restrain yourself. A deep sigh when Mr. or Ms. Right walks past, a long wink at a meeting, or a knowing look are dead giveaways. Resist the temptation to neck in the supply closet, and when someone asks how you spent the weekend (you were at a romantic hideaway) say, "I was with friends."

As we saw in the last chapter, you need to develop safe ways of communicating. Whether it's using E-mail, telephone, conversational codes, or carrier pigeons, select the most confidential method. Your working hours should be completely off limits for any type of romantic exchange; and talk about your weekend plans after work. Stay discreet, maintain a professional image, and keep your work separate from home.

When to Go Public

As we've seen, couples generally wait some time before they let the word out. At a bare minimum, they must be sure that their relationship is solid, committed, and mutual. This time period will be different for each couple, depending upon their timetable, the company climate, and how fast the word gets out anyway. However, no policy demanding the disclosure of these relationships will force couples to go public before they feel that they're ready.

"Going public" doesn't mean you announce it in the company newspaper or tack the news on the office bulletin board. It happens when you confide about your relationship to just one person at work—one is all that you need for the news to become public. As one chagrined female office worker said, "It turned out that my best friend knew more about my romance than I did. She'd been sidling over to my lover and drawing out every bit of information from him that she could. She then told her best friend. You can't tell anything to anyone—it'll be around the office in five minutes."

Each decision can only be made after weighing all the facts; evaluate the office politics, company climate, coworker reactions, and whether your career "exit routes" are in order. If you're in a prohibited chain-of-command relationship, you'll want to have the responsibility realignment readied or transfer completed, a new outside job taken by your lover, or both of you ready to go, before you let the news of your romance out. The problem occurs, of course, when someone finds out the facts before you're ready—your boss, for example.

Don't Wait Until the Word's Out

A senior editor at a leading technology-oriented magazine said, "I know of an affair going on right now down the hall from me, although they've been trying to keep it a secret. He's an editorial assistant and she's an editor. I have to hand it to them, they're being discreet, but I think more people know about it than they realize. I really think we're respecting their attempts to keep it a secret and away from us."

These words ring true. When people suspect or think something's going on, some may gossip. But if they aren't sure, you may earn the benefit of the doubt—at least, there should be limited complaints. "There's no need to draw unwanted attention," said Karen. "And people seem to understand that." But remember that you still must be careful of the office hyena and the other animals that skulk in the shadows at work (this is treated further below).

As Harry said: "Who's doing it to whom? That's interesting news and gossip to everyone. Somebody's always boffing somebody else. And it makes no difference whether you're a paramedic, lifeguard, actuary, or some big 'hot shot' executive. Just ask any secretary who's been around at all. It's the women who seem to know; at least that's the way it was with my company. It was fun to talk about it, provided it wasn't carried any further than that."

Although people try to keep it a secret, coworkers eventually figure things out. Nancy commented: "People compare notes, and there's a tremendous amount of gossip out there. You do notice things. A lesbian couple has been romantically involved for sometime. I would see them in the hallway, and, then, I said to myself that they seemed to be acting together more than just girlfriends. There was this look that one gave the other, just a look and that was all I needed to decide for myself. It was then confirmed by two of my friends, even though this couple had gone out of their way to keep it to themselves. Another romance involves a department manager with a roadrunner [someone who wholesales cars to dealers], so they're not in a reporting relationship. Basically, no one really cares as long as the romance doesn't interfere with getting your work done professionally and on time."

Jenny is a lawyer in a Miami law firm. She said: "A relationship is happening now between two lawyers who work on different floors from me, even though both of them are married. They're staying with their spouses, at least for the moment, because of the children and finances. They met when they smoked together at the designated smoking area. It was easy to spot that one when I discovered that she was parking her car every morning in his parking area, not in the one where her department parks. They spend their lunches together, many times away from the office complex. What cinched it for me was seeing him give her a very sensuous back rub one day in the smoking area. Then a coworker confirmed all this to me. You can usually figure it out on much less."

The time comes, however, when you can't wait any more. Your romance is committed and sustaining, you've even discussed marriage or a long-term arrangement. It's tough to keep a secret for long, especially in small corporate towns. Moreover, most companies expect a boss-subordinate relationship to be brought immediately to management's attention. And friendly coworkers could be miffed if they hear the news from the office hyena or busybody before you tell them in person.

Donna ran into that problem when her best friend spread the news around the company. Suzanne and Jeffrey had a similar experience with the human resources manager who was unexpectedly badgered by Jeffrey's ex-wife. However, Lyle and Vi were lucky in that they talked to their supervisors before a coworker got the goods on them. Although the decision depends on the particular couple, there is a commonsense rule. A couple should go public when: (1) the relationship is committed and mutual; (2) your "exit routes" are in place; (3) both lovers have been discreet and professional to that point; and (4) there's no additional reason to hold back.

The Decision Might Not Be Yours

People can pick up on the looks between you and they might talk, but companies typically won't respond to rumors. Randall, Jerry, Jacqueline, and other executives were nearly unanimous in emphasizing that their companies don't follow up on rumors. They respect their workers' rights to and feelings of privacy. Unless they receive a formal complaint of favoritism or some other charge, they'll look the other way.

Nevertheless, to some extent it depends on your corporate climate, as well as what you're doing. Christian, the head chef of a prominent hotel, said: "I've had this problem with a waiter of mine. He dates other waitresses, assistants, and the help in general. He first became involved with an eighteen-year-old high school senior who was waitressing to earn money for college. They broke up, but she didn't complain. If she had, I would have written him up because of her age. He went with someone else for a few months, then they broke up. She complained that he had tried to kiss her and 'pushed' himself on her, after they had broken up. Well, I gave him a written warning for that one. It said: 'Stop, or else you're gone the next time.' One more complaint and he's out. I've had it with him." Management will balance the rumors against the concrete complaints. That is the nature of this beast. It's the complaints that give you trouble, not the fact that you're in a relationship. Taking the time to analyze your situation, decide on the best route, and then sell your boss and coworkers pays dividends.

Suzanne and Jeffrey

We first met these two in Chapter 5. Suzanne gave us a close, detailed look at their story: "I was in love with Jeffrey but he hadn't responded to me yet. Then both of us were working on a Saturday morning. I sent him an E-mail on a work issue, and the telephone rang immediately. It was Jeffrey; he was also working that day. We started talking, then drank some coffee together. He told me later that was when he decided he liked me in a romantic sense—I don't know what I did or said that day that made such a difference. He invited me over to his house that Saturday.

"We drove over; the rest of his family was gone. We talked and he then said to me, 'I think there's something here between us.' I was upset with him, because I wanted to hear more. I left upset, then rethought it, finally concluding that he said this because he was grappling with being married. This is just a problem we're going to have to deal with, I thought. Then there was this question of integrity for me—his wife, him, and his family. He had to do what was best for him.

"One evening, we were walking around the buildings. The weather was chilly but there was a gorgeous, red sunset. We talked about our feelings and ourselves. I began crying, because it was such an emotional time for me and equally for him. One week later, we set our first date: straight to a hotel. There was no need to fool around, as we already knew where we stood with one another. The hotel was close to work, but we chose an afternoon when there was a company-wide meeting.

"We had to keep it from everyone at first. His wife worked at the same company.... How do you keep it from others? My experience was that people in general don't trust themselves, or they don't think about what they see. Perhaps, they don't want to see, or they keep their suspicions to themselves. Although we were discreet, Jeffrey and I differed on this. I wanted to go public as soon as possible, and he wanted to keep it quiet. I could see that he had much more at stake, so I went along with his feelings.

"We talked about when, how, and whether we should go public. Then I left some friends and found my own apartment close to work. We would make love there, rather than at the hotel. We would talk quickly in the hallway as to our time availability and go to my apartment. Jeffrey soon left his wife. They weren't getting along at all, and I had simply made it easier for him, and for both of us.

"We told about our relationship to a friend of his, who wasn't in our group. He was a project manager who was then having an affair with one of his female coworkers—it does depend on the company, doesn't it? She eventually left her husband, and they have had an off-and-on romance since then. We told the news to another friend who was also sleeping with her boss, and they eventually became married. All in all, we told three friends, but Jeffrey for obvious reasons couldn't tell his wife.

"She became suspicious, however, as she had her own office affair with Jeffrey that had ended in marriage. She hired a private investigator. Once her suspicions had been confirmed, she stormed into my office and confronted me. She was hysterical and crying, waving around the family pictures of Jeffrey and his children. It was a difficult time for both of us, but she finally left my office.

"She ran next to the HR department and complained to the vice president about our relationship. However, her words were four-letter ones about our sleeping together. Jeffrey and I were lucky. Before she got into all of this, we had managed to arrange a lateral transfer for me to work under a friend of his on a different project—we weren't boss-subordinate any more. He had decided to arrange this before we told our three friends, and Jeffrey was right. As I think about it, someone got that information somehow back to Jeffrey's wife.

"His wife wasn't through yet. She went to a friend of ours and scared the hell out of him. The word got out and the wrong people found out about our affair. The entire situation was now entirely out of control. A coworker of mine complained to the HR department and with this second complaint, things were getting a little rough. He complained that the only reason I had received a lateral transfer, which didn't involve any extra job benefits such as a raise or even time off, was that I had been sleeping with the boss. And the only reason he complained was that I had turned him down when he wanted to sleep with me—and he was married too.

"He argued that even though I didn't receive any work benefits from the transfer, that he didn't have a chance for the same transfer, due to my relationship with Jeffrey. I don't know what his trouble was, because he didn't want to go to that department when he was asking me out. So, this HR executive comes and meets first with Jeffrey, then meets with me.

"My meeting involved the HR guy and some woman I hadn't met before. The exec said, 'You can't keep doing this. The relationship's affecting business. It looks to others like you were promoted over that coworker of yours.' I told them to forget it, that even the manager who took me couldn't understand why I was transferring to his department. There was no favoritism involved at all, I argued.

"However, he said they had decided Jeff would stay where he was, but that I would have to retransfer to another department. They would reverse the chain-of-command transfer. Some people would say that I was lucky there was another opening, but it didn't really turn out that way. This transfer was down a notch from where I was with Jeffrey, then with his friend. And I had to work for that woman I met with the HR officer, whom I've affectionately named the 'bitch.'

"Everything calmed down after that. I did really good work for about four to five months. But with the way they handled this, I wanted to leave—and get out soon. However, I wanted to leave together with Jeffrey and not by myself. Then more company politics came into play. The old VP had let Jeffrey do exactly what he wanted. The problem was that a new VP replaced this one, and he was more hands on. He and Jeffrey didn't get along.

"Jeffrey was passed over for an obvious promotion. Although he had successfully completed a project showing there was a market for the new hardware and that it could be commercially developed, he wasn't put in charge of that product. Jeffrey then decided to leave the company. I was so excited when he told me this, that I ran straight down to the 'bitch' and told her I was quitting too."

It's hard to say whether Hollywood or the real world has better scripts.

Soul Mates or Not?

Jeffrey and Suzanne acted like soul mates in their responses to an indifferent company. When partners decide to go public, they're making a strong declaration of their commitment to one another. You don't make an announcement of any relationship unless you feel that it's the right one. You must have a committed relationship before you're willing to take the risks and go public.

The word sometimes gets out before you can do this, and it can be an awkward time, at best. Sam, a New York City real estate broker, was called by the owner into his office and asked about his relationship with one of the managers. She was married at the time but considering a divorce; Sam was single and not committed to anyone. They had started seeing one another, and it was then a "purely physical" relationship. Sam was caught on the spot when the owner said another employee had seen the two of them together "dancing cheek to cheek." Sam replied that they were only friends, she was having marriage problems, and she needed someone to talk to about her problems. Although he continued to see her, it was embarrassing to Sam to defend his relationship—especially when he knew that the owner didn't believe his story. But he did.

Selling the Boss and the Company

Selling the company on your relationship is no different from any work-related campaign to get a raise, promotion, or advancement. This time you want the approval to keep both your soul mate and your job. By this time, the uncommitted affairs have gone by the wayside (or should have). You know that you have to go to the highest person you can for support, whether it's a corporation, police station, or a law firm.

As Suzanne and Jeffrey did, you should have your exit routes in place before going public, especially if you're in a reporting relationship. If the company frowns in a deadly way on office romances, you'd better have another job already set up for one of you. Before you tell your best friend, decide whether you should first tell your boss and find out how your coworkers are seeing things.

Try to talk with your supervisor before a coworker gets there with the news. What type of a person is your manager: is he or she conservative, or more likely to work with you and keep a good employee within the company's fold? Is his or her philosophy different from the company's, and if so, in what way? Is the manager's informal way of handling these situations different from what's written down as formal company policy?

For example, Lyle's boss was less supportive than Vi's. In Jeffrey's case, the first vice president was quite supportive (things continued as before, after Suzanne retransferred) but the second one caused the problems.

Donna

Let's look at Donna's experiences. She said: "I had been at my job for two years and it was okay. The affair with George, I have to admit, was better. We'd have dinner after work, but never ran into anyone we knew. We didn't hold hands at work and kept our relationship low key when we were there. Once we got to his place, we'd jump in bed and have great sex—we couldn't wait. Or have fun times, somewhere else. The only problem was when I told that friend of mine what I was doing. She then told two other secretaries in my department, who in turn filled my boss with the details.

"I had been promoted by then to working primarily for one office, and my boss was a decent enough guy, but he was older and in his sixties. George was in his mid-forties, ten years older than I was. Although we didn't talk about it, I started getting the feeling that my boss disapproved of what I was doing. He didn't say anything to me about it, but he stopped giving me some of the more exciting and interesting work to do. My job began to become more detail oriented and less challenging.

"I would ask about transferring, and he would say there wasn't anything open. I checked around and discovered he was right. Even though my workload from him decreased, I still got work from other departments who liked what I did. My affair continued, although I started wondering where it would go. The rumors about us continued, but no one complained except for my boss's reaction, and life went on."

Christian and Amy

Others have better experiences, because so much depends on the company, its climate, the situation, and the supervisor's disposition. Christian, the restaurant head chef, had met Amy, the hotel manager, nearly two years ago at a company get-together for the employees (one of Amy's ideas). They dated, fell in love, and started living together at Christian's house. It helped that Amy was the "head honcho" for that hotel. It was a landmark building in the area and served also as the operating headquarters of the company's extensive national network of hotels.

Amy would fly regularly to Texas, where the organization's executive offices were located. She told her boss at the appropriate time about her relationship, that she and Christian were going to marry, and that they were being discreet (as well as working in different departments). "No problems," he told her. Amy and Christian began to make their wedding plans.

Put Yourself in the Boss's Shoes

Remember that supervisors don't want their jobs endangered by what their subordinates do. You're in love and want the best of both worlds for yourself and your partner; your supervisors simply want to keep their bosses off their necks and to advance according to their career objectives. Both of you need to sell your bosses on how good a job you'll keep doing. Convince them that your relationship will be good for both you and the company and that you're both committed to being a member of the team. If you sell your bosses on what you're doing, everything else can fall in place.

Selling doesn't guarantee that the two of you will stay, get married, and live happily ever after with two dynamic careers at the same place—although it can happen with pro-interactive companies. Your boss may allow you sufficient time to get your plans in sync with the company's policies. If yours is a reporting relationship, lateral reporting (or evaluation) changes may be made. However, accept the fact that changes will occur.

Paula and Chuck

Paula and Chuck were police officers, and Paula didn't want to date fellow cops, although she had been asked out by enough of them. The department's rule was that couples, whether they were dating or married, couldn't work out of the same district. Paula liked where she worked and didn't want to get hooked up with someone who had a "Wild West" mentality. The problem was that the nonpolice guys she dated had problems relating to her, simply because she was in law enforcement. Under the department's regulations, she carried a gun in her purse, and that by itself made a few of her dates nervous. They didn't understand Paula's work or her.

She met Chuck at a department party, and he seemed different from the other cops. Chuck was "polite, nice, and interested in me as a person." He, in turn, liked her "smile, easygoing attitude, and her attractiveness." They had similar interests, such as camping and the outdoors. They started dating and became heavily involved. However, they were careful to keep their personal matters at home, and they talked only about work at work.

What they liked best about their relationship was that each understood the other's job pressures and stress. Chuck and Paula each knew instinctively when the other should be left alone after a bad day. They understood the long hours and stress that came along with the territory—a fringe benefit of their partnership.

They kept looking for any openings at a different district. When one came up, Paula with her background was the better candidate. However, she wasn't accepted when she applied for it. As rumors of their involvement became louder, Paula's supervisor asked her about it. She confirmed their relationship and mentioned that they were looking for a transfer. Her supervisor agreed to "turn a deaf ear" to the rumors until one of them had worked out an agreeable transfer.

Chuck's turn came up, and he applied to work in a different district. When his transfer was approved (one year after they had started dating), they still kept their affair quiet. Chuck, however, told his superior what was going on. On the day that he first reported for work at his new job, with both supervisors told in advance (and grinning), Paula and Chuck sent out their wedding announcements.

Working With Coworkers

It shouldn't be too difficult to figure out how your coworkers will react. It will depend on the company's climate and the personalities of those you work with. Steve and Alice were fortunate: their boss-subordinate affair was not only tolerated, but support came from the top. Although Suzanne and Jeffrey ran into a buzz saw of complaints, what's important is that neither was fired; in fact, their company's climate tolerated a variety of workplace affairs. *Unless a reporting relationship exists, most coworkers won't be a problem, provided the two lovers are discreet (like Tommy and Nicki).*

The Reporting and Complaining Coworker

When a coworker cries "foul" and you're in a boss-subordinate relationship, the reporting element of the relationship must be changed.
This can become complicated, as with Suzanne and Jeffrey's relationship; other companies enact policies ranging from the simple "either
the romance goes or one of you needs to choose who goes" to the
more pro-interactive "we'll work it out, somehow" or transfer evaluation responsibilities to another supervisor.

Complications can arise when one coworker works with one lover
but reports to the other—so you should be on the alert for this situation. For example, Adam and Bill work together, and Adam reports to
Connie, his boss. If Bill and Connie are having an office romance,
Adam might worry about what Bill says about him to Connie when
they're in bed. If Bill works directly for Connie, the standard chain-
of-command reporting problem is present as well. Even if Bill doesn't
report to Connie (he works for someone else), Adam might still complain. The bottom line is that if no one complains, you're in good
shape—and perhaps a little lucky. It's what happens when somebody
does, that you need to anticipate and be ready for.

Remember that Bill and Connie could be the fairest people on
earth, but Adam might still complain in this situation. For Bill and
Connie, Adam's complaint would be hard to swallow, especially if
they're being fair; however, it might be entirely different from Adam's view.

Adam's insecure feelings could be handled by a meeting between
Bill, Adam, and Connie—or between Bill and Adam, or even between
Connie's boss, Bill, and Adam. A facilitator or mediator could be used.
If Adam's being too sensitive and unrealistic, management should in-
stead talk directly with Adam. What's important is not just feelings,
it's what's right and fair in light of all the facts.

If favoritism is present (for example, Bill receives promotions
while Adam doesn't, and they have equal abilities or evaluations),
then the pendulum shifts. However, pro-interactive companies must
look at their work relationships from a fair and equal perspective—
not by trying to please everyone who makes a complaint. There aren't
enough reasonable people in the universe to accomplish this feat.

*The bottom line: Handle coworker problems according to the situation.
The alternatives are: work with them, talk with the boss, "lie low," end the
affair, transfer, use your exit plan, leave, or some combination.* Try working
with your coworkers, when the word's out. They may just be worried

that "things might change" or that the two of you might shift the office balance of power. Take your time and decide on the best approach— it's all within your control.

How Committed Are You?

Commitment is all important. One employee in his late twenties was asked whether he was involved with a woman in the department. Although he kept denying that there was anything between them, one coworker commented, "Everyone else was thinking, 'Sure, sure, sure.'" He finally said to one employee, "We're just together for the sex. Neither one of us has much around now." This wasn't a very gallant statement, and these lovers soon broke up.

Lyle and Vi

Lyle's boss hesitated to endorse his romance with Vi, and this caused them some concern. They had had few problems with their coworkers because their friends were quite supportive. It helped that they were in different departments and didn't report to one another. Lyle said, "Understandably, it would have been more difficult if one of us re-ported to the other. We then would have had to stay underground until one of us located a transfer or another job."

Because Lyle and Vi were concerned, they took pains to do the best jobs possible at work. They kept all meetings to just business. However, they would stroll out separately and meet for lunch when they had the opportunity. They were careful to limit lunch to one hour, but they enjoyed the break.

They weren't ready for their coworker's complaint. The employee who had surprised Vi on the phone at Lyle's apartment complained to Lyle's boss. He argued that the relationship had no place in the office and gave Lyle an unfair advantage—that Vi in public relations would tell only Lyle about the important developments yet to break that concerned the company. This employee worked in finance, and Vi and Lyle had no idea why the coworker was so bothered.

Lyle asked his supervisor if they could meet together. Once to-gether in her office, the coworker seemed to be embarrassed by what he had said. Lyle coolly explained that his relationship with Vi was permissible under the company's policies, that they were being quite discreet, and besides, he said laughing, how could public relations have anything to do with collections. Lyle's supervisor unexpectedly sided with Lyle, apparently because of his calmness in dealing with the situation.

Office Hyenas, Busybodies, and Hatchet Men

These predators exist in nearly every organization, large or small, from doctor's and lawyer's offices to universities and corporations. It's a fact of life when you work for somebody else. And regardless of the term used, both men and women are equal to the task. These people seem to have nothing better to do than to stir up trouble. They'll argue against a romance, not because they're affected directly by it, but on vague general grounds: "This doesn't belong in the workplace" or "Committed couples give an unfair advantage." They aren't guided by business considerations, but by some personal ax they need to grind.

These potential complainants must be taken into account in your deliberations. If they do appear, then act coolly and be businesslike. For example, if the boss says that he or she's received a complaint, answer the contentions. This is another aspect of the delicate balance between going public and staying underground. If you've told the highest, appropriate person before the word goes out (or the office hyena can get to work), then you're in an excellent position. The problems occur when the hyena gets there first.

If the objections to a romance aren't truly work related, they may reflect factors of permission, control, or even office politics at its worse. What a complainant may really be saying is "these people don't have *my* permission, or the company doesn't have *my* consent to this policy." This is quite different from a reasonable complaint about favoritism. The lovers, and the company, must be able to distinguish between the two. Also, you'd better have your exit routes down, just in case the hyena wins that round in the company's court.

Hell Hath No Fury

The reactions of nonworkers must also be considered, especially if one partner is still married. This doesn't mean you shouldn't fall in love with someone who's married, but you need to understand the possible complications.

Suzanne was concerned about integrity, but she still ended up in an emotional confrontation with the ex-wife. We've seen several examples already of spouses who complained to employers on num-

bers of grounds. People are caught, whether it's the telephone numbers on cell phone bills, notes left in pockets, confidences to a friend,
or simply a spouse's suspicion that something's going on.

It turned out that Sam, the real estate broker, was turned in by
the husband. Even after Sam told his lover about his meeting with the
boss, the two decided to keep seeing one another. Their relationship
eventually did wind down, in part owing to the boss's meeting with
Sam. The wife divorced her husband nonetheless, later learning that
he was the one who had called Sam's boss. The ex-husband had been
following her around, finally spotting her and Sam together in a restaurant. She and Sam stayed friends, although they met and married
others.

Alex and Samantha

We were introduced to Alex and Samantha in Chapter 6. Alex was the
older English professor, Samantha the much younger student. Alex's
wife called the dean and nearly sabotaged their relationship. They
were forced to stay underground with everyone, not only due to the
university's climate but also because of the unromantic administration's worries about potential harassment charges. However, as long
as Alex and Samantha stayed together, Alex couldn't be hit with a
sexual harassment charge, no matter what his ex-wife did or the university worried about.

Alex said: "Both before and after my ex-wife went nuts, our deal-
ings with everyone were that we, as a couple, didn't exist. We'd drive
miles to see movies in another city to avoid stumbling upon someone.
We didn't go to hotels, and instead we went on picnics in remote
parks. Samantha was living with her parents, because she didn't have
enough money to live elsewhere.

"One day, we went to a restaurant for lunch, and she looked at
me with a weird look and said, 'Those are my parents' best friends.'
We hadn't even told her parents yet, and they would have hit the ceiling then with that news. We were in the booth behind these people,
and a photographer took their picture for our local paper. There we
were behind them on the front page, but no one noticed or brought
this to our attention. I still can't believe it.

"My ex-wife, after I told her about us, not only called up the
dean, but also threatened to make a big scene at Samantha's graduation from the university. At the last minute, my ex relented and said
it was okay for me to go. I had to go, because I was in the commence-

ment ceremonies as part of the faculty. She then said she would instead meet and talk with us.

"We agreed to talk in her car. When she drove up, she said that she'd only talk to Samantha, but Samantha wisely refused to get into the car with her alone. When we all got in together, we couldn't reach any type of an agreement. Samantha said simply that she wanted to spend the rest of her life with me. My ex then looked at me strangely and said, 'Well, if I can't get any more money out of you, then I'm going home. . . . If you want each other that bad, then you two can have each other.'

"The administration didn't support us, even after we married. When I would talk with them as part of my responsibilities on academic committees, they would be noticeably cool to me. Some faculty members are still reserved about our relationship. We've been married now for ten years and had our first baby two years ago. We're a very happy couple, and we'd do it again, no matter what the problems were. It was worth it."

Everyone has problems that run into their relationships, whether they are in-laws, not enough money, job transfers, or objecting friends. Work is another problem, potential or otherwise, that a couple must deal with in its commitment.

The Five Airplane Transfers

Carrie is another hell-raiser whom we've met before; she's the female equivalent of Tucker, the accountant. Carrie had met Frederico, another manager at the agency, and carried on a turbulent affair with him. Then she transferred away, and Frederico married his present wife. While having marriage troubles, Frederico sent Carrie a Christmas card and she answered it. They talked on the phone several times, deciding to spend a weekend together in Palm Springs.

Carrie met him at a Palm Springs hotel, and they were getting reacquainted with each other when the phone rang. Frederico picked it up, and his face went white. After an abbreviated conversation, he put the phone down. Carrie looked at him and knew that his wife had been on the other end. Frederico explained that she only had to make easy arrangements to board their horses and pick up mail, then his wife would be calling their travel agent. She had decided to join him at the Palm Springs "conference" he was now attending.

While he talked, Carrie repacked her bags, checked into another room, and unpacked. She came back to Frederico's room and found him sitting on the bed with a big catlike smile over his face. "She won't be here for another twenty-four hours," he said. "I called up my friend who's the travel agent that we use. He's booked her on five flights, telling her that these are the only flights that can get here at this time. With all those plane connections, she'll be coming in when you're heading out." He reached over to Carrie and drew her close to him.

After a wonderful twenty-four hours, Carrie's plane had started its engines when Frederico's wife's flight landed and taxied to its gate. Frederico greeted his wife five minutes later, but Carrie didn't care because she had enjoyed a "great time" and was thinking about putting together another fun time with somebody else. Frederico's wife later divorced him, but by that time Carrie was with that someone else.

Enjoy Your Romance

Being alert for the problem situation, worker, or spouse, doesn't mean that you don't enjoy yourself and your partner—of course you do. Work at the office and put on your work mask, but leave it there when you walk in your front door. It's time to live, no different than if the two of you were working at separate places. This may well eventually happen, so start the party now and enjoy yourself.

Laura said, "We took walks together and drank wine at an outdoor café. There were embraces in the moonlight and walks through the countryside. We made a rule: when there was a problem to solve, we would solve it. When that was accomplished, we would enjoy ourselves and savor the moment."

Enjoy an Irish coffee or a glass of wine together in an intimate setting after work. Savor that wonderful Sunday brunch people rave about, and don't ruin that special time by any thoughts about work or being discovered. Life is to enjoy, not fret about. Barbecue at home, head to a skating rink, picnic together at the park, or take in your favorite museum's latest exhibits.

Sally, a doctor in her late thirties, told her physician lover to met her at an inexpensive café for dinner. She left a note with the waitress to give him when he arrived. The puzzled lover was directed to a nearby park by the beach. When he found it, Sally had a chilled bottle of champagne waiting with two cold glasses and appetizers. They walked on the beach barefoot to a popular restaurant to eat cracked crab and continue toasting with champagne. As we've seen before, lovers have been pulling off these romantic overtures since the start of time.

Donald, a software engineer, arrived at his partner's apartment before her. He arranged three floral bouquets in the living room. He wrote three love notes with one sentence that had been broken down into three phrases. When his lover arrived, she put the phrases together and it read, "We're flying together over the weekend to ski at Lake Tahoe, February 12th to 14th, all expenses paid. I love you so much, Donald."

Although kissing and embracing aren't recommended for the workplace, make up for that when you're off work. Needing to be discreet at the office doesn't mean that you can't write a romantic note, leave a bouquet of flowers, or give a secret glance when you have the chance. Savor your romance and seize these precious times.

Chapter Twelve

When Love's in Full Bloom

Relationships at this stage of the game should be mutual and committed. Whether they last forever or not depends on "the lovers' attitudes, human behavioral skills, level of commitment with each other, and just plain luck," said one marriage counselor. People seem to come in two basic types: those who find the right partner on the first or second attempt, seeming to know instinctively how to make their relationships work regardless of personality differences, and those who cycle through different partners until they eventually find an association that lasts longer than the others.

After having time to mature, most romances based on "impure" work motives fall by the wayside—they don't last very long. If sex is being traded for power, the other partner usually picks up on it and the involvement hits difficulties, if it hasn't already fallen apart (see Chapter 9 again).

The affair or "fling" has by now run head-on into the wall of reality. For example, an executive with a steel fabricating company had an intense sexual relationship with a corporate trainee. She was fifteen years younger, kept fit at the gym, and loved the game playing involved in keeping the affair away from their coworkers. The deception was grating on the older man, however. He tired of "showering and changing at the athletic club, then coming home in a cold sweat after seeing her." The executive decided that he wouldn't be able to face his kids if there was a divorce. His younger paramour, who worked in another department, wanted to know where they were going. He chose the wife and kids. She was a "little disappointed" to hear the news, but it turned out she was seeing someone else at the time any way.

A manager and her assistant had an affair for several months; she ended it, deciding that he spent too much of his time talking about work when they were on "our personal time." Two firefighters had an intense relationship, but they agreed to break it off when she felt he was "too insensitive" and he believed "she was too status conscious." A post office employee dated his supervisor but ended the involvement when she wouldn't marry him. Relationships start and they end; they begin again with different people and some last. It makes no difference whether they start at work or not; all at the same time have the same sense of fragility and of strength.

There Are Challenges

You've tried to keep your work at the same level and to maintain the same basic routine as before. Life at the office may have become complicated by your romance, especially if you've had to go underground with your lover due to the company's policies or your need for privacy. Communicating in code, determining who's for or against you, and selling the boss and your coworkers does take its time and energy.

Numbers of relationships aren't this way, but you need to consider clearly some of the potential problems. It's easier to win when you know what could be ahead of you. For example, a female attorney fell in love with a fellow lawyer. Although they tried their best to keep it quiet, the news of their relationship eventually surfaced. Unfortunately, their affair ended owing to "personal differences." He left after receiving a better offer from a larger law firm. At about the same time, a lead partner didn't assign her a corporate account that she thought she should get. She's still at the same law firm, having realized before that there could be a risk if it didn't work out. She's waiting for simply enough time to pass, then "things will be easier." She's also not sure if there weren't other political factors for why she didn't get that prize corporate account.

Even when the romance is going well, there can be casualties other than potential job and career impacts—for example, the injured spouse in an extramarital affair. Spouses who are left behind can become especially bitter (which is understandable from their point of view). We saw this happen with Suzanne and Jeffrey, Alex and Samantha, and it also occurred with Steve and Alice.

Steve's ex-wife became vindictive, not only in contesting the property settlement but also in being ultracritical about him with his children. As Danny DeVito said in *The War of the Roses,* "A civilized divorce is a contradiction in terms." When a relationship ends because one spouse has found a "better" mate, the spurned spouse can easily become vengeful. Who doesn't think about joining a "first wives club" (or a "first husbands club") in these situations?

You can't blame them for their feelings. Battles over the division of property, child support, and spousal support aren't rare today. This can be a nearly expected complication when you fall in love with a married person, whether at work or not. These battles don't necessarily have to happen; some couples are able to handle the details of their severance in a "civilized" manner—but don't bet your bank on it.

But Look at All the Benefits

People who haven't had an office romance, or who have been happily married for years, might wonder about the benefits. "When I felt insecure about my office's reaction, I would talk with Jeff about it. We would console each other and make new plans," said Suzanne. "I'd think about how lonely and unhappy I was before meeting Karen," said Frank. "Then work and any of the problems completely paled by comparison." "The days were a problem sometimes, but the nights were heaven," said another.

It's the companionship, mutual support, and love that helps people overcome the rough times at work. They remember what it was like before they met their lover—spending nights alone, microwaving frozen dinners, and falling asleep in exhaustion before a glowing TV—with no one to share their thoughts or company. They remember that work wasn't all it was cracked up to be, especially when it was all they had. People have a reason to put their relationships over their job: romance is better.

It's not only the strong positive attraction between the sexes that pulls people together. Togetherness is better than being lonely, having nothing to do on the holidays, and having no one around to talk with. "Friends just go so far," said Roberta. "It's just easier to get through life with two people, starting with two incomes and the same rent." These are strong motivations.

As Alex said, "My relationship with my first wife was so bad, it was depressing to be in the same room with her. I was so lucky to have met Samantha and to have her in my life. I gladly took the problems that came along with it." Karen said, "I would do it all over again, even with more problems, just to have what we enjoy now. I love him and my life's good." Take a look at all of the relationships you know about that started at work and where the people are now. People are choosing love and companionship; they believe that "two heads are better than one" at overcoming whatever problems get in their way. It's beautiful to see this happen.

Most important, many office relationships don't have the problems we've been highlighting. Whether it's Steve and Alice's romance, Joanne and Tom's, Bill and Vicki's, or Ed and Beth's (and there are many more), there are numbers of couples who have missed these troubled waters. We've discussed Christian and Amy, Paula and Chuck, Bob and Betty, Tommy and Nicki, Karen and Frank, and so many others who have enjoyed smooth sailing. The point is that office romances don't always have problems, and for those that do, many couples pull together and choose to stay with each other rather than accept their company's interference with their relationship. Keep in mind that at least one-half of all work romances end in long-term relationships or marriage.

There Will Be Ups and Downs

Any relationship has ups and downs, whether you've met at work or not. One man had a tiff with his girlfriend on their way to work and dropped her off one block away to keep up appearances. When he walked into his office still steaming, a process server strolled up and served him with his wife's divorce papers. One week later, life seemed to be better: his girlfriend agreed to live with him, and he had received a promised raise.

There are emotional highs and lows simply by having an office romance. People do experience love, passion, and the overall "just feeling great." As well, lovers can experience guilt, worry, and anxiety, whether due to legitimate concerns such as the boss or an office hyena, or owing to feeling insecure over the unchartered waters being crossed. You'll need to share these feelings with each other. Be honest but share a closeness with your lover at the same time.

It can become tiresome to use code to communicate with another adult, especially when you're paid good money to make big-time business decisions. One couple used notes, knowing stares, and phone conversations in their own private code. Since their company discouraged office dating, Kate and Howard left work separately to meet later at parking lots or designated rendezvous points, then went on dates as a "normal" couple would. They didn't hold hands outside work and even made vacation plans that allowed them to avoid anyone from work. They spent their weekends "with friends," never "with one another"—a typical way of life, especially at companies with restrictive policies. This was a "downer" for them at times (although others like this game), but it was their love for one another that kept it all worthwhile.

Since their corporate climate discouraged workplace relationships, both of them started looking for other jobs. When Howard found one that paid the same money, they told their higher-ups. Howard said bluntly that he was accepting the new offer so that Kate's position wouldn't be jeopardized. In a policy reversal, the officers decided they wanted to keep both well-trained workers, allowing Kate and Howard to stay at their present positions. Howard turned down the job offer, and they're both still there—but now married. It was a "little tense" before then, but both were pleased with their company and its change of mind.

How Do They Do It?

What is the secret of successful couples? Why do their office romances work out? Those who have gone through this before share their thoughts with us.

All Work and No Play Makes . . .

Even if you keep your personal life away from work, you still may have to bring work home—and all that work can make "Jack a dull boy." Harry observed, "Carve out some time for yourself and enjoy each other. That's why you're working so hard in the first place." Another executive said, "You can get into a very selfish mode if all you do is think, eat, and dream work. It doesn't leave much room for anybody else in your life."

Whether your workloads are legitimately different or not, the one with more free time can become uneasy. Too much work can be too much of a good thing, and there's more to life than just work.

Jennifer was the office manager in a small firm of architects; John was the managing architect. Their most important rule when they became involved was: don't bring your work home. As Jennifer relayed: "We recognized that most important for us was that we needed time to be just 'Jennifer and John.' We agreed in the beginning, don't bring any of your problems from work to our home. If work was down, or people not getting along, then all of that stays in the office when we walk through our front door." We will visit them more in Chapter 13.

Be as ruthless with your personal time as you are with your work. It's nice to be able to share your work experiences with someone who's been there, but you do need to carve time away for you as a couple in love. Work hard at the office, so you can take some time off together. *Steal time for your romance.*

Make Romance a Priority, Just as You Do Work

If after a particularly long period of work pressure, make romantic plans for your better half, then steal him or her away for the weekend. Decide whether the work you're bringing home is really that important. Can *some* of it can wait for another time? It makes no difference whether your partner is at the same office or not, a key to any lasting relationship is to make the other person feel as important as anything else in your life.

It is romance that offsets any pressures that could be arising from work on your relationship. The companionship, love, and closeness is the cure to any "what ifs" or insecurities. It is the sharing of experiences with someone you love that is why you're in it—so show that it has that importance to you.

"Don't take your romance for granted," said Laurel. "Work at your relationship, just like you do with anything else. Make having a great relationship your goal." For example, Christian occasionally brings Amy a bouquet of flowers and a card with a love note. Amy will buy a small gift for him when she goes shopping for clothes or incidentals. Herb will surprise Mona with tickets to a show she said she'd like to see some day—and Mona will go out of her way to surprise him with one of his favorite, home-cooked meals when he comes over.

Do Those "Unexpected" Things

Romance is when you do something unexpectedly for the other person that simply brightens their day. If the opportunity presents itself, leave a present, even if it is at work. Steal a kiss in the elevator when no one's around. A lawyer crept into the office of his lover and left a gift in a desk drawer. He called her on the telephone and told her to look through her desk. When she did, she discovered and unwrapped the present. It was a small teddy bear.

One couple was having a particularly difficult time getting together due to their work demands. The man made a Caesar salad, cooked pasta, and took the complete meal over to his girlfriend's house. He was there when she came in, tired and hungry. He heated up the pasta, poured some wine, lit the candles, and gave her an unexpected gift.

This approach is especially appreciated when you've been together for some time or are married. Unexpected gifts are more than trips to the countryside for a weekend romantic adventure—they can be sleigh rides in the park during winter, a bike ride to the beach or a park, ordered-in Chinese food, or whatever's appreciated. A woman waited for her husband to come home from work. She put on romantic music, chilled a bottle of wine, and put on a sexy dress. When he came to the door, she didn't strip in front of him and drag him off to bed. She drew him a hot bath, poured him a cold glass of wine, and handed him the newspaper. They jumped into bed later. Follow these basic approaches and keep your romance percolating.

The Little Things Do Count

It's when you're the busiest that doing a thoughtful act without being asked makes so much of a difference. "Taking the trash out, doing the dishes, vacuuming the floor, helping with the wash, or just helping out when work becomes a little too much," said Trudy, "makes you really appreciate your other half. Those helpful little things just make your day."

For example, Chuck had a tough day on the beat and dreaded coming home to mow the lawn, as he had promised Paula that morning. When he arrived home, she had already done it. Betty said, "I had one of those days that you could only confide to a close friend about—nothing had gone right and I was in a foul mood. I couldn't believe it when I arrived home, but Bob had seemed to anticipate it. He had baked a casserole and it was in the oven; my favorite pie from the local bakery was on the kitchen counter. He had left a note on the refrigerator door that read, 'Just thinking about you, love Bob.' He scored big points with that one."

Whether it's changing the oil, washing the car, giving the dog a bath, or cooking dinner, the little things do count. Try to do one simple, thoughtful act a day for your lover or spouse and watch the dividends multiply.

This Is Your Day

This could also be called the "King or Queen for a Day" winning strategy. Set aside one day when the other person gets to do whatever he or she wants. Put the answering machine on (you're out for the day) and do whatever your partner wants. For example, one woman wanted to stay in bed for the morning, have breakfast in bed, sip an espresso later at a café, followed by a movie and a walk through the nearby flower gardens. Her guy asked for and received love in the morning, lunch out, and then love in the afternoon. One fiancée asked her lover to help her clean up the apartment in the morning, then see a play in the afternoon. The man got to sleep in late, eat a late brunch, and then fish in the afternoon in return. You alternate with each other, but try to keep the requests within reason. A friend of mine called me up asking "how do you make tortoni?" I had to look the word up in the dictionary—it's a type of ice cream.

Both Count

It almost goes without saying that both people matter, regardless of what each does. In one household, the wife is the senior editor of a leading computer magazine; her husband operates from their home a painting and remodeling business. He's also the househusband or Mr. Mom to their children. She's as supportive with his career as she has been with her own. A Harvard MBA has worked for the largest of companies and been in a variety of interesting careers; he's been as proud of his wife's career as a postal clerk because of her work record, ethics, and approach to life.

Have Some Fun

The Two Programmers

Mona and Herb both work as software programmers for the Federal Government in Washington, D.C. She's in her forties, tiny, lithe, and as a friend of hers said, "You could carve a diamond on her body." Herb is in his fifties and overweight, but they met in the same department at work and began dating. They wanted to keep their involvement a secret from their coworkers, so they went to great lengths to accomplish this. Their rule was: no glances, secret looks, or personal talk at the office, and all vacations would be to faraway places. When they jetted to vacation at St. Marten, a beautiful island in the British West Indies, each told their colleagues that they were heading to a different place. After a week of sun and suds at this exquisite place, they were ready to head back to Washington.

Not missing a trick, Mona bought a T-shirt at the Miami airport that read, "I Love Puerto Rico." Herb didn't buy anything, telling everyone that "I just laid back on the beach in St. Marten." They also told their coworkers different dates for when they were on their "separate" vacations. This worked out well, even after their second trip, when Mona again gave out her Puerto Rico T-shirts.

Later, Herb came down with a sinus infection and went to see a doctor about his condition. After he had returned to his apartment and was in bed, Mona answered the phone, thinking that it was the doctor calling them with a new prescription. It was a coworker checking up on Herb's progress (a common enough occurrence).

They decided afterward to go public and announced their plans to be married. Mona subsequently received a promotion and transferred to another department. They soon married and honeymooned, of course, in the British West Indies. Their friends keep asking when she's going to give them more "I Love Puerto Rico" T-shirts. However, Mona and Herb keep returning to St. Marten, where they now own a condominium.

Steve and Alice

Although they enjoyed both their romance and working together at the real estate development company, Alice was the first one to leave, joining another brokerage company that offered a better commission split. They continued to spend every night together at her house, with an occasional weekend away and enjoyed their relationship. Once Alice was working elsewhere, their involvement was no different than if they had met through a singles' ad. They traveled to Hawaii and the more remote island of Maui on one trip, took long weekends now and then at Big Sur on the Northern California coast, and enjoyed vacations from Death Valley to Yosemite. Life is to enjoy and live—here's to life.

Think About the Other

When you think and do what makes the other person happy, you have discovered the key to a successful relationship. If both of you are this way, you'll stay together as a couple as long as you share this approach. The common thread of long romances is thinking about the other—doing the little things, as well as the larger romantic adventures and vacations. When couples are this committed, they'll nearly always choose their partnership over their careers. Businesses must understand that putting roadblocks in the way of couples today simply means that valuable workers will find other organizations that do want them.

Enduring Relationships

"You need to share basic common values for any romance to become a long-term commitment: honesty, kindness, loyalty, and an unselfishness toward one another with what's left over being the icing on the cake," said Robin, who's celebrating her thirtieth wedding anniversary. This is over and above the work-related rules of being discreet, separating personal feelings from the workplace, and the other commonsense rules we've been discussing. Sharing values, work ethics, company experiences, and income expectations seems to balance the pressures from working together at the same office—stress that's absent in nonwork involvements. This doesn't mean that the partners over time will continue working there; in fact, the odds are that they won't, given the average of eight different jobs that people enjoy today over a lifetime.

Other factors should be present for a relationship to endure. An important one is knowing the difference between "what you want and what you can get," as Harry said. This starts with knowing yourself, then your partner.

What Do You Really Want?

You need to know what you want a partner of yours to have or be. This means that you know what's really important to you. The problem is that couples don't think about this when they're head over heels in love. "People seem to come together so quickly, that they don't think about these things. When romance is in the air, who considers the differences? It's later when they decide that they can't make it, all because they're so different," said Betty, an executive with a large bank in Los Angeles.

Betty continued, "I want my partner for life to be my intellectual equal, use correct English when he speaks, have a sense of humor, and have a little more money than me so that I know he's not after mine." This is a real laundry list, especially the criterion that he speak "correct English," but what's important is that this is how Betty feels and what she wants in her lover. Mary, an energetic middle-aged es-crow officer, needs her man to be "financially independent, active, nice looking, and like to jog." She might give up on the jogging, but she wouldn't give up on the active part or being financially indepen-dent. Judy wants her partner to be "sensitive, brighter than me, and have a sense of humor."

Pierre wanted a woman who had a "firm body, looks like a model, and no dependents." I know that this sounds sexist but that's what he said and what Pierre wants for his partner. On the other hand, forty-two-year-old Sabina said, "I'm still at that stage of my life where I might want bacon and eggs in the morning, but Eggs Benedict on another. I like my men to be as different as I do my meals." She also said, "Men who aren't good looking and without money need not apply." Louie, an older middle manager for a financial services com-pany, wanted a woman who was "kind inside, loved animals, and thrifty." Tony would like a "gal who's attractive, gives me a sense of freedom, and has personality." All these types are out there, along with the types they're looking for. Whether they find the one who best matches what they want is another question.

What's Your Partner Really Like?

"The perfect man or woman doesn't exist. If you're looking for one, then you're going to be spending a lot of nights at home by yourself," said Harry. "Your job, no matter how important you are in that organi-zation, isn't going to be much of a help when you're alone. I know of some executives who are so busy at work that their dog's lonely. And their private lives aren't any different."

The characteristics you're looking for can be an absolute criterion, or they can be simply what you like in a person. Your requirements can be that the person have a sense of humor, or be physically attrac-tive, artistic, educated, thin, tall, strong, bright, or spiritual, love people, love money—whatever's important to you. Regardless of what yours are, check them out against the person you're involved with at the time. Then have that person do the same thing with you.

No one gets everything that they want. It may turn out that being sensitive and bright is more important to you than having a great sense of humor. Speaking correct English may not be as important as showing kindness. In business you would call this "prioritizing objectives." Checking out what you want before committing is simply another way to ensure that you're meeting your needs.

These basic qualities go beyond what you might see in someone at the office. Whatever's important to you, be sure that your partner meets the most valued ones; otherwise you would be advised to go more slowly with your present relationship.

The Test of Time

Gary, a psychiatrist in Beverly Hills, said: "A relationship needs 'speed,' quality, and depth to be strong. Speed is the chemistry or physical attraction between the two lovers; quality is the ability to enjoy positive, shared experiences; and depth is the capacity of these people to become closer together due to their common experiences. Over time, speed decreases as the people have more experiences together and the 'newness' of one another fades away. Hopefully, this is offset by an increase in the quality and depth of their relationship."

In addition to these ingredients, the emotional ability of the individuals to give to one another and their ability to enter into a relationship are equally important. As we observed, Mike, the managing paralegal at the large law firm, couldn't make a commitment. Although he was honest about this with the women he dated, he still wasn't good, long-term material. Be aware that the "walking wounded" are out there—and this, of course, includes those at work.

As Gary maintained: "Commitment is almost a by-product of having the love, physical attraction, and experiences that I've talked about. If both really want the relationship to work and are committed to that goal, then the details will fall into place." At times, one person's ready and has to be patient for the other to get there (as with Suzanne and Jeffrey). If your lover doesn't want to make a commitment, you're better off heading in a different direction, especially if you're at work. As Laura said, "If you really love someone, then you don't want to share them with anyone. Why have the pain?"

People have the luxury of looking back to see where their past romances went awry. Perhaps you didn't know what you really wanted in others; or you didn't know what you wanted in yourself. Look inside yourself to see what's within your control and what isn't.

The crazy times we live in and conditions at work put pressures on any relationship. Among couples who work together, and among couples who don't, the most common subject of arguments is (as you would expect) finances and money: Who spends what? Does it benefit both? And what do you do when there's not enough to go around? It makes little difference whether you're married, living together, or dating, this issue always exists. Then there are the emotional needs of both, the demands of children from prior marriages and in-laws, and the normal differences that all of us have. It takes commitment, love, and energy to make a relationship work, and *these considerations are totally separate from work.* Although working for a pro-interactive company helps, whether a relationship succeeds or not is up to you.

Chapter Thirteen

Good Things Do Continue

After finding love in the workplace, numbers of people continue their relationships long term or marry, and the proportion appears to be trending up from the one-half already reported. A doctor marries her patient; a contractor ties the knot with his customer; a manager marries an assistant. Policewomen wed other cops, and lawyers become betrothed to other attorneys and paralegals. A company founder leaves his wife to marry a vice president with whom he worked closely.

It's not uncommon for one partner to leave his or her job for another company, continuing the relationship and then marrying—workers meet, leave, and tie the knot, because relationships last longer than jobs. Whether it's a small dentist practice, a hospital, or a Fortune 500 company, the results are the same.

Married couples seek jobs with the same company, and, if they're lucky, both are able to land positions with that business. Two married professors decided to leave the East Coast for the West, agreeing to head off as soon as one of them had secured an acceptable position. The wife was the first to get an offer, accepting a position teaching psychology at an Oregon university. Her husband couldn't secure a position at that same time; he instead started his own consulting practice in the town. A new dean accepted a position at the same university, provided his wife was offered a teaching position—this was granted.

Spouses condition their acceptance of jobs on positions or assistance given to their partners. This opens up different opportunities, or dilemmas, depending on what happens. In other cases, one spouse may accept a particularly lucrative new job while the other spouse stays behind, the transferring partner accepting a long-distance weekend commute in return.

The situation is different when we're talking about people who meet and try to continue their careers at the same company. As we've seen, one impulse is to keep the relationship quiet, secure a transfer or new position outside the company, and then go public with the news—depending on how restrictive the company's climate is. Jacqueline indicated that the rule at her company was, "Employees know the rule if they become and stay involved here—one leaves."

The transition at many companies from what existed before is striking. Nancy, the senior manager at Ford Motor Company, said: "Two decades ago, it was forbidden around here for two people to marry, as one had to quit. You couldn't even work in different divisions, and this rule didn't make any sense. Now, employees can marry and work while at Ford, but not usually in the same division. There isn't a formal dating policy and no specific rules or guidelines. Each Ford manager, therefore, has discretion in this regard. The company doesn't police the workforce on work romances, although it doesn't approve of chain-of-command or conflict-of-interest situations.

"With all the movement to our various subsidiaries, people are promoted and transferred to numbers of out-of-the-way places every-day, whether they're married, in love, or recently divorced. What happens is that the couples try to work within the company, but this depends on who management wants where and by what time. You take your chances—but people meet and get married at work every day. It's the way the world is."

Married Couples in the Workforce

Before one bank changed its rules against married couples' working together some years ago, the husband in one situation was forced to transfer to a branch in a different part of the state. They're still married, although the weekend commute was a headache. Taking advantage of today's trends, Tommy and his wife, Nicki, not only met at a bank, but both allowed to work as usual in the same department.

Xerox even permitted a top executive, Joe Laymon, to move his office and staff from its corporate headquarters in Stamford, Connecticut, to central operations in Rochester, New York, so that he could be with his new wife, Dianne Jones, also a top Xerox executive. However, she resigned later so that she could spend more time with their children. What happens in any specific case depends on a number of factors, including how the lovers sell their bosses.

The Trends

The 1992 *Sex in America* study (completed by Michael, Gagnon, Laumann, and Kolata) surveyed a statistically representative sample of 3,500 adults, aged eighteen to fifty-nine. The study found that people who knew their partners longer before having sex were much more likely to become married than those who didn't. This makes sense, because taking the time to first become friends would seem to make any subsequent romantic involvement stronger. What's surprising is the extent of this: 50 percent of couples who waited more than one year after their first meeting before having sex subsequently married; only 10 percent of couples who had sex within the first month of meeting married.

The research concluded that people usually had sex with people who were like themselves, similar in education, race or ethnicity, and age, whether their objective was marriage or not. Ninety percent of all couples, whether they were married or not, were of the same race or ethnic group; more than 80 percent of couples had attained approximately the same level of education.

Other studies (including the 1994 University of Chicago, *Sex in America* research) reached the same conclusion that work relationships have strong foundations that help them last. The reasons are straightforward: coworkers have time to create a friendship before becoming involved; employees with like interests and values tend to come together; and personnel must bond together in projects and alliances to succeed in an organization.

Family life has changed considerably over the past twenty years with the rise in numbers of working women and numbers of dual-income families. According to the U.S. census, two-income families rose from 42 percent to 64 percent of all families between 1975 and 1993. Marriages have accordingly become more egalitarian, as have workplace romances.

The economic contribution of women to their partnerships is striking and accounts further for the strong trend towards long-term relationships arising from work. A 1995 study by the Families and Work Institute in New York determined that women earned about half or more of the income in 45 percent of two-income homes. When separated and divorced women (including single-parent households) are added in, the number climbs to 55 percent of all homes. A Louis Harris & Associates survey conducted at the same time indicated that wives share equally with their husbands in supporting their families—48 percent of married women say that they provide one-half or more of their family's income.

We are talking about joint partnerships and an "equal say" in today's relationships, especially in workplace romances. This equality has carried over to marriages as well. There's no question that long-term relationships at work will continue increasing, and that organizations will need to reflect this basic fact. Companies with outmoded policies will have to discard them in favor of more progressive ones, including day care assistance, flex time arrangements, and social flexibility.

The Irony of Becoming Married

What's ironic is that couples already married have a better chance at striking a deal at numbers of companies than couples who meet inside, marry, and then try to stay there in well-matched career paths. Why? These companies fret about potential sexual harassment charges until the couple's married (then breathe a sigh of relief), possible concentrations of power in the spouses' hands, or conflict-of-interest situations between the two lovers. When trying to hire attractive candidates (either together or as part of a working team), organizations do seem to behave more flexibly than when a more "troublesome" office romance pops up and is transformed into a marriage. At many firms, a couple who dates secretly can continue at the firm (provided there aren't serious complaints and it isn't a reporting relationship). However, as soon as the couple surfaces and announces marriage, different rules apply.

For example, the 1997 Romac International study indicated that 62 percent of responding companies had policies in effect controlling the hiring of spouses, relatives, or significant others; 75 percent regulated situations where spouses worked within the same department or work group. The report stated: "Some firms feel that such a policy is unnecessary. The overwhelming majority stipulate that 'employees related by blood or marriage may not hold positions in which they are in a reporting relationship.'" Only 9 percent of these companies had policies in effect regarding dating among coworkers (and 62 percent allowed supervisors to date an employee). Things can change when a couple dating or living together decides to marry—being discreet has its advantages.

No wonder couples go to such lengths to keep their romances

secret until they're ready with their plans. It is amazing that companies are surprised at this, especially when it's their policies that are responsible for this underground behavior in the first place. Given that companies have different formal policies and informal interpretations that apply when their employees meet and marry, you'll need to check on yours before going public and then make your plans.

Some of the Situations

The transition from dating to marriage has interesting implications. The first questions involve the company's climate (whether it's pro-interactive or not), which partner has the better career opportunities, and whether it makes sense for one or both to stay. The partners over time will need to make continuing decisions over their work, relationship, and separate careers. For example, what happens later if after a transfer one lover is directly or indirectly reporting to the other (which has happened)? Or is transferred to another operation in a different state? Will the company accommodate the other spouse?

It Depends on the Company

Given the wide variety of companies and industries, what happens can depend on the luck of the draw. If a business is large enough, people can be transferred as easily as "one, two, three."

Don, a senior financial services manager, commented: "As I think about it, a young man with us in his late twenties was having an affair with a woman in her mid-thirties; then he began living with her. Both worked for us in the same division. When management heard about that relationship, and I think there was a complaint, they transferred him from San Diego to Twin Cities, Minneapolis. They found a job for her in Twin Cities, as well, but it was a demotion from her responsibilities, although they kept her at the same salary level.

"The couple landed in Minneapolis in the dead of winter, and they couldn't sell their house in San Diego. They hated it there, the climate, the job, everything. Both of them quit their jobs with us, and came back to San Diego jobless. By then they had married, and he became an insurance broker. She found another job in sales with another firm, and both are doing well and loving it in San Diego.

"Then a father, quite high-up at our New York City headquarters, arranged a job for his son. The young man was married at the time, and both he and his wife came here to work. They divorced after a year or so, and his ex-wife, Bianca, was promoted to our Denver office. Another man in his thirties, Lanny, joined the company in San Diego, then also was transferred to the Denver office. Lanny met Bianca at the Denver office; they began dating and became quite involved. We then promoted Bianca to another position, but this time to our main office in Dallas.

"Lanny wanted to transfer to Dallas to be with Bianca, but we had no openings there for his position. So what did he do? Lanny quit the company to head to Dallas and be with Bianca. He looked for a job with another company and found one with a smaller business there. Meanwhile, Bianca's first husband stayed and was promoted back at our San Diego office. You never know where the pinball lands after it stops bouncing.

"If you're married, then you still take your chances at companies, especially if one of you receives a promotion to another region. A husband-and-wife team, for example, was based in New York City, and then the wife was transferred to San Diego. They endured a one-and-a-half-year separation, before she was transferred back to New York City. It's now entirely possible, given the global economy we live in, for one partner to be transferred to another country, let alone another state.

"I do have my suspicions about a woman who just transferred here from our San Francisco operations. Since she doesn't know anyone here, she's been hanging out with some of our single employees, going out for drinks and dinner. She's in her early thirties, is an account supervisor, and goes bicycling with the field managers who are above her in rank but below me. I have a feeling that there's more here then she's saying. I've heard that she's been having an affair with someone in the company and that wouldn't surprise me. But that's the way it goes.

"If it works out between them, managing two careers together here and staying at this location would be difficult. If the romance ends, it won't affect either career—provided there's no harassment complaint. Typically people who are married or in long-term relationships have problems continuing their careers together at the same place regardless of the company, especially if they're heading up the company's ranks. It could be different if you found a job niche and were able to stay there.

"As you would expect, the office predator is definitely out. There's also more mutuality these days when two people get together. In fact, they're taking their time to get to know one another before becoming involved. As our workforce becomes younger, it tends to be single with recent college graduates. They're more into dating their coworkers, especially at the office since they don't have much time anywhere else. The company becomes their home. As one heads higher up the corporate ladder, however, the middle managers and executives become more discreet with their relationships.

"Our San Diego divisions recently relocated into the same building. You're consequently now aware more that romances are starting up. An employee before would have to drive to attend a half-hour meeting across the city at another division, then head back here. There was limited opportunity to continue something, even if they had the interest. Now it's easy to come up with an excuse and walk two minutes over to chat with whomever you're interested in.

"In the early eighties, involved workers were transferred away. This wouldn't happen today. Now, they could see each other, both at work and home, and that would be fine. They'd have to be discreet, out of respect for their coworkers, but there would be no problems here in today's culture."

Tommy and Nicki

When Tommy and Nicki married, their bank's policies on married coworkers came into play. Tommy later received a promotion, so that he was reporting to Nicki's boss. As a result, the executive vice president needed to decide whether there was a conflict of interest. He decided that there wasn't, because Tommy and Nicki were responsible for different functions, Tommy in data processing and Nicki in marketing. He's twenty-eight now, she's thirty-two, and both recently were promoted to assistant vice president—congratulations!

They're still discreet in their working relationship at the bank, understanding that as a married couple, they must still meet the informal standards of their coworkers and supervisors. From the executive vice president's decision, it appears one of them is being groomed for a promotion to another department, and Tommy and Nicki believe that will be Nicki.

Tommy's advice for couples makes sense: "The first rule is professionalism. There should be no public displays of affection, whether you're dating or have been married for some time. That just does not make any sense. You can't act differently toward one another than you would with any other employee. Some people will be cautious about your relationship when you go public, despite all of your precautions. You must keep your work standards high and professional.

"Next, you want to keep it quiet until the right time. You need to see how both your careers will be going, whether one should stay, or both, or one transfer. Don't go out on public dates; keep them private. Even if coworkers figure something out, you won't be as threatening to them by keeping a low profile.

"This brings us to another important rule. Get the blessings of the highest person at the highest level in your company before you go public. You will need his or her support, and you'll want someone who can go to bat for you if some problem or difficulty occurs. In my case, I went directly to the executive vice president of the bank, and she was very helpful. When Nicki's boss was hesitant at first, my boss and the executive vice president stepped up to bat for us. The company as a whole is very supportive now.

"Keep in mind that your work standards shouldn't change when you date or marry. We still are hard-working, career-minded individuals. My wife kept her last name at work, not adding mine to it, to lessen the impact and keep people from being threatened. We go out of our way to be professional at work. However, we love the fact that we both work at the same place. We love our work and talk about all that day's developments that affect us. As our days take different directions, we love to talk about our work once we are home—although that may change over time.

"There isn't any better place to meet someone than at work. You see how they relate on a day-to-day basis with people; you get to know their likes and dislikes in a natural way. You find out their goals, how they work, and what motivates them. I'm surprised that most people don't find their mates at work."

Christian and Amy

Amy and Christian felt comfortable. Her boss in Texas had agreed she could stay involved with Christian, both their jobs were going well at the hotel, and they planned to be married. They bought a house and began fixing it up. Then company management decided it wanted all of its operations to be centered in Dallas. This would involve consolidating all their centers, including the operational nerve center in Illinois where Amy and Christian worked.

Amy was asked by headquarters to transfer to Texas, and she asked how Christian could be included in the transfer. Her boss looked around and said he could work as a chef at its headquarters, but that his responsibilities wouldn't be as great. Amy and Christian talked it over. They decided to accept the job transfer, because the career opening for Amy more than offset the potential worsening of Christian's position.

They took trips to Dallas, and Christian inquired about openings at two of the most prestigious hotels. A managing chef's job was open at one, and he decided to accept its employment offer. They put their house up for sale; when Amy transferred, they'd buy a new house and marry. Christian would then tell the company he was leaving to work for another hotel.

Bernie and Lucy

Bernie and Lucy were managers in their mid-forties at a software company in Denver who met, fell in love, and became engaged. After the usual "diving underground" period, they talked with their boss and received his permission to stay in their present jobs. Although they occasionally worked together on group projects, they operated from different departments. They married quietly and continued at the company.

A headhunter later contacted Bernie and told him about a small, growing software company in Boulder. An easy forty-five-minute drive from Denver on the Boulder-Denver Turnpike, Boulder is a quaint technology center and the location of the main campus of the University of Colorado. Bernie would be the company's vice president in charge of product development with much wider responsibilities than before. He was ready for a change, and Lucy agreed with his decision to accept the new job. During the next several months, Bernie worked long hours and knew he was right—his new firm was going places with its software.

Lucy was also happy, as she was due for her annual evaluation and felt she had done a good job to date. The evaluation interview, however, was an unwelcome surprise. Instead of talking about her good work, her boss asked how Bernie's software work was going and whether she had heard anything about it. Lucy said she was sorry but couldn't help him there, because Bernie "kept those things to himself." Her boss gave her an "okay" evaluation, not as good as in the past; it seemed clear that he was bothered that Bernie was working for a competitor.

Lucy and Bernie checked with an attorney who told them that

firms had legal problems firing a worker for dating or being married to another who worked for a competitor, unless the worker was passing trade secrets. Later, Lucy received a raise, but it was much less than what she felt she deserved. Lucy couldn't prove anything, but the apparent lack of trust disturbed her. One month later, she left to work for another software company that wasn't competitive with Bernie's.

Suzanne and Jeffrey

Suzanne and Jeffrey left their old company to form their own business. As Suzanne said: "Jeffrey was ready to leave when he did. I'm sure that if we had been treated fairer by the company that both of us would have stayed. However, that wasn't the case. He had his stock and savings from his high-income years, so we were safe. I could always go to work somewhere else and help us make ends meet. He started a company that consulted with firms on product design and marketing. As we believe in people, we decided to invest in ourselves. We married eight months after we left, and our business has grown well with several contracts from major companies.

"What's hard to believe is that companies who are so hardheaded when it comes to business matters, can be such 'softies' when it comes to making the right decisions on office romances. They're scared to death of lawsuits—what's idiotic is that you would think they'd want to keep their best workers, even when they're in love. These people are responsible, energetic, and totally committed to the company's goals.

"Businesses should want their employees to be involved with one another. You want them happy, contented, and not out cruising the bars late at night. You don't want them nursing a hangover in the morning; you want them in bed talking with someone who's also committed on how they're going to meet the firm's goals. That's what is so unbelievable."

Lyle and Vi

After Lyle met with his boss, he talked everything over with Vi. They had to figure out what was best for them. Vi was in a good position; her boss was pleased with her progress and quite supportive. Lyle wasn't so sure about his. He remembered that his boss had him spending more time on collecting the smaller, more troublesome accounts. Lyle decided he should look for another job.

It took him a few months to find another job that was just as good. Lyle accepted the position, and he and Vi married the next month. For the first year, both enjoyed their jobs and their marriage. Then a management change and a disagreeable boss put Lyle's new job in jeopardy. Vi checked with Lyle's old boss: his replacement wasn't working out, and she would love to take Lyle back at a better salary. That they did. The moral of the story: don't fly away too quickly unless you know well where you're going to land.

Jennifer and John

Jennifer and John worked for a close-knit, prominent architectural firm in Seattle. He's in his late thirties and was the managing director, while Jennifer is still the office manager. Jennifer joined the firm first, followed by John, and they were friends for the first three years. During this time, they realized that they liked each other but didn't act on this because John was "technically" her boss. They would go out with the same group of architects and friends for drinks, dinners, and parties on the weekends. John was going through a divorce then, and as he recalled, those "times were difficult."

Although both were single, they didn't date because they worked together for the same small firm, and they held to this, even after John received his divorce. They even talked about it, concluding, "We'd do it, if it wasn't for the fact that we worked and talked together so much at work."

Jennifer added: "It was John who made the first move, and I then followed up on it. We had gone out for dinner and talked about going out together. Again, we decided that we shouldn't due to our close working relationship. We headed back to the office, so that John could make a phone call to his cousin. Once we were there, he turned around and kissed me. I knew that type of kiss, because my knees buckled. I looked at him and said, 'There's no turning back now.' We didn't and started dating right after that kiss.

"We knew that there was something here. We had been working together for those years and had become good friends. We talked about this, but kept dating, always saying that we'd keep our friendship, no matter what happened. In a month, I was going on a family vacation to Cannon Beach, Oregon, and I invited John to come along. Up until then, we didn't have much of a problem keeping everything quiet at the office, because it was always business as usual. However, how could we make our vacations coincide without causing too much suspicion?

"First, we didn't leave or arrive back on the same day. John left the day after I did, telling everyone that he was seeing some friends. He stayed with us at the beach, then left two days before I traveled back to the office. Our relationship changed, as we became more deeply involved. I wanted to live together before he did. John wasn't sure about this development, but he was honest in telling me that the divorce had scared him from making this type of commitment."

John commented: "We dated on weekends and went out with the group, but we were pretty cool about it all—pretty discreet, in fact. We had a couple of close calls, and it turned out that a few of our friends had picked up on what was going on between us. One time, we were out having drinks, and I put my hand on her leg and gave her a smile. All of a sudden I realized what I was doing and snapped my hand back, made a funny look to Jennifer as if I didn't mean to be 'fresh.' However, the others hadn't picked up on it.

"After nearly two years of dating, I agreed with Jennifer that we should live together. It was a major decision for me. Before moving in, we wanted to see the America's Cup finals in San Diego. So we worked out this deal where Jennifer was flying to San Jose to see some friends, leaving on a Thursday, and I was heading to San Diego to see the finals that Friday.

"The owner of the firm sat back and put 'two and two together.' He wondered if we were going down together. He asked a friend of ours who worked there whether we were traveling together. My friend answered that he should ask me. Well, that did it: no denial and 'ask John' added up to the fact that we were a twosome. When he asked me, I told him the truth. He was worried about whether I was being honorable about all of this, because he didn't want the sexual harassment liability if we didn't make it.

"I told him we had been dating for two years, and this blew him away. He couldn't believe we had been together that long without him finding out, but he was very supportive of us. We were friends and all of us, including Jennifer, had worked closely together for several years. He started laughing that he hadn't caught on. When Jennifer and I moved in together, I made my lasting commitment to her. We married soon afterward, and we invited everyone we knew, including those at the firm. We continue to keep work and home quite separate from each other, so that our working relationship is always and absolutely above board."

Jennifer continued: "When the owner asked John about our relationship, it was time for us to get caught. It already had been two
years, and we began talking more personally in the office. We began
taking our lunch together every day, but we limited our romantic
involvement to one kiss in the elevator after lunch. That was it. We
tried to be as quiet as we could around the others, but when you get
so close to one another, you can accidentally switch to your 'at home'
level. Once I said loudly across the office to John, 'Hey, *honey*, could
you come over here.' A friend of mine pulled me over, and asked if I
knew what I had said. I didn't.

"The owner didn't worry about us, once we had confirmed what
was going on. He trusted both of us. He was more concerned over
whether I would quit, because we had kept it quiet for so long. I told
him we kept it a secret to be sure that our relationship would work
out. That it did. However, we were close friends before we started
dating.

"There are a few rules that we follow. The most important is:
'Don't bring it home.' When things are bad in the office, we leave it
there, so that John and Jennifer have some time together. We spend
enough time with one another at the office. The second is that we
keep our romance at home. We limit our personal agenda at work to
lunch together and one kiss in the elevator. The third is that 'work is
work' and 'home is home.' We keep them totally separate.

"There is a real life for us after work. We do so many things together—and apart. John just returned from a trip to Alaska where he
fished with his friends for salmon and steelhead. We have the normal
areas like everyone that we discuss and disagree over, but we have a
close relationship and a wonderful one. And we both love cats.

"We have needed to separate our relationship at work distinctly
from the one at home. For example, if he tells me to photocopy something personal at work, I'll get irritated. I talk to him about that, saying
that I'm his wife. However, I'll go along with what he tells me to do
in public; it's just that I'll talk to him in private, when I think he should
have used with me a different tone of voice or approach. However,
we'll work it out. It's our ability to communicate that solves our problems, whether we're at work or home.

"We're very much equals at home, although I tease John that 'I'm
the boss' at home. I'm the neat one in the house, so I ensure that he
picks up after himself, makes the bed, and helps with the dishes. So
I guess in that respect I *am* the boss. Right now I'm having him pick
up a little in the house. We won't fight in front of anyone at work. In

fact, our new employees are surprised to hear that we are married. They'll look to see if they can catch us necking by the Xerox machine, but we don't do that.

"I'm not a bar scene person, and neither is John. When you get to know someone as well as we do, then meeting at work is the best way to find and have a relationship. And we don't have a problem from working or playing so many hours together. In fact, I've gotten to the point where I'm so used to seeing him around me that I have to adjust to his absence when one of us is off by ourselves.

"Romances at work have really grown over the past several years, especially with the long hours now required by your job. In fact, John's brother met his wife at a company office party, and they've now married. It has certainly worked out for all of us."

As a postscript, John left the firm later to accept a position with a development company. Jennifer is still with the small architectural firm, loving her work, as well. Our congratulations to both of them.

Chapter Fourteen

When Good Things Come to an End

"**W**e worked together so well, and he liked my ideas and how I thought. I woke up feeling so alive each morning, dressed sharply, and thought I looked as I felt. It was such a total turn-on," said Demi, a fifty-six-year-old project manager. "I couldn't believe how low and angry I felt those short months later when our relationship fell apart." Ruth, a twenty-five-year-old, marketing coordinator, said, "Our intimacy started at work when we drank coffee, batted PR slogans back and forth, and worked late at night. Having an intense sexual affair later was almost a foregone conclusion. When this fell apart, I wanted to hide in my office and never come out."

"I couldn't believe I was working with someone so sexy but who had such street smarts about people. She just knew when someone was lying," said Robert, a thirty-four-year-old cop. "She told me some months later that she was going back to her husband. I couldn't handle that and put in for a transfer." Ted, an older but now wiser doctor, said, "After trying to put my life together after my divorce, I thought that she was the 'forever and ever' one. We kept it quiet at the hospital, spent quality time together, and I was ready to settle down—but she wasn't. When she said it was time to call everything quits, I had the hardest time of my life trying to adjust to that. For some reason, this was even harder than my divorce."

Carl, a management trainee in his late twenties, said: "What a great place to meet gals, I thought, as I first looked at all those great-looking trainees. You see what they're like, get to know them, and see whether they want the same things you do. The only problem was that I fell in love with someone who was more into where you were going in the company. She dumped me when she found someone who was heading up the corporate ladder faster. What a tragedy. When I saw her, I wanted to curl up and crawl away, but I didn't. I just gritted my teeth and started thinking about the girlfriend I had left for her. That did it, and the ex and I got back together. It was then a real blow to my ego, but I survived.

You Can't Hide

Breaking up has all the problems of any romance that ends, but with one complication: you can't stop seeing each other unless you're in different departments—and you can't always depend on that. Let's look at the stories of Sue and Marianne on this.

Sue

Sue is a forty-two-year-old financial manager who said: "On the first day after we ended our affair, I stayed in my office and asked my assistant to do everything, including getting my coffee, duplicating, and even running down missing reports. I used the telephone and hibernated—I felt so terrible inside. I wished I had been the one who ended it, and then I wouldn't have felt so hurt inside. It was a monstrous blow to my feeling of self-worth.

"When I ventured out, I looked for any signs of my ex-lover, and if I saw him, I would turn the other way. Just as we hid our romance from everyone else, I now was trying to hide from him. I tried my best to avoid any meetings that I knew he'd attend. I tried to get my work done as quickly as possible, then get away from work as fast.

"After a week of talking to friends, avoiding him, and holing up, he called me at home and said that he also was feeling bad. My hopes rose that we'd get back together again, but he dashed them by saying 'it was too bad things didn't work out between us.' He suggested lunch later that week so that we could work things out.

"Lunch didn't help much, as I tried to get back together with him. However, that changed as soon as he admitted he had met someone else. I was so angry that I shot up and stormed away from the table. We never interacted socially again after that. My feelings changed to where I just didn't like him at all.

"It took several weeks, but I finally got over this anger. Time is a great healer, and I returned to my normal, even way of looking at things. I met someone new at a wedding, and that helped me to heal and forget. Both of us are still with the company and we work together okay now, but I still don't trust him."

People handle breaking up differently, and this does depend on whether you were the one who ended it or not. These reactions also vary with the lovers' personalities, their reasons for being in the romance, and how much they see one another afterward at work.

Marianne

Marianne is a thirty-one-year-old assistant to the president who had an affair with a product manager. She said: "I was lonely at home and there was nothing in my life except work. When I met Randy at the corporate gym, we became buddies. Randy was a product manager, and I liked how well we talked together. We liked trading information on who was doing what and where the company was going. We fell into that affair. I woke up one Saturday morning after the first night together and thought, 'Oh, my God, I'm involved with someone at work.' That bothered me, because my career is important to me.

"However, I liked that I had someone to be with. We could go out to dinner, laugh, and make love. There were no ties or commitments. I thought I would try it and keep the best of both worlds: a career at work and no more lonely nights or eating alone at nine o'clock at night. Then the president called me in and said he had heard rumors that I was seeing Randy. Someone had spotted us at lunch and concluded that we were more than work buddies.

"I didn't lie to him and confirmed that we were seeing one another. The president said it was my decision, but that it could hurt my future at the company. He said some workers might not accept it and would look at my affair as being unprofessional. He simply asked me to think it over.

"That was a tough decision. Randy wanted me to commit, and I was being told that it would hurt my career. After enduring a sleepless night and talking it over with Randy that weekend, I reluctantly concluded that I couldn't have both—so I chose the career. Randy tried to get back together with me, but I stood my ground. He argued with me that evening on the telephone until I told him that he was making everything worse. Randy just found it difficult to take no for an answer.

"The next day, he walked into my office and said we had to talk. I said no, and he left angrily. I didn't know what to do, so I sat down with the president, told him that I had decided my career was more important, and that Randy wanted still to stay together with me. He said I had made a wise decision, then left to talk to Randy. I don't know what he said, but it worked. Randy never tried to contact me again. He left a few months later, and I was promoted to being a vice president two years later."

More Than Work Is Involved

Breakups entail financial, as well as emotional, problems. Think about someone you've known who has been in a divorce. In fact, employees go through divorces all the time. Unmarried couples have all the complications of a divorce, except for the need to file court papers dissolving their marriage—they buy property together, become jointly obligated on apartment and car leases, buy TVs and furniture on installment plans, and open bank accounts together. Dealing with these financial ties is an unfortunate part of any ending.

Bob

A few years before he met Betty, Bob had been involved in a long-term relationship with Delores. She worked for a real estate lender, and Bob had met her when her bank agreed to lend on one of his development projects. Bob and Delores started dating and eventually bought a house together. "When we broke up," he said, "we had to work out how much my half was worth. I was having financial problems at the time, which was the reason she ended our relationship. She was into maintaining an image, and I couldn't keep up my end of it.

"I couldn't buy her out because I was broke. We had to work out what she could afford to pay me for my half. She talked with an attorney. We eventually agreed on this, but I didn't get much out of the deal. It was a difficult time, both personally and financially for me." This isn't much different from what married people go through when they divorce.

Ending an affair involves a loss, especially for the one who didn't make the decision. It takes time to heal, and some people need more than others. A friend of mine went through such a hard ending; she said, "I felt then so lonely that my bones were cold." These strong emotional reactions need to be handled, ranging from feeling numb to the "normal" painful feelings of rejection, hurt, and depression.

As Silvia said, "The rough times were here. I had gone through this once before, but this didn't make it any better. I felt down and depressed from being alone again and the rejection. I tossed and turned at night, then I had to pull myself together for work. I couldn't face seeing my ex-lover during the day."

Donna

Donna was becoming uncertain about where her relationship with George was heading. She reflected: "One day, I went over to his house to wait for him to return from work. I played back his answering machine to see if he had left a message for me, but discovered instead this sweet female voice leaving a message. She said it was so nice meeting him over lunch that day, and that she wanted to see him again. I began thinking about our relationship and decided that there wasn't a whole lot of kindness here. It had been fun in bed, but we really didn't have anything else.

"I broke it off, although he wanted to stay together. What made this easier for me was that I had made the decision, and that we worked in very different areas. I stopped working on those public relations matters in my off-hours, so there were limited reasons for us to meet. Although we were in different departments, we did work in the same building. The problem became to me more of a 'public relation issue': how should we act now toward one another when we met in the hallway?

"I handled this by telling the same 'friend' that I had ended the relationship but didn't mention the specifics out of a sense of propriety. The news spread as quickly through work as the first gossip that we were together. George and I tried to be decent to one another afterward, and we even met over lunch to keep intact our limited working relationship. The lunch was cordial enough, although we both were somewhat distant. After then, we'd say, 'Hi, how are you?' and the 'Fine, and you?' type of stuff, but we were uncomfortable with one another. I was uncomfortable because of the phone message, and he was uncomfortable because I had ended our relationship.

"I had tired of receiving less interesting work, even though I was on salary. I stayed with the company for six months after breaking up with George, then left to take a better job as a manager with another firm. George married the woman whose voice was on his answering machine. It turned out that she was a local TV anchorwoman. He had met her in his public relations work for the company, so George ended up with two office affairs, one with me and the other with the woman who ended up as his wife."

Endings Don't Have to Be Earth-Shattering

Carrie

To say that Carrie is a conformist is like trying to say Picasso "painted by numbers." Carrie at one time worked for the agency in Atlanta. A tall man in his thirties, Hal, worked in the office next to her. Carrie said: "Hal was unhappily married. He'd tell me what his life was like, then say that he was so unhappy. He and his wife hadn't made love for several months. I don't know why I became interested in Hal, but I think it was because he was so sexually needy. I had just broken off with someone who had given me an ultimatum to marry or part—that was a mistake on his part. Even though I loved that one, I decided to 'part.'

"Hal and I had been friends for months, along with this budding sexual attraction that I felt for him. We started dating and eventually he left his wife. He, in turn, started working out to put tone to his body, wore smart clothes, and started wearing some great aftershave lotion that I had given him. I couldn't believe that his wife didn't catch on, but she probably didn't give a damn.

"We were able to keep it a secret. We kept it so well that the woman working next to him at the agency became interested in him because of his new act. She started putting moves on Hal and flirting with him. She followed him around at work, trying to seduce him. She'd come up to me and tell me she was going to get him to go out with her. She never got him, because during that entire time Hal had been with me.

"Sex with him was great, even though he was much less experienced than I was. However, I couldn't say anything that would convince him that sexually he was more than just 'okay.' This, however, began to get old, and he began to sabotage the sex. We had less sex as he withdrew more, but he would still complain about our not having enough time together. It was true, however, that I was on a fast track at the agency and worked a lot of hours.

"So I called in some favors to get a three-day weekend off, and

Hal was thrilled. I cooked and stocked the refrigerator with quiche, cold lobster, pâté, and the best champagne. Even though I wore ridiculously sexy clothes, built a romantic fire, lounged around making sexual suggestions, and asked him to please not trim the hedges, he still spent that time fixing the car, working around the house, and even rotating my tires. He was finally ready for me on the last night—seven hours before I had to be back at work, and I was into some stressful activities then at the agency. I broke up with Hal soon afterward.

"Although I was careful to avoid any romances with subordinates for sexual harassment reasons at the office, I felt freer when on trips, at seminars, or at any classes taken away from where I worked. I was propositioned by two of my instructors, including one who was so hot looking that other women kept chasing him. This one was so downright, knockdown gorgeous that women who hardly knew him would hand him their room keys in the elevator. I seduced him by being nice but not showing any real interest. He was intrigued because we would talk during breaks and at lunch, but I would never suggest anything more. It's the old story that I wasn't the prettiest thing around, but I was the only one who wasn't coming on or seemingly fascinated by him.

"He was a real sweetie when we got together. He sent me two dozen, long-stemmed roses without the thorns. Can you believe that, he even had the thorns cut off from the stems? When we were an act, he wrote me incredible love poems and three to four letters a week. He was a good one.

"Another one that I met on these trips was Felix, who was a criminal fraud instructor. I think I got interested in him because he was a very bright guy, then I decided he was also nice, protective, and cute. He had the room across the hall from mine at the hotel where we were staying and training. However, he was married then and still is, so we only talked and I respected that.

"What was ironic was that another instructor at the same time also became really interested in me. So I spent the night together with him, and what an acrobat that man was. I was exhausted from our night of gymnastics. In fact, after nearly six hours of continuous sex, I told him that I was going to sleep but that he should feel free to continue without me. I think I accepted him to work off the lust that I was really feeling for Felix.

"By then, Felix had decided that he had made a mistake by not following up with me, but unfortunately the seminar was already over. Felix and I called and sent letters to each other for some months afterward. I had already ascertained that Felix had enjoyed several affairs, and he then wrote me saying we should make up for lost time. Well, that was like telling a thirsty woman there was champagne on ice, chilled and waiting—and I was never, before or after then, more in lust than with Felix. He was living at the time in Miami, and I was residing in Washington, D.C., so we decided to meet up in Santa Barbara. We planned that trip's details down to the clothing that each of us was going to wear.

"When we settled into bed in Santa Barbara, Felix said he couldn't believe that all I wanted was to have sex with him. He couldn't believe that I only wanted his body, not him, but that was the truth. He began talking this way just as we were getting very steamy. He then freaked out when I became more amorous; Felix basically chickened out, all after such a promising beginning.

"I put on my clothes, packed my bags, and moved to another hotel room, which I thought was nice of me—to simply smile and leave. Felix made it clear that I was welcome to stay platonically, but that seemed to me to be an awkward arrangement. I had no hard feelings, but there were a few frustrations. I told him that if he changed his mind, he could call me. Then I went down and started making new friends in the lobby.

"For four days, we didn't see each other. I saw him at the airport when he was heading home. He had decided that he didn't want to leave his wife, which was the last thing I wanted him to consider. I had thought the whole idea was to have some fun and then go back to our partners. He had done that before.

"I've lived a good life and have had a lot of experiences. That's what life's all about, isn't it? I've been engaged several times—but I'm trying to break myself of that habit. The problem is I'm attracted to men who say they're independent and don't want a commitment; what happens is they always seem to change their minds and then want to marry me. However, when it comes to walking down the aisle, I just chicken out. For now, I have my woods, a nice house, my cats, my career, and I'm getting a much-needed and well-deserved rest."

Vincent

Vincent is a hardworking MBA who follows the straight-and-narrow path. He's worked for several companies and is now with a software firm. He said: "I was working as the vice president of finance for a manufacturing company. An attractive woman, Kyle, worked closely with me. She was having a spell at the time of the 'lonelies.' We had worked closely for a year, so I said I'd buy her some dinner and she could talk to me about it. She had just broken up with some guy and she was a little down. We ended up drinking over at her place and making love until early in the morning.

"When we arrived the following morning at work, we didn't say anything about that evening. It was as if nothing had happened. We went to an office party that night and didn't even talk to one another—it was as if we had violated some aspect of our friendship. At the time I was married, but that later ended up in divorce.

"A few years later, I was on vacation with an old girlfriend, and I saw Kyle on TV. She had married in the interim, and a fire had burned through Malibu and destroyed her house. A TV reporter was interviewing her about the fire. On returning to L.A., I ran down her telephone number and called her up. We got together and began an affair that lasted for several months before we called it off again—we began arguing with one another, and that wasn't the way we used to be.

"A few years later, we got together again. I had moved north to Montecito, a rich suburb next to Santa Barbara on the California coast. She had come through, looked me up, and again we started up an affair. We had a long distance relationship between there and Los Angeles, then Kyle called me up and said she had met a wealthy accountant. I congratulated her, because that was the way we were with each other. I threw her an engagement party, and then they took off back East to live. That was the last time I heard from her. I still think about Kyle and wonder how her life is going. We had good times and she was a good person."

Why Did It End?

If you've recently lost a relationship, asking why it happened is probably an academic question. Donna simply said that her "relationship wasn't going anywhere, and the answering machine message tipped the scale." The experts and the studies indicate that both lovers' motives are an important factor in determining whether the affair lasts or not and what happens afterward. As Professor Pierce observes:

There are three basic motives for a workplace romance: love, ego, or job related. What happens later depends upon which one of these reasons is present. Mutuality is a big factor. For example, if I've asked someone out because I like her, then that's one thing—and when it's mutual, then the setting is ready for a good relationship. However, if it's job related, such as wanting a better evaluation or a promotion, then that's where the problems begin. Ego-satisfaction reasons, such as getting back at ones spouse, also spell trouble for the new romance. Insincere motives are more likely to lead to problems than sincere ones. Mutual, sincere reasons for entering into a romance are necessary for any relationship to last.

Love is what has fascinated romance writers for centuries: those feelings of deep affection, personal attachment, or sexual passion and desire for someone else. Romances based on love last longer and usually work into long-term commitments. *Ego* is typically identified with lust, sexual gratification, "one-nighters," and flings. Ego makes people date on "the rebound" and count their sexual conquests the way an angler adds up the trout caught on a fishing trip. *Job*-related motives are just that: seducing someone due to the perception that some benefits at work will be gained, such as a salary increase, promotion, lighter workload, increased vacation time, job security, and the like. This includes the standard sexual harassment charge of where sex is demanded for job benefits (or keeping whatever's already there), along with luring the boss into bed so that you gain some work benefit.

If two partners are "in like," they will more than likely be friends. Friendship provides a stronger bond than simply coming together for sex, control, or ego gratification. It's easy to see that love lasts longer. If one partner has a different reason for being together than the other, that affair may very well run into difficulties. If one lover wants a long, satisfying and committed involvement but the other just wants the ego satisfaction of an extramarital fling, then it's easy to see that romance won't last. If one falls in love but the other doesn't, you know there will be troubles. And if one or both simply want job-related benefits, even trading sex for control, the potential for sexual harassment charges rears its ugly head in full force.

Jack, who worked for a high-powered consulting firm, seduced his boss. This affair quickly faded and he left for another job. Carrie and Tucker were interested in "fun, sun, and no involvement"—and that's what they got with no long-term romances. We learned about office wolves such as Mike (the paralegal) and black widows such as Debbie (the postal worker), along with Mindy's avarice and Brown's unreasonable pursuit of Ala. But then there were the committed love affairs of Herb and Mona, Christian and Amy, Alex and Samantha, Suzanne and Jeffrey, and all the others.

Everyone has his or her own reasons for love, but the "pure" motives count when it comes to romance and commitment. Even so, they are not always enough, as we see from Donna's story, where the romance seemed to be ending anyway. As Harry, the ex–general counsel, observed, "Some workplace romances just seem to run out of gas, like what you see with those that arise outside work. Some people cycle through romance and relationships during their entire life, while others stay with the same person for years and years—and they are the lucky ones."

We can't forget the role of women in these developments, including the changes in the workforce, company policies, and partnering of office romances. As one career woman observed, "Women have changed the roles. There are the aggressive ones who are too much for even other women. Some just say 'let's screw' and that's all they want then, but most people eventually desire committed, long-term relationships. Women today are not only entering into affairs, they're breaking them up, with more of these relationships from work lasting long times."

When It Happens to You

Emotions are such strange, but powerful creatures. Your heart can be singing when everything's going right, but then be crushed when your lover leaves you. Whether you initiated the breakup or not, take time to listen to your feelings and figure out what you need to do to heal. "Try to crystallize where you are and what you need to do, but don't rush into making too hasty a decision," said Harry who cycled through one romance at work.

At First

It takes time to heal. If you ended it, you're usually the one who's less hurt—but you still may need to think about some damage control. When you meet each other at the fax machine, or in the elevator, try to be courteous. One senior financial analyst commented, "After the affair was over, I first hid in the office. Although I had ended it, there was this concern over what he would do when he saw me. He worked in the marketing department, so my life didn't have the complication of having to work together. Later in the day, we were walking towards each other in the hallway, and he continued past me without even giving me a nod. 'I can handle that,' I said under my breath when he disappeared around a corner."

If you were the one rejected, the times are more difficult. "It was so hard at first," said Demi. "Where once we were giving each other secret looks, now we were looking the other way. You wanted to reach out and scream 'what's all this insanity about'; but you keep your feelings in check, at least that's what I did, and feel terrible inside. Then you go back to your office and think about what you should have done or said to your ex-lover at the time."

A Cooling-Off Period

"At first, you're better off giving each other some space and distance to cool off," said Ruth who went through this. "If you were the one dumped, then you're really into trying to avoid the other and hopefully not trying to get back together. Give yourself some time to get over the initial shock, anger, or hurt; try to put the breakup in some sort of perspective. Go about your work, as best you can."

"When you're not in constant contact, then all you can do is try giving a half-smile and keep going," said Carl. "The problem's when you're in such close contact with one another. The next day, there she was in the same room with me. It was almost unbearable. I would think that I'd show her how wrong she was, that I was going to make it in the company. I would grit my teeth and focus on being professional. You try your best to focus on your work, someone else, the boss, anyone except for that person. I thought to myself, one day at a time, that I would make it that day. Then the days began adding up to weeks; you do what you have to survive."

Some are able to do this, and others can't. "If you can't handle it, then that's what happens," said Robert whose affair with his lover ended. "I told her the next day that I couldn't work with her, and she said she understood. I guess she 'understood,' since she was the one who screwed everything up. I blew up and told her to get away from me. She went to the sergeant and said that we had an argument over some matters and needed some space. He rotated us around, and then

I transferred the hell out of there. I couldn't face the others, since some of them knew what had been going on between us. It was just best to leave."

Working It Out

Give the cooling-off period time. After you've settled down from your first strong reactions, think twice about trying to work it out with your ex-lover. Trying to make a friend of an ex-partner looks good on paper, but it's much more difficult in the real world. The first overtures usually are made by the one who broke it off, but be careful of the ex-lover's feelings. Ruth endured this and observed, "I thought Bill's attempts to say 'let's be friends' were presumptuous. 'How nice,' I replied sarcastically. He convinced me that we should try this for the 'good of the company,' and I agreed to have lunch with him. It really didn't work, but at least he tried and I felt somewhat better due to that."

It's obvious you don't want to make a "date" to work things out, because this approach only fuels the fire more. If your ex-lover refuses to meet you, accept that and go on from there. Beth was able to work out some accommodation with her "Dufus." Her lunch with him did help, although she wondered why she had gone out with him in the first place. It depends on the person, but sometimes the breakup starts to seem acceptable when you decide you shouldn't have been together anyway.

Marcia was the manager and Rob the assistant manager of the production end for a small toy manufacturer. She ended it because she didn't like keeping everything a secret and "all the lies" they had to tell to be discreet—Rob was also married at the time. When Marcia suggested they stop because she didn't like what they were doing, Rob was relieved. He was tired of the stress, as well. Sometimes things work out when you have the right reasons.

If It's Interfering With Work

As Robert experienced, if you work so closely with someone that you can't work it out or "gut it out," talk with someone you trust at work and get their advice. Follow the company's policies, especially if it's a pro-interactive company. See if using mediation, consulting a therapist, working an intervention by the company, or requesting a transfer is possible. It is all within your control.

Ted, who worked at a hospital as a physician, was crushed when his romance didn't work out. In his profession, there's no room for not concentrating on work. "I called in sick the first day, because I couldn't get out of bed and felt so bad. When I came back, I made my rounds at the hospital. I focused my thoughts on my patients, as they deserved nothing less. It worked until I ran into Jamie when she was working on a patient. I fled into the coffee room and drank two cups to refocus.

"I managed to get through the day. A friend of mine asked me how it was going and I said, 'tough.' Without thinking, I found myself heading toward the human relations guy and without knocking walked right into his office. I told him that I had a problem and needed his help. He looked directly at me and said, 'It involves Jamie, doesn't it?' I didn't know how he had heard, but word gets around fast.

He first talked with me, then called Jamie in. He worked out a way where we could treat our patients without always running into one another. It was his working with us that allowed me to handle my patients; the nights at home were something else, as I replayed in my mind any chance meetings we had that day."

Just as people have a right to their private affairs, whether at work or not, companies in turn have a right to expect their employees to get their work done professionally and efficiently. If you can't work together, after all the options, there's only the transfer or "one quits" alternative left.

Dorothy managed a small bank branch in a rural town and Max assisted her. They worked closely on all aspects of the operations, and Dorothy was going through a bad divorce at the same time. It wasn't long before Dorothy and Max were having a hot and heavy affair. When the divorce finally wound down, Dorothy began wondering about Max and her. He seemed to becoming more distant, and one evening she asked him why. He said he was finding it difficult to work for her during the day, and then switch roles and be her romantic equal at night.

They decided to end their relationship. Although it was "mutual," Dorothy was still hurt by going through two relationships that had ended. However, she had to pull herself together. It was tense at first, and the temptation to restart was there. Max asked her for a transfer, and she gave him the good recommendation he deserved. It took one month; this time was not a good one for either of them, but they made it through without a blemish on their careers.

It's uncommon for broken romances to end up in sexual harassment litigation when job-related motives aren't present, but it can happen when one ex-lover wonders just why he or she got involved in the first place in a reporting relationship. Fortunately, according to the experts and the interviews, most ex-lovers try their to keep their work relationships going, despite their angry and hurt feelings—provided they entered into that romance for the right reasons.

Where the job wasn't as important when they first fell for one another, it can become more important afterward. As Demi said, "My feelings were so bruised by that ending, that they were nearly raw. I didn't like seeing my ex-lover, but even with that, it was better than my crying at night. And at work I had something to do. I ended up deciding I at least had my job, and if I did have one, then I better do what I needed to keep it."

Damage Control

Damage control is important to both ex-lovers, not just the one who ends it. It's a real plus if the two ex-lovers can work things out and act professionally around one another. If the word is out, they'll need to assure their coworkers and the boss that their good work will go on as before. This is another reason most couples try to keep their romance quiet as long as they can and until they're sure their relationship is the right one.

If people only suspect your affair, you might let "sleeping dogs lie." However, if the ending was bad and an ex-lover overreacts, one of you will need to talk to the boss or someone in the organization who can intercede. If the boss knows, then he or she is the one you'll have to tell about the breakup. You will need to think about first (and even rehearse) how to approach and what to say to that supervisor. Remember that unless you're quite close to your boss, he or she probably doesn't want any more headaches that don't involve strictly business.

In larger companies, the alternative to simply talking with the boss is going to the human resources department. "I worked for my lover, and the HR manager stepped right in when I complained that she wasn't being fair to me afterward. He wasn't happy at first that we had been in a prohibited relationship, but he did mediate the problems and we were able to work out our differences. I can't say that we were friends during this period but we at least got our work done."

Leaving work is also an alternative if the company and you can't come up with an acceptable alternative. This is also not the end of the world. "When we broke up, we worked so close that there wasn't any place to hide," said Kelly, a benefits manager. "There were no transfer openings, and our supervisor wasn't that helpful. In fact, the company looked on the breakup as a 'bastard child.' I left for another job, as soon as I could find one. I soon felt much better."

Not Taking "No"

Problems occur when one ex-lover tries to patch up the romance against the other's wishes. What makes this situation so difficult is that relationships have normal ups and downs. *Couples do cycle naturally through good and bad times, even breaking up and getting back together again (sometimes more than once and regardless of whether the lovers work together).* All of us know of relationships where two lovers broke up, then patched up their difficulties and renewed their romance. Attempts at reconciliation can be successful, even when one of the ex-lovers is doubtful. When these attempts are successful, no one complains. However, the problems are created when one partner knows the relationship is dead, but the other doesn't realize this. Hope, unfortunately, springs eternal. Given the current organizational climate, this human behavioral fact is generally ignored; the likelihood of job penalties today is greater, even in cases that could never meet the legal tests for harassment.

EEOC regulations state that the complainant in a soured relationship "must clearly notify the alleged harasser that his or her conduct is no longer welcome" after a consensual relationship has ended. It also provides that if this conduct continues, the failure to bring the matter to management's attention, or the EEOC, may be evidence that the new approaches were, in fact, *welcome.* Moreover, as we've seen, a single incident usually is not enough to establish harassment. Trying to get back together by itself isn't an actionable crime, although restrictive companies with their fears of harassment lawsuits treat it as if it were.

A hostile working environment claim may be made, of course, even after a consensual sexual relationship has ended; however, proving this claim does depend further on the facts and applicable case law. For example, a male worker brought a sexual harassment suit against his female boss, claiming that after their consensual sexual relationship had ended, she began treating him badly. A short time later, the employee was fired. The court admitted that that employee was treated unfairly, but the judges decided that he had not proved that illegal sexual harassment had occurred.

The one who broke off a relationship is the one who enforces the decision. If you ended it without any "rights of appeal," show some feeling and understanding: put yourself in the shoes of your ex-partner who now has egg on his or her face. After waiting a reasonable amount of time, ask your ex nicely how you can make things easier. If that doesn't work, ask a mutual friend to intercede. If that doesn't work, send your ex-lover a letter saying that you're sorry things didn't work out, but that's the end of it. The letter is practical, and it also serves as legal documentation. Typically, a note that states "the next step will be to take a copy of this letter to your boss" may be enough.

If this doesn't work, you'll need to ask your supervisor for help. This doesn't mean filing a formal sexual harassment complaint. Why not? You can always make that complaint later; most workers just want the conduct to stop, and formal procedures will involve you, as well as your ex-partner, in the game of "charge, countercharge." The boss's informal intercession also may very well do the trick. If it doesn't but your organization employs a mediating approach independent of its sexual harassment policy, use it—invoking the charge-discipline-fire sequence associated with sexual harassment complaints can also hurt you in the eyes of your coworkers. If all else fails, go over the supervisor's head to his or her boss. If that doesn't work, *then* you'll be one of those rare people who complains to the EEOC. But remember that six out of seven of such complaints are ultimately dismissed for lack of prosecution, proof, or other reasons.

Although lawyers constantly worry about harassment charges from ended romances, most aren't brought, even when there's persistent pursuit or a severely damaged working relationship. Workers generally understand that a breakup is a relationship problem, not one that involves true sexual harassment. This charge typically comes in breakup situations when one worker is later demoted or fired, that worker's lawyer then arguing that this bad result was made in retaliation for the broken romance. See Chapters 5 and 15 for more on the "not taking 'no'" problem.

Nonwork Considerations

Whatever you do, let yourself grieve. Talk about your feelings with friends during off-work hours; don't hold them inside to stew and make yourself miserable. The rough times are here and will continue. Get some rest, even if you put more effort into work. Talk to a friend, go for walks, try to stay active when at home, and start the healing process.

It's normal to feel down when you think you've lost the "love of your life." However, if your sleepless nights interfere with your work or routine, or other signs are present (continued lethargy, not eating, or mood swings), then consult a physician or counselor. Be gentle with yourself and, if at all possible, don't make any major decisions, such as changing jobs or relocating to another state. It's not the time to bar-hop to "get even" or to buy an expensive new car. You need to keep the traumas and stresses of everyday living to a minimum. You'll have to go through a state of mourning, unless you're one of the few, lucky ones.

If you have a religious or spiritual foundation, be sure to use this. Counselors are the first to emphasize the positive effects of this solid grounding. And stay away from the drugs and booze. Substitute instead the more positive addictions of jogging, working out, or even gardening—whatever it is that relaxes you. It takes time to heal while you're also adjusting at work.

Fortunate people seem to have the ability to grieve and then get on with their lives; they apparently have an inner strength to rebuild their lives with activity and renewed vigor in a short span of time. Talk to others who've broken up and find out what they've done to adjust. As one ex-lover put it, "Afterward I could say that the time was a 'learning experience.' When going through that period, it was just plain hell."

What's the Company's Approach?

Organizations usually ignore breakups—until there's a complaint. The problems between Katherine and Eric on their breakup would have been overlooked if the company hadn't received a complaint about her reconciliation attempts (even though it was probably Eric who complained).

Businesses take a variety of approaches depending upon their policies (see Chapter 16, "Companies Are People, Too"). It helps if the organization you work for is "pro-interactive" and has a reasonable policy in place. For example, one firm requires that *all* ended romances be reported to a supervisor and that both workers undergo mediation if work problems persist. Of course, what people actually do will vary from what any organization advises. In this case, two of the company's workers didn't report an ended romance; the company only learned about the problems when a coworker complained. However, the firm interceded with professional counseling, and the problems were solved.

Pro-interactive companies will intercede like restrictive ones because they're worried about harassment complaints; however, these firms also realize that the "warn and discipline" route isn't the best way to end what is fundamentally a human relationship problem. Organizations that trust their employees, but know employee problems occur in the most efficient of workplaces, will have more proactive but less punitive policies that work. Try to work for a company that has such policies in place.

Pete and Peggy

Pete and Peggy met at a hotel near Malibu, California, where Pete was a waiter and Peggy was a waitress. They started dating and became lovers. When they came to know one another better, Peggy began backing away because of Pete's temper. When she broke it off, they were working in the main dining room of an exclusive seafood restaurant on the beach. They continued to work together, even though it was difficult. When times were slow, Pete would approach Peggy and ask if she was dating anyone else.

One day they were working together on the typically packed Saturday morning shift. He asked her out again, but Peggy politely declined. Pete walked past her and hissed "Bitch!" at her. Peggy explained to the manager what had happened. She said that she didn't want to make a complaint but wanted him to talk to Pete and help out. He did, and that was the last time Pete talked to her. Each ignored the other when they worked together, but there were no further working problems.

Fraser

Fraser is the vice president of human resources for an integrated health care company that also owns several hospitals located in the southeastern United States. He has thirty years of executive experience in several industries. Fraser observed: "Companies should try to mediate office problems, whether they're coworkers who can't work together for personality reasons or ex-lovers that just broke up. Usually we won't do anything if we hear a rumor that two people are together. We don't do this because it's none of our business. We will intercede if we receive a complaint or some information that productivity or performance is being adversely affected.

"We've had cases where one employee has filed a restraining order against another when there was a romance breakup or divorce involving coworkers. In that case, we tell both employees to go to the judge and work it out—to tell the court that they're both working here and that it's their problem.

"If two parties are feuding over a broken romance and one of them has complained, then my director of employee relations sits down with them and tries to intercede and mediate the problems. If that doesn't work, then I'll go down and say something like, 'If you don't work out your differences so that work can go on around here, then both of you are fired.' That has always worked.

"The smaller the firm is, the less the transfer options. This means that in smaller companies, more of a premium is put on working out these problems, and that in turn requires that mediation is brought to play even more—perhaps on a mandatory basis. As the firm becomes larger, then it's easier to transfer within that organization. This doesn't mean that you use less mediation and intervention, only that you have another available alternative.

"One policy that I have changed around here is our antinepotism law. We have always avoided the appearance of preferential treatment due to family members working in the same department or one family member supervising another. Now we have extended the nepotism concept to include domestic partners. As with most firms, we don't prohibit dating, since you couldn't even if you wanted to. However, if the relationship becomes more committed, then one of them has to transfer or leave; and we give them ninety days to decide which one of them this will be. I am looking to change this policy to where the "transfer or leave" only applies to conflict-of-interest or reporting situations.

"Broken romances are much more prevalent than sexual harassment complaints—and by a wide margin. We handle romance problems administratively through my offices with the mediation and 'drawing the line' approach. We also use a preventive approach with our policy on antinepotism."

Transfer, Leave, Demotion, or Promotion?

From Katherine and Eric to Andy and Vicki, we have seen some of the "tough love" handed out by companies to employees who have broken up. It doesn't make sense at times to apply legal sexual harassment standards to what are basically no-fault human relationship problems.

Whether a company works with (mediates), transfers, demotes, or fires someone for what happens after a relationship has ended depends entirely on its policy. What's ironic is that the same actions are taken at less progressive organizations when an office romance is simply discovered and nothing else has happened. See Chapter 16, "Companies Are People, Too," for more on this.

Who Loses More?

Older academic studies typically concluded that women "lost" more (promotions, relocations, or terminations) than their male partners did when an office romance ended—for example, Quinn and Lee (1978), Quinn and Judge (1984), Driscoll and Bova (1980), Devine and Markieticz (1990), and Anderson and Fisher (1991).

However, these studies were completed before the Clarence Thomas U.S. Supreme Court nomination hearings and the 1991 Civil Rights Act's effects (see Chapter 4, "The Law of Romance"). The ensuing legal onslaught resulted in an evening of the results between the sexes (according to the experts, later studies, and surveys), with many of the interviewed human resources executives saying that men were now as much at risk. As Professor Pierce comments, "Given that back in the 1970s and 1980s a greater number of women were in lower status positions, it may have appeared that gender was the critical factor, when really it might have been job status and how expendable one was in the organization's eyes. This has changed significantly since then, and more research is definitely needed to fully address this issue."

The consequences of a breakup are now decided case by case. Women being fast-tracked up the corporate ladder will, if involved in a breakup, be treated the same as their male partners—at worst. If you're fortunate enough to be working for a "pro-interactive" company, this subject won't come up. The point is: regardless of sex, you're better off thinking about how to deal with your specific situation, than being concerned over academic arguments (that now go both ways) as to which sex loses more in a general sense.

More Stories

When we're discussing romance and endings, we're talking about real people and what they do. Here are a few more:

The "Burnout"

An attractive, thirty-two-year-old woman, Cecilia, worked as the assistant to the jury commissioner of a Miami courthouse. She was married, had no children, but became bored. Cecilia began an intense affair with a maintenance man who was in his mid-forties. They kept it going for two years. She made excuses to her husband for being out on certain nights, saying that she was at a lecture series, a painting class, or whatever worked. She and her lover would take "nooners," and all in all, it was a satisfying relationship. Cecilia told everything to her best friend, which was a mistake because this friend was again telling everyone else.

However, Cecilia decided that her affair was really an attempt to hide something from herself. She saw that her romance was keeping her tied to a life that wasn't really giving her complete happiness. The relationship became a symbol of a life that was "on hold." Cecilia broke off the affair and soon left her husband. She also quit her job and headed to a smaller city in Florida to be a modern dance instructor. Cecilia had a "thirties" burnout. At last report, she is happy and quite contented.

Going "Postal"

Henry was happily married to Tippy, and both worked for the post office in Montgomery, Alabama. Tippy worked in the back office, sorting mail, while Henry was a carrier who delivered it. They had been "married for years," had five children (ages ten to twenty), and were both in their mid-forties. Henry didn't think much of the fact that Tippy changed her schedule so she could work later and on a different shift than Henry.

She began arriving home late, saying she had worked more overtime. Henry didn't really notice whether she was because Tippy handled the family's finances. However, when they weren't able to pay all their bills, Henry checked her pay stubs and discovered that Tippy wasn't doing that much in the way of overtime.

He began checking out what happened after hours. He watched Tippy leave on time in her car, then followed her a few miles to an apartment building. He watched her get out, walk up the stairs, and disappear. An hour later, she returned but was followed by a younger man, Manny, who Henry knew also worked at the post office.

He confronted them, but Tippy shouted at him to get away and Manny scampered back into his apartment. Henry couldn't believe it. Tippy was having an affair with a man who was fifteen years younger than Tippy and who worked with him as a carrier. She moved out of their house and served him with her divorce papers.

Henry was beside himself. He confronted Manny the next day and lunged at him. Other mail carriers interceded to pull him away; during the fight, a loaded gun fell from the back of Henry's shirt and clattered to the floor. He was put on administrative leave and then quietly retired from the post office. Tippy obtained her divorce, married Manny, and the new couple transferred to Salt Lake City.

The Chutzpah of the Year Award

As an example of how office affairs can become complicated, one single investment banker recalled that he began dating a "quite attractive woman" who was the travel coordinator for the firm. The only problem was that when they had an argument, he would have problems getting his travel arrangements confirmed in time. After two months, he discovered that she also was having an affair with the married CEO of that same prestigious Wall Street company—and who had also just discovered the competition. After deciding to end the relationship (and just before being warned by the general counsel, the CEO's friend, to get out of the way), our single friend discovered again that he had problems scheduling his business trips.

Eventually, he left the company, in part because he doubted that the CEO (who's still with this Wall Street firm) would deal objectively with his annual bonus or further advancement—probably an accurate assessment. However, the chutzpah of the year award has to go to the young travel coordinator, merrily dating men much higher up the corporate ladder, at the same time, traveling around the world with all of them, and without any apparent concerns. Life is just an attitude, isn't it?

Chapter Fifteen

Read This (Before You Hire a Lawyer)

Your relationship just crashed on the rocks. It was great at first, but now your time together doesn't taste right, especially since the relationship had been with your boss. Or a coworker has persistently asked you for a date, but you don't have the slightest interest. The company hasn't done anything about your complaints, or, if it did, you were the one who transferred. Worse yet, down the road you were the one who was fired.

You remember the newspaper and television stories about those large sexual harassment awards. Then you came across one article that insisted the average award for these cases is at least $250,000. Companies settle because they can't afford the disastrously high legal fees. It's time to hire yourself an attorney. Right? Wrong—don't make the decision yet. You need first to talk with several experienced lawyers about your case, analyzing its strengths and weaknesses and deciding what it is you really want to accomplish.

The Role of the Media

The problem with the media is that it sensationalizes the rare, easy to prove, debasing cases of sexual harassment that do win big—and should. However, in this area, it is always someone else who wins these large verdicts. You have the same chances of winning $500,000 in a harassment judgment as you do in winning that much in your state's lottery. And winning at lotto involves fewer headaches and bad times. An experienced litigating attorney said, "People go by what they read in the paper or see on TV. That's not the real world. The media only reports what will grab readers' interest, like a $1 million verdict. They don't tell you about all the cases that go nowhere, that are dropped, where the judge rules against you forcing the lawsuit to be dropped on some technicality, or where you don't get enough money to cover your expenses and the lawyers' fees. The media has no interest in what happens day-in and day-out in the real world, because it isn't newsworthy enough."

Not only that, the odds are against your winning a case, whether you rely on the EEOC, your state human rights agency, or your own lawyer. For starters, the EEOC has no enforcement powers. It can decide in favor of either party or simply issue a "no decision" right-to-sue letter. Even when it issues a ruling, it cannot administratively enforce that ruling but must sue in court to enforce it. As a practical matter, it only sues in class actions or multiple-party cases. Thus, in most cases, claimants have to hire their own lawyers, even after filing a formal complaint with the EEOC. This, as you would expect, takes some time.

Next, factor in the costs of the lawsuit, the attorney fees, and the out-of-pocket expenses, and you'll be shocked at what you receive—the bottom line, after all, is how much you receive after everyone else is paid off. Further, the odds of prevailing in a broken romance or persistent suitor situation are much less than when you have a clear-cut sexual harassment case. The same lawyer said, "Plaintiff attorneys count on putting enough pressure in these cases on a defendant so that they'll settle. We're on a contingent fee [no fee is paid until there's a settlement or judgment] when the defense is charging their client for each hour they expend. The hourly rates can range from $150 to $350 per hour and up, depending on the lawyer and where you are. These forced settlements don't always happen, and when they do, they may be fairly less than what the client was asking for or expected. And you do have expenses to pay."

Forget about the large verdicts you read about in the newspapers. That isn't the real world. This chapter will go into the details of what actually happens and what you need to do.

The Procedures

We assume at this point that you couldn't work out some accommodation with your ex-lover and you feel your company wasn't any help—

in fact, they made it worse. Let's say that you broke up with your superior, he or she stayed on, and the company fired you for poor work performance. This is about the worst outcome anyone could experience from a workplace romance.

Under Title VII, you must file your complaint with the EEOC within 180 days after the occurrence of the alleged discriminatory act. However, in states or localities where there is a fair employment practices board and an antidiscrimination law, your complaint must be presented to that state or local agency. In these jurisdictions, you must file your charges with the EEOC within 300 days of the harassment act, or 30 days after receiving notice that the state or local agency has ended its processing of your charge, whichever is earlier.

Pay attention to these time limitations, because if you miss them, you won't be able to sue under Title VII (you can sue under other theories but not these friendly ones). You must file an administrative complaint before filing a civil lawsuit under Title VII or under various state fair employment practices acts. As this is a complicated area at best, you'll want to consult with an attorney on which approach is best for you. And it's better to talk with several lawyers, if you have the chance, because their opinions can differ as to what alternative is best for your case.

Many cases are filed with the EEOC, rather than a state agency, due to local regulations requiring this, attorney preference, and the higher profile of the EEOC. The advantage of these administrative interventions, whether by the EEOC or a state agency, is that the agency in question will act as your free civil rights attorney—and they can facilitate settlement. You have no legal fees to pay when you use this route. The EEOC will notify the employer about your charges. If after investigating your case, the agency believes your employer is guilty of your charges, by law it's bound to try to reach a reasonable settlement of your complaint. If it can't reach a settlement, the EEOC will either bring a legal action on your behalf against your employer (which is quite rare) or issue you a right-to-sue notice authorizing you to sue on your own behalf (which is much more likely).

Basically, the EEOC rarely sues because most of its offices are clogged down with complaints, and it's nearly impossible to investigate all of them adequately. As Lloyd Pearcy, an experienced Denver litigator, explained: "After receiving a charge, the EEOC has six months in which to investigate. Immediately after the filing, the EEOC notifies the employer requesting certain information. Often this letter and the company's response, if any, are all that's in the file after six months. At the end of six months, the complainant has the legal right to demand and receive a 'no decision' right-to-sue letter."

There is a 90-day deadline following receipt of the right-to-sue letter for filing in court. As attorney Pearcy explained further, "This is the most unforgiving statute of limitations [you can't file your suit if you miss this deadline] that I know of. So there are two deadlines that must be monitored: the 180-day or 300-day deadline following the aggrieved event for filing the EEOC charge and the 90-day deadline following receipt of the right-to-sue letter for filing in court." Sounds simple so far, doesn't it?

However, if you also have a state or local agency with the ability to represent you, the EEOC will defer any action on your complaint to give that local agency time to act on your charges. The EEOC will take over if your state or local agency doesn't, and keep in mind the varying time limits within which you must respond with your complaint. It's best to contact the EEOC without delay when you have a harassment charge that your company hasn't handled properly.

A right-to-sue letter from the EEOC or your state agency gives you the legal right to sue under Title VII or the state law equivalent, but you have to hire your own attorney at your personal cost and responsibility. You can immediately hire your own attorney without going through the EEOC, but then your lawsuit can't invoke Title VII and its provisions. Your lawyer will be relying on other causes of action for your case, such as a breach of an implied contract of employment, the duty of good faith, public policy, other applicable federal and state statutes, and other employment law theories.

Now you always must factor in the attorney fees and costs. Your lawyer will tell you what his or her charges will be and whether they will be on a contingent fee basis. Don't forget to consider the out-of-pocket costs mentioned above. Lloyd Pearcy explained: "In Denver, the costs of getting one of these cases to trial is $10,000 minimum. Figure $5,000 to $15,000 per expert witness. You need to have an economic expert who calculates the damages for your client, plus medical and psychiatric experts. A well-prepared case could cost $70,000 and up—and that's before any attorney fees." These numbers could be higher or lower, depending on where you live, but it's better to estimate higher from what you're told because that's the direction expenses usually head.

The bottom line is that you must discuss your specific situation with an experienced attorney. Whether you complain to the EEOC, go to your state or local agency, or file a lawsuit in federal or state court, this decision can only be made by weighing the pros and cons of your case, after discussing all of the facts with experienced lawyers in this field.

The Statistics Are Against You

By the EEOC's own statistics, the large majority of complaints filed with the agency don't go very far. About 60 percent of all EEOC complaints are rejected for lack of sufficient evidence, and another 25 percent are closed because the worker withdraws the complaint, declines to cooperate, or can't be located. Typically, 12 percent are settled in the employee's favor without a formal finding of discrimination or harassment. This leaves only 3 percent of all cases, on the average, that are strong enough to take into court under the EEOC's procedures. Overall, only one in seven complaining workers has their EEOC complaints resolved in their favor, and even then, there are long waits—it can take up to a year and a half or more just to have the average claim rejected or resolved.

In the past six years, the agency has pushed only 991 cases to the threshold of a lawsuit. These aren't overwhelming numbers. Some 16,000 sexual harassment complaints are filed annually with the EEOC—or approximately 15 percent of all claims (including Title VII discrimination complaints) so filed. The numbers represented by broken romances or persistent suitor situations are estimated at some 3,000 each year (or the approximate number of quid pro quo cases filed), or 3 percent of all cases filed.

So for practical purposes, assume you'll be hiring your own attorney. Your chances for winning can be better with an attorney, although it depends on your case. Depending on the survey quoted, plaintiffs lose from 50 to 60 percent of all the cases that they bring on sexual harassment charges. A survey by Orrick, Herrington & Sutcliffe, a respected law firm in San Francisco, indicated that plaintiffs won only 40 to 50 percent of the employment cases filed since 1990, down from 60 to 70 percent during the 1981–90 period. The study indicated that this decrease was due to the fact juries weren't finding that employers engaged in the types of conduct found so outrageous as in earlier years.

Harassment litigation isn't the "dialing for dollars" that many people are led to believe by the media. The EEOC reports that in recent years the settlements there have averaged between $15,000 and $20,000. Although the surveys of what's secured by the lawyers indicate higher awards, the average amounts wrung out aren't earth-shaking—especially when you factor in the attorney fees and expenses usually paid by the client such as filing fees, depositions, expert witnesses, travel, jury expense, and other out-of-pocket expenses. The reason so many people file first with the EEOC is that their activities are free.

The *Dispute Resolution Journal* in its Oct.–Dec. '95 issue published a comprehensive study by Dr. William M. Howard of three judicial alternatives used in employment discrimination cases: litigated cases in federal court during the two years ending in 1994, as compiled by the Federal Judicial Center; American Arbitration Association awards for terminated employment cases for 1993–94; and awards in cases arbitrated before the securities industry's self-regulatory organizations.

Among litigated cases, if the highest 10 percent of the verdicts were eliminated (which skewed the statistics), the median award (or the award in the middle of all verdicts) for cases litigated without a jury was $35,000; the mean (or average) judgment was $58,000. If the highest 10 percent again were eliminated, the median award for cases with jury verdicts was $106,500; the mean was $417,000. Now, that's getting better, you might say.

However, when you factor in that only 10 percent of all cases ultimately proceed to trial, the rest being settled or dropped for lack of prosecution, and that employees won only one out of every four cases tried before the judge (two out of five before a jury), *the conclusion was that there was only a 2 percent chance of obtaining these plaintiff verdicts.* Further, although 70 percent of the cases settled before trial (employers, although winning the majority of court cases, would rather not risk a multimillion-dollar judgment), other studies indicate that these settlements average from $35,000 to $40,000—and don't forget the attorney fees and expenses. Studies conducted more recently support these conclusions and major findings.

Let's take a hypothetical example of a $200,000 judgment that isn't appealed and that amount is paid (which doesn't necessarily happen in the real world, as defendants go out of business, don't have the money, or just won't pay it). If the lawyers were on a 50 percent contingent fee after the trial, and the expenses of the litigation were $50,000 (a not unreasonable number), the plaintiff receives $50,000—not the amount that would be reported in the newspaper. Remember the long-shot odds of getting one of these awards are about one in fifty.

When cases were arbitrated rather than litigated, the awards were less than when tried in court. Arbitrators usually aren't subject to the wild emotional swings juries can be; arbitrators must be agreed to by the parties, which works a compromise on how conservative or not they are. The findings: employees won in two-thirds of the cases, but when eliminating the highest 10 percent of the awards, the mean award was $44,000 and the median was $25,000.

When reviewing the securities industry arbitration data, the mean was $31,000 and the median was $22,000 (again, eliminating the top 10 percent). A survey of National Employment Lawyers Association attorneys by Dr. Howard indicated that attorneys screened their clients in order to take only the best cases—minimum provable damages of at least $60,000, a retainer of $3,000 plus, and a 35 percent contingent fee (which can increase when in trial or if an adverse verdict is appealed). His studies indicated that nineteen of every twenty employees who felt they had an employment discrimination claim, in fact, weren't able to obtain a lawyer's representation for that claim because of the selection process used by lawyers.

The bottom line: the odds of winning a skyrocketing verdict are almost nil. Although the median award in jury trials was $106,000, there's only a 2 percent chance of winning one, given all the claims filed. And then there are the legal fees and expenses that must be paid from the proceeds. Nearly 70 percent of these lawsuits settle before trial, the average settlement being $35,000 to $40,000, again before paying the lawyers and the legal costs. Further, sexual harassment insurers say their settlements average "$25,000 to $50,000," again for those cases they settle. These settlements, after attorney fees and costs, reduce down to $5,000 to $15,000. *Be aware that lawyers in numbers of situations don't want the risk of contingent fees—they will charge you on an hourly basis. And these statistics include all of the flagrant, no-borderline sexual harassment and discrimination lawsuits—not the broken romances we've been discussing.*

Incidentally, the survey of lawyers indicated that while the plaintiff's fees were usually contingent, the defense costs average $100,000 in litigated cases, but only $20,000 in arbitration, which is a simpler and less time-consuming process. Although the awards for arbitration were less than for litigated cases, employees won a greater percentage of the cases. Mediation and arbitration are quicker, faster, less expensive, and less negative processes for clients to use. This area is treated further in the next chapter, "Companies Are People, Too."

The lack of success of the average sexual harassment case may be due in part to the "frivolous" and borderline complaints that are filed.

"Many times, sexual harassment claims aren't raised," said Liz, a re-spected defense attorney, "until the employee has been threatened, demoted, or discharged for some work reason. The employee's attor-ney then argues harassment or discrimination was the reason for that discipline or termination. Frequently, harassment is made as a claim by an employee trying to reverse that punishment, and in numbers of cases, the two simply aren't connected and they can't prove it. I have seen various sexual harassment cases that were truly meritorious. The problem is that this knee-jerk reaction by lawyers is trivializing what's an important civil right."

In cases where the attorney is arguing that the harassment brought about the employee's termination or discipline, the jury or judge must decide first whether the alleged conduct in fact occurred. If so, then they must decide if this conduct met the legal standards for actionable sexual harassment. As part of this, the court must decide whether the harassment bore some relationship to a term or condition of employment. This process narrows considerably the extent to which harassment will survive as a valid claim, not to mention any actions brought in connection with workplace romances.

A Few Cases

Although the statistics prove the long odds sexual harassment com-plaints face in obtaining meaningful cash settlements, there are the publicized wins. A female civilian security guard sued the U.S. Army for $300,000 in 1993, alleging that coworkers made crude sexual com-ments to her and the army retaliated against her complaints by as-signing her to a trailer. The army agreed with the EEOC's finding of harassment. An attorney represented her, and the army agreed to a $60,000 settlement in late 1996. This was unwelcome sexual harass-ment, period.

A female fundraiser filed a sex discrimination suit against a uni-versity, however, alleging that the institution fired her for dating her boss, while he kept his position. The chancellor stated he told both employees to end the relationship, or that one of them would need to find employment elsewhere. The woman said she would find another position in two months, but when she couldn't do this, she was fired. The boss kept his job, but he didn't receive a merit pay increase the following year, as the details of that relationship had been inserted in his file. The woman sought more than $50,000 in damages but settled the lawsuit for $5,000. The settlement came when the jury told the judge that it was having a difficulty reaching a verdict. The university didn't have a specific policy that barred supervisor-subordinate relationships, except between professors and their students. Using sexual harassment policies and procedures in these cases makes no sense at all.

A woman was having domestic problems at home with her husband, and she entered into an affair with a coworker. Her work performance deteriorated, and both of the workers were indiscreet about their relationship. The company fired both for lower work performance, the effect on their coworkers, and bad office evaluations. The woman brought a sexual harassment lawsuit for $250,000, alleging that her firing was due to having complained about sexually offensive behavior by the two top company officers. She alleged that one CEO had asked her for a date, stared at her, and made lewd comments, among other inappropriate behavior. The evidence presented by her coworkers was to the contrary. The jury rejected all of her claims, finding that the company and its officers were blameless. The CEO commented that his staff, even with the win, would have difficulty overcoming the stress that the plaintiff's allegations and trial had placed on them.

On the West Coast, a $1.5 million lawsuit was filed against the owner of a beauty salon by five ex-employees, each alleging unwanted touching (such as back massages) and other sexual harassment allegations. Two plaintiffs were dropped by the judge from the lawsuit, and they are appealing not only that decision, but also the award against them of defendant's attorney fees. The jury awarded the remaining three plaintiffs $500 in actual and $9,500 in punitive damages, or $10,000 each. If you factor out the assumed contingent fee payable to the attorneys (given that they accepted their full fee), the costs of trial, the out-of-pocket costs for depositions and transcripts, and other expenses, these plaintiffs more than likely lost money. The defendant then appealed the decision awarding even those amounts—and we're not even talking about romance and relationships in this case.

Litigation is not an enjoyable process for most people, and please keep in mind it's not what you win, but the net amount received that counts. Even assuming that a favorable verdict is received and paid, there are the contingent fees, trial expenses, and out-of-pocket costs that must be paid. Further, even if you receive a large verdict, the other side may very well appeal, putting more pressure on you to accept a lesser amount in settlement. "We're not talking about morality in these cases," observed one lawyer. "We're talking about money, pure and simple."

If You Want to Go Further

Don't Make the Decision When You're Upset

Take your time in making any final decision. The best decision isn't made when you're angry, upset, or want to get even. Don't make a short-term decision that has strong long-term implications. Wait, talk to friends, and when in a calmer state of mind, then make your decision. Liz, who experienced years of litigation warfare, said, "The worst decisions are made when someone's emotional about it. You need to make a decision only after you've weighed all the facts. You must prove your case in court, have the law on your side, and be working with a reasonably competent lawyer. If you don't, then you're in for a bad experience."

Have You Done All That You Could?

Ask yourself if there's anything further you can do at the company about the broken relationship or amorous advances. Most important, you must have put the actor on notice that what's happening is now unwelcome and must stop. If you've been in a consensual affair and it's now over, you should send your ex-lover a letter, stating specifically that the romance is over. Keep a copy for yourself so you can prove later that your ex-lover knew new ground rules were in effect.

Have you talked to the officers at the highest level who have the final say on your complaint? Be sure that you've exhausted all administrative remedies under the company's policies and procedures. Given the lack of success people experience as they go further down the legal road, ask if you've done everything that you could. Look at mediation as an alternative if all else fails.

One female employee became upset when her supervisor didn't do more to separate her from an ex-lover, telling them instead to "work out the problems or chose who leaves." The two ex-partners met at lunch, not accomplishing anything except cold stares. She didn't want to leave, and neither did her ex-partner. One attorney said she had a case in suing her company; another lawyer said, "she had some problems" and needed to go further with the company.

After a sleepless night, the employee decided to go straight to the top and plead her case. She sent an E-mail message to the company president, telling the business reasons why she felt her ex-lover should be the one to transfer. The next day, the human resources manager talked to both. Within the week, her ex-lover transferred away and eventually left the company. She's still with the organization and has been receiving her normal merit increases.

Remember that the EEOC, a state agency, or your lawyer must review the entire record. The complete circumstances of the case, such as the nature of the advances, the extent of the relationship, whether it was consensual, the context within which the alleged incidents occurred, the motives, whether the allegations arose after the relationship was over, among other personal considerations, all must be analyzed.

What Do You Really Want?

We're talking about people and their feelings. It's important that you decide what's important and what you really want. Do you really want to sue or punish someone? Do you want an ex-lover transferred, monetary damages, an apology, or just what? The interviews, studies, and common sense indicate most people simply want the conduct stopped so that they can continue with their careers and advancement, just like everyone else who has a problem at work.

If the motive is to get even and punish the actor, then take your time before you make that decision. Reread this chapter and talk to several attorneys about the merits of your case, all before making any final decision. Think about the best way for you to become vindicated, as well as what's best for your career.

Liz, who handled a variety of sexual harassment cases, said: "The emotional levels run high, and I don't blame them. However, being vindictive paints a bad picture about you to your company. Think about your career and what's the best approach to take for it. If you feel you haven't anything to lose, then go for broke. However, be sure that you've looked at all the legal aspects of your case. Talk to friends at work and get as much feedback as you can. If possible, find out if someone else has gone through a similar episode there and talk with him or her. You need to get as much information as you can in the beginning. It's too late, once you're in the thick of the briar patch and then feel you've made a bad decision."

You Have to Prove Your Case

Being wronged isn't enough—you have to prove your case. And you need both the law and facts on your side. Check with an attorney as to whether the law is on your side. For example, if you were in a relationship with your supervisor, then broke up, remember that you must prove your boss's conduct met the applicable legal standards for sexual harassment (see Chapters 4 and 5 in this regard).

The fact that you had an affair and it didn't work out is not enough. If you were demoted because you ended it, then the law is on your side. However, if you still received fair and reasonable evaluations as before, you probably don't have a case—even if you're still upset and angry over the broken romance. Feelings do matter, but not when it comes to clinically evaluating your case.

It's also important to "document, document, document." Write down what happened with whom, when, who was present, and what was said. Be very specific—the more specific, the better. Construct your case using your personal notes, supporting office memos, and corroboration by others. Liz reasoned: "Think about who was present, if at all, when the unwelcome conduct occurred. If no one was, then see if you can put together memos or correspondence showing that both of you were in the same place at the same time. Make copies of work policies and procedures. Talk to your coworkers for their recollections and see if others had similar problems as you did, because there's strength in numbers. Perhaps they even can join you in your complaint. Make copies of everything and keep it at home, in case you're fired and can't get back to your desk."

Talk to Several Attorneys

What amazes the experts is that individuals will take the longest time to check out consumer items like computers, cars, and insurance; however, they'll jump with the first attorney that appears to take an interest in their case. Talk to several attorneys about your case: the problems, strengths, how long it will take to proceed, the costs, and the attorney fees. Don't settle for less. These problems will take a long time and lots of effort to be solved legally. Be sure to obtain courtesy, no-charge consultations. If the lawyers are looking at whether they'll accept your case or not, it's only fair that they don't charge you for that time.

About Attorneys

If you can't work things out within the company and want to pursue your case legally, then search for the best legal value. This means talking to several attorneys and finding the best one who's experienced but at an affordable price. Be sure that the initial discussions are free, at least up to the point where the lawyer can decide if he or she will take your case.

Interview the lawyers you talk to. They're deciding whether to accept your case, and turnabout's only fair play. Rate them on several factors before you make up your mind: a detailed conflict check (that the lawyer hasn't represented the other party on any other matters); the attorney's experience with your type of problem; the attorney's time availability; the costs and expenses that you're responsible for; the attorney's malpractice coverage, just in case that lawyer makes a mistake; and your compatibility in working together.

Look for that lawyer who has a genuine interest in your case, will work with you on fees, and is compatible. There's nothing worse than looking for a Godzilla and finding one that doesn't know the difference between attacking the other side and going after you. Sometimes the best choice isn't the least expensive (that lawyer really doesn't know the area) or the most (you're paying for all of the expensive surroundings you see in that law office). Be sure to get in writing whatever agreement you have with the lawyer you finally select. And if you don't talk about how mediation can be used, be ready for a long, expensive process.

Mediate, Don't Litigate

The legal process can be quite inefficient in this area. Simply reread the statistics on what actually happens when you head into court. Arbitration still depends on a court-type process, and unless there's a contractual or judicial provision mandating its use, this requires the consent of the other party for its use. Although mediation also requires the other party's consent, the beauty of this process is that it isn't binding until you have an agreement. If the mediation doesn't work, you can always head into court—and even use it later if things get bogged down again in legal maneuverings.

Mediation is especially useful when there's a continuing relationship, such as at work. Suing a company makes more sense after you've left. Mediation is an informal proceeding wherein an impartial, third party shuttles back and forth, determining the areas of agreement and minimizing the differences. The mediator is motivated to find common grounds, not take positional arguments as the law does, which simply accelerates an already bad situation. This process is used in every conceivable situation, ranging from solving divorce and child custody problems to automobile accidents, debt collection, medical malpractice, union problems, and contract disputes. Companies are using mediation especially in harassment cases where the complainant simply wants the conduct to stop.

One lawyer who switched from litigation to become a full-time mediator said: "It doesn't take you too much time before you realize that the existing judicial system is a terrible way to solve disputes. The process tears up people as much, if not more, as their initial differences. The time it takes, high costs, loss of privacy, bad publicity, and stress all take their toll. Mediation is the only sane way to solve problems." Another attorney commented, "Clients walk into a lawyer's office and have no idea what's best for them. Some attorneys would never recommend mediation, just because they don't understand it, don't like it, or can't do it. First-timers then fall into the long, expensive court process of trying to beat someone else down to get a win. They learn much too late about all the insanity that's taking place there."

And what do attorneys think about mediation? A 1996 sampling of members by the American Bar Association (ABA) indicated that:

- 51 percent of attorneys actually *favored* mediation over litigation for resolving disputes, while 31 percent preferred litigation;
- 77 percent said that their clients willingly use mediation;
- 51 percent believed that mandatory alternative dispute resolution (ADR) techniques such as mediation should be encouraged (18 percent said that they should be discouraged, while 28 percent didn't take a position);
- 39 percent said that clients find mediation more satisfying than litigation (46 percent equal or less); and
- 85 percent said that they weren't worried that less expensive ADRs would reduce their practices' revenues.

These are very supportive statistics. Additionally, nearly all state courts provide for mediation in some way, as do most federal district courts. Businesses have discovered the advantages of using mediators for especially sensitive problems.

As just one example, the president of a medical testing laboratory called me in a panic: his two top workers were in a dither. The woman, Candy, had just stomped into his office, calling her male coworker, Eddie, a harasser, male chauvinist pig, and a few choice four-letter words. Eddie was speechless. The two worked alone for ten hours a day in a lab set far away from the others for safety reasons. Candy complained that Eddie had talked offensively to her. My client was perplexed because the two had worked together for months without any problems.

We began following their standard sexual harassment policy: talk to both parties together, then alone; advise each about their rights; ascertain the facts; and work toward a penalty phase of a written warning, transfer, or demotion. Before this went too far, thankfully, we agreed that using a mediator made much more sense. We hired a trained specialist in the work relationship field.

She met with them individually and together. By the end of the morning, she had discovered the problem. Eddie had used new words in a different context that had set off Candy. It was a communication problem: Eddie didn't realize their effect on her, and she had misinterpreted those remarks. The mediator worked out ways for them to communicate more effectively. Eddie and Candy still are working together in that isolated laboratory, without incident, by themselves, and three years later.

An attorney observed, "Folks should really consider using mediation in the harassment area, especially when there's problems with proof and given the cases that the defense wins." As another example, a supervisor tried persistently to get his subordinate, Jane, into bed. He made sexually suggestive remarks and stroked her hands when she told him not to. She didn't like his continuing advances, told him so, and argued with him strenuously about that. When this didn't work, she simply quit one day. The company had a sexual harassment policy that was used; however, she didn't think about that on the day she left.

Jane had more proof from a coworker who had seen some of the goings-on, but this potential witness had been fired later for poor work performance. Jane lodged an EEOC complaint, and later filed a lawsuit against the company, its owners, and the supervisor. Although it was stipulated that the business and its owners didn't know what had happened, it had a liability exposure due to the supervisor's conduct and the upcoming jury trial. The attorneys, after several lengthy and expensive court hearings, agreed to use mediation.

Jane had reduced her demands to $70,000, the company had countered with $10,000, and there each party stayed. Two sessions later, the difference had narrowed to between $50,000 and $25,000. The mediator asked Jane if she had ever seen a court case before and knew what a trial was like. She said she didn't. Jane's attorneys arranged for her to observe a trial where cross-examination took place; she talked to a woman who had gone through a harassment trial and a defense verdict. Her attorneys were in favor of this, because they wanted her to understand what could happen, should the mediation not be successful. Jane realized she didn't want to go through this process. At the next mediation session, she and her ex-company settled for $35,000. From this, Jane paid her lawyers and the expenses.

Another ADR is called arbitration (which we will address more fully in the next chapter). Arbitration is more like a court proceeding, except there's limited discovery or fact-finding; the parties choose the decision maker (the arbitrator); the arbitrator doesn't have to follow the rules of evidence; and the arbitrator's decision is binding, whereas it isn't in mediation. The same ABA survey of lawyers indicated attorneys were less enthusiastic about arbitration, with 31 percent preferring it to litigation (41 percent preferring litigation). This isn't too surprising, because arbitration more closely approximates litigation but doesn't have all its attributes. However, it is quicker, less expensive, and more flexible than outright courtroom trials. As one lawyer observed dryly: "It's litigation, but less—and without the rights of appeal."

An Overview

A lawyer friend of mine, when asked what motivated him to take sexual harassment cases, said: "The money, my friend, the money." You won't find many lawyers saying this in public. They will claim on the record that their motive is fighting for the principle, and there are attorneys who do this. However, as my friend said later: "Come on, get real. If I couldn't make money at this, do you think I'd be doing it?" This doesn't mean that lawyers shouldn't be able to earn a living while enforcing the rights of everyone to work in a "hassle free" environment, it's just that when attorneys take on the marginal cases, the risks are (as Liz said) that very important civil rights become trivialized and diluted. And romance, when it runs into problems, gets thrown into this process.

Litigated cases can take years to settle, and as we learned before, you'll have to hire your own lawyer for nearly all the cases. Remember that attorneys and all the expenses get paid from the first proceeds, and that no case is an automatic winner. You have to prove your claims in a court of law.

You must look at what happened with a cold, objective eye before making any decision to file a lawsuit. Remember that clients generally are personally responsible for paying their out-of-pocket costs, even when the lawyer is on a contingent fee: win, lose, or draw.

Look closely at using mediation when the other party has a similar view. Mediation can be used whether an attorney represents you or not. Let the mediator contact the other side to see if they have an interest in this alternative, or see if your lawyers would agree to use it.

Making the Final Decision

We discussed the case of Dawn in Chapter 1—and she still isn't a happy camper with the legal system. "Even when you win money, the taste can still be left in your mouth," said Liz. "This isn't an area where people feel good, starting with what caused the problems in the first place."

Like Dawn, your likelihood of prevailing depends on the attorney you get, what he or she does, what the other side does, among a number of factors that aren't within your control. As we've discussed before, the great majority of harassed workers (not to mention broken romances) don't receive the large judgments or settlements you read about in the newspaper. People are fired, transferred, and demoted for unjust and lousy reasons, just as people are sexually harassed with no justice received. And broken relationships, whether at work or not, have the greatest uphill battle of all to win in court. Most don't win a cent.

You need to consider, How bad am I feeling? How long will suing take me? What will be the remedy, and what will this cost me? Balance the pros and cons. Is there someone else in the company that has had a comparable experience? Does he or she feel the same way I do? Remember that there's strength in numbers, especially when someone has solid proof or will sue along with you. This is a real personal judgment. Don't be railroaded by your friends, one way or the other. Make the decision that's right for you.

Who's the Real Winner?

The broken romance, harassment, or lousy experience is bad enough. You then pile on the time, money, and energy spent trying to rectify this legally. However, the real winner is whoever can best put the bad experience behind them, regardless of who actually wins the legal battles. It hurts. It's bad, whether you're at fault or not. But the reality is, you have to get on with your life and put all of this behind you. The one who does this, regardless of whether money's lost or won, is always the real winner.

Chapter Sixteen

Companies Are People, Too

The evidence is compelling: companies can grant workers the freedom to enjoy social relationships at work, still surpass corporate goals, and fall into less expensive courtroom battles over harassment charges. The concept of "pro-interaction" was explained in Chapter 6. This discussion isn't limited to the business world. Romance includes police departments, law firms, accountants, universities, the post office, nonprofit agencies, in short any place people work together for mutual goals and joint purposes.

No question about it, the "one-size-fits-all" sexual harassment approach plus a "victim's" or nonresponsibility mentality that afflicts some of us can create problems for coworkers and organizations alike. It's also obvious that relationships can end up in only two ways: a continuing long-term romance or marriage (where at least one-half of all work affairs head) or a breakup (where the other one-half end). It's also impossible for the owners of a business (whether it's the public with its police department or the shareholders of a company) to know how different people will react to a breakup, because this is so interwoven in closely guarded, internal psychological factors. Unfortunately, the law chooses to become mixed up with sexual harassment concepts in regulating affairs of the heart when it has very limited reasons for doing so.

Let's take a look at just two examples, in addition to what's been discussed so far. An officer of an East Coast–based company became involved with a female subordinate. This was definitely consensual; they not only had problems being discreet (their coworkers complained about favoritism), but they began living together. This was the happy time, and their relationship seemed solid enough even to outlive their careers at that company. Unfortunately, they ran into relationship problems and she threw him out of the house. It was tense at work, so the officer fired her (a poor decision), although unsatisfactory work performance records supported his action.

She sued the company on sexual harassment grounds, including alleging that her supervisor forced her into having sexual relations (we don't know what her actual motives for the romance were), made improper advances, and assaulted her in his office. The company fired him and settled out of court with her.

A small police force in a coastal California town was hit with a sexual harassment complaint. The woman alleged her supervisor made improper advances while trying to establish a sexual relationship. There was no way either one could be transferred, as this was a small police force. At first, the town relied on expensive legal advice from an attorney, including that the complainant "be bought out," since she was the lowest person in seniority. Morale at the department began to plummet. Fortunately, the police chief remembered a mediation firm practicing in the region, contacted them, and sold the two police officers on using mediation. The mediation worked, the lawyer was paid, and the officers are still working together on the force.

The question becomes why natural human relationships at work can be so condemned by some on general policy grounds (aside from the complications)? One argument is that women shouldn't have to endure unwanted sexual advances at work. No question about that. The argument continues by presenting the numbers of sexual harassment incidents in the workforce (both reported and unreported) and declaring that this must be stamped out. Who would argue with that? The problem is that the baby is being thrown out with the bathwater when we consider consensual relationships and the natural ebb-and-flow that occurs between people in relationships. Not to mention that reasonable advances, even if spurned, aren't grounds for sexual harassment and shouldn't be.

However, the one-size-fits-all philosophy rears its ugly head. So what's a company to do? Outlawing office dating doesn't work. Telling coworkers to keep their feelings out of the office sounds nice but doesn't work in reality. However, there are effective business strategies to employ. Pro-interactive companies don't have the problems that restrictive firms have, even when both enforce strong sexual harassment policies. It's a question of basic company attitudes to their workforce.

It Starts With the Company's Climate

Pro-interactive organizations don't have the lower morale, employee turnover, and lower productivity associated with restrictive ones. *"Employees just don't operate well in a climate of fear,"* said Randall, echoing the thoughts of other human resources executives. "Instilling a meaningful sense of corporate loyalty makes more sense. A workplace should be pleasant to work in, even with the long hours and stressful conditions. Workers should feel free to interact and relate to one another, even with the problems, without the fear that they will be punished for those relationships. A company has the duty to support its employees in a progressive way that enriches their lives, the employees in turn giving their whole-hearted efforts and support of the business and its objectives," added another.

This is strong preventive medicine—but this philosophy doesn't mean that the organization's emphasis is on dating, socialization, and wild parties. The loosening of social relationships is simply an outgrowth of an entity's underlying attitude toward its employees. Pro-interactive companies find that a pleasant, sometimes fun environment, is more productive. A chain of ice cream stores creates a fun culture for its employees, including costumes and theme nights (such as romance, disco, pajama parties, science fiction, and so on) at their stores. A bank designs various "forgot the business suit" days for its employees so that they can wear informal attire (which is appreciated by its workers). A fire department puts together a "get-together" every three months for its employees and their families or partners.

And there is more. As Johnson Wax believes, employees are a company's greatest asset and they are to be trusted—we've already seen how it supports its workers with employee-friendly programs. The founder of Quad/Graphics, Harry Quadracci, takes his "trust employees" concept so much to heart that each year he puts on a Quad University where his managers leave the plants running in the hands of their hourly workers for up to three days. Bankers Trust sponsors special child care camps for its single and working parents when children are on school vacation and no one is at home to take care of them. It, like other pro-interactive companies, has put in place different philosophies when it comes to its employees.

Bain & Company, the venerable management consulting firm, expects its workers to put in long workweeks for the excellent compensation that it pays. In return, it works with its employees, including organizing various social events, accepting office romances, and even transferring people so that they can be with their significant others.

Robert DeMallie, the director of external communications for Corning Incorporated, commented:

> As women came into the workforce, they needed changed policies from expanding benefits such as child care, elder care, and flexible workweeks to having a more flexible approach taken with personal relationships in the workplace. It's natural for people to pair off, especially when they are so committed to their job. At Corning we have 6,000 employees headquartered in Corning, New York—a town of only 15,000, including those of us who live here. In recognizing this, our chairman and CEO, Roger G. Ackerman, launched a formal program to enhance the way our employees work together with a prime objective of addressing the needs of the individual worker.

Springfield Remanufacturing (see Chapter 6) encourages employees' socializing and married couples' working together at its operations. It supports activity committees for its workers, including fitness programs and personal trainers, among other programs. Odwalla (also mentioned in Chapter 6) puts mutual trust at the top of its list. Its employees "self-organize" with their own picnics and softball games—socializing is important at this firm, as two of its founders even married afterward.

Tom's of Maine, like many small companies, reflects its founders' philosophies and attitudes. Created by Tom and Kate Chappell in 1970, the business is motivated as much toward its mission in life as toward obtaining sales growth and profits. With a $5,000 loan and a belief that products could make money but didn't have to pollute, they created and marketed ecologically friendly products such as all-natural toothpastes and deodorants. A start-up operation in the beginning, they created a company that employs over seventy-five workers with sales in excess of $20 million (and these numbers are climbing fast).

Their commitment to the environment has received accolades in the press, as has their belief that it's possible to make money at the same time that you're bettering the world. "You don't have to sell your soul to make money" is their creed. The company donates 10 percent of its pretax income to charities, offers its workers three months of paid maternity leave, provides child care subsidies, and encourages employees to spend 5 percent of their paid work time doing volunteer service (and 80 percent of their workers do).

What's important is that *these entities trust their employees, earning this in return, and there isn't uncertainty woven in their working environments as seen at less forward-thinking companies.* Recognizing that office romances occur as a positive fact of life is an important management tool and helps to foster an enjoyable work environment.

These organizations understand that demanding long work hours creates in turn strong social and relationship needs for their employees. Companies that don't actually force their people to look for companies that do—regardless of the state of the economy or how plentiful jobs are. Dissatisfied employees will simply bide their time until an opportunity comes their way. Pro-interactive policies are a matter of keeping well-trained employees with your workforce, not with your competitors.

A Reasonable Office Romance Policy

The *Romac Report,* created by Strategic Outsourcing (see Chapter 3), presented the results of its extensive survey of personal relationships at work in February 1997. Only 9 percent of the 592 responding businesses said their company had enacted any policies on office dating. As the report mentioned: "Most respondents felt it was impossible to legislate and enforce any rules without employees feeling their liberties were being infringed upon. Also, for many people, the workplace is the only social outlet to which they are exposed and feel comfortable."

Surprisingly, two-thirds allowed supervisors to date an employee within his or her organization. Despite concerns about coworker dating, as described at Chapter 3, three-fourths of the respondents had *not* had a "serious problem" with consensual office romances that ended in an unfriendly manner (70 percent of companies with over 500 employees had the same result). *Definitely, the fear of these problems is greater than what actually happens.*

A better alternative than relying on sexual harassment policies would be to take a positive stand: try to solve the anticipated problems arising from coworker dating but recognize that employees have a right to their relationships, provided their personal life doesn't interfere with the company's operations. This policy would include a statement that the entity recognizes that workplace romances occur, but that it expects the participants to be discreet and avoid excessive public displays of affection. Workers should endeavor to maintain a professional work image at all times and leave any relationship "ups and downs" at home.

A specific individual (usually the owner in a small business or the HR manager in a larger one) would be designated as the person to whom problems in relationships could be reported. The following situations would be reported:

1. One party wants to enter a relationship, but the other doesn't;
2. One party wants to end a relationship, but the other doesn't;
3. All relationships involving a boss-subordinate or potential conflict-of-interest situation (such as an important customer); and
4. Someone complains or problems occur in the workplace due to a relationship.

This designated person, or "ombudsman," would be empowered to iron out the difficulties confidentially and creatively.

Keep in mind that these procedures don't just apply to single employees. Married couples working for the same company can also have relationship problems that carry into the workplace. These policies would apply similarly to married couples experiencing difficulties or divorcing. Employees, whether married, gay, or single, would be treated the same way with regard to their workplace romances.

Boss-subordinate relationships are the primary cause of worries for companies, as also documented by surveys such as the *Romac Report*. Three-fourths of the respondents in the 1994 AMA study agreed that it was okay for coworkers to date, but the numbers reversed (three-fourths disapproving) when bosses and subordinates dated. It's presently within a company's legal right to banish these relationships outright, especially when problems such as favoritism are being caused. However, as we've seen, this restrictive approach simply drives workers underground and can create further unresolved problems. For example, the relationship may surface only when it's over and an ex-lover is bringing a sexual harassment charge. Well-trained workers may leave to work for more progressive employers.

A better alternative would be to require boss-subordinate relationships to be disclosed confidentially to the couple's supervisors. The company, if at all possible, would strive to retain both workers. Responsibilities would be realigned, evaluation functions reassigned, or transfers arranged. Should a transfer not be available, the partners could maintain their relationship (provided favoritism was not present) until a transfer opportunity arose—but a neutral, third-party executive would make all job evaluations. Concerns as to supervisorial control on the subordinate are met by emphasizing the right of the subordinate to meet directly and confidentially with the highest ranking officer at any time, should difficulties occur on the job or with the relationship. Of course, the firm always has the right to fire either or both workers if job performance plummets, disruptions in the workforce occur, or coworker morale and productivity suffer.

A business can tailor its approach to specific situations. As bigger entities have more flexibility than smaller ones, a small company's policy could simply state that its option would be "to make such adjustments as management decides to be in the best interests of the company, including termination if no other opportunities develop, work performance has suffered, or coworkers have a continuing genuine complaint owing to the effect of the relationship." Companies do not lose their power to take strong actions when merited by adopting pro-interactive approaches.

However, just how do you force people to report relationships, when in fact they don't do that now? The point is that you can't force them, but you can create a climate that encourages problems to be reported and solved before the lawyers are contacted. You can put a positive procedure in place to handle work relationship problems, whether due to a romance or not. What some companies do instead is to throw an iron curtain down on any conduct that's complained about, rely on a sexual harassment charge being made, and then follow their sexual harassment policies to enact various disciplinary measures. That's ridiculous.

Reasonable workplace romance issues should be treated as relationship problems and not as sexual harassment grievances—although true sexual harassment situations must be handled promptly under these policies. It doesn't make sense to use harassment procedures for all reported problems. If you wait long enough without taking a balanced, problem-solving approach, guess what? You will have a tough, expensive sexual harassment charge on your hands.

This doesn't mean that inappropriate words can be used—they can't. Nor does it mean that pursuit can be unreasonable. Of course it can't. It just means that relationship problems are acknowledged at the beginning as what they are. Sexual harassment policies stay in place as they are. Inappropriate behavior is still out, but in the early beginning, problem phases, or ending stages of any work relationship, employees have a place to go that doesn't involve a charge and countercharge atmosphere.

The emphasis is on solving, not punishing, with an integral part of this process using mediation, rather than an internal company court. However, the penalty harassment procedures are still available for clearly unreasonable conduct.

It's goofy to use corporate punishment as the stick to "make problems go away," rather than taking a more positive approach to solve the problems and minimize workforce disruptions. Numbers of businesses treat office romances the old way divorce used to be handled: identifying a culprit (or culprits), proving wrong conduct, then punishing (with divorce then by asset distribution). In today's world, divorce is seen as the relationship problem it always was—recognizing that it occurs due to no one's fault. The emphasis of "no-fault" divorce is on solving the problems from the breakup, rather than the ancient way of searching for past guilt and then punishing. Office romances will be handled the same way. Mandatory mediation and conciliation concepts will be used more extensively (as with no-fault divorce), rather than outmoded, punishment-oriented concepts. It's only a question of time.

In essence, a written office romance policy would:

1. Recognize that office relationships exist;
2. Establish a mechanism whereby relationships and problems are to be reported confidentially;
3. Solve boss-subordinate relationship problems with solutions tailored to the company's situation and retaining those workers;
4. Employ mediation to solve relationship problems, but still reserving the use of warnings and extreme discipline measures (such as suspension or termination);
5. Separate romance from sexual harassment, but retain the discipline measures for unreasonable or serious noncompliance;
6. Rely on seminars to counsel workers on the pluses and minuses of workplace romances, including the company's climate and its procedures; and
7. Create a general environment of trust and support for its workers.

Appendix 1 presents a model office romance policy. Please note that the applicability of these provisions and procedures will depend on the company, its size, philosophy, and industry, as well as other factors. Although lawyers prefer to put policies down in writing, the important concept is always the philosophy. An organization can establish an informal process whereby an ombudsman helps employees solve work relationship problems, and mediation is required first, but not put anything further in writing—however, these policies would have to be communicated to the workers. In any event, an organization should discuss these concepts with its attorney, weigh the pros and cons, and then make an informed decision.

Jay Waks is a partner and the cochair of the Labor and Employment Law Department at the New York law firm of Kaye, Scholer, Fierman, & Handler, LLP. He represents corporate clients in employment litigation:

Ten to fifteen years ago, it was the subordinate who typically was the woman in a corporate reporting relationship and who was fired due to an office romance. Today, it doesn't happen that way. Both employees are counseled as to how best to eliminate the supervisory aspect of the relationship—and today, taking into account the legitimate business interests of the corporation and those of the involved parties, it may be the boss who is transferred. What's important is that you don't peremptorily fire well-trained people, and that instead you manage these relationships rather than ban them.

Any company's stated policy on workplace romance would normally assume that there's a strong sexual harassment policy in place, signed off by senior management, and including three major points. First, that employees in a relationship can find themselves in a situation that may adversely affect themselves and others in the workplace, should they break up. Second, that they have an affirmative responsibility to tell their boss when they have a reporting relationship and are romantically involved—then, one of them must transfer or the supervisory aspect of that relationship must be transferred to some other superior. Third, should the relationship end and either of them is unhappy, that they must work out their problems so that the workplace is not adversely affected—otherwise, they may have to choose which one should be reassigned or should leave the department or company.

Companies which have well-articulated work philosophies in place, sensitive to the legitimate private relationships of their workers, will have fewer significant, irreconcilable problems with internal romantic relationships between coworkers and avoidance of sexual harassment complaints. The creative philosophies of

progressive companies emphasize flexibility in handling office relationships creatively and swiftly, solving the expected employee
problems which inevitably arise from these relationships and their
breakups, in order to ensure a mutual respect between the company,
those who are romantically involved, and the coworkers.

Using the Policy

How this policy would be used in specific situations will depend on
the individual circumstances. The basic questions are: What is the actual work environment of the company (pro-interactive or not)? Is the
romantic involvement disrupting the workforce? Has the company
had situations like this before and how were they treated? Can the
firm accommodate the partners in their present positions, balancing
the company's needs with those of the lovers and their coworkers? Do
the lovers feel isolated, thus requiring a dialogue with their coworkers?

For example, if two coworkers are rumored to be having an affair but there are no complaints, the company has no interest in becoming involved. Even if a spouse or a lover (from outside the company) complains, unless there is a clear conflict-of-interest charge
(such as a patient and physician), then there still wouldn't be sufficient reason to intervene. Only if coworkers complain or a boss-
subordinate relationship is involved are the dating policy provisions
to be invoked.

In dealing with boss-subordinate relationships, it's important that
businesses don't adopt a policy of reassignment or resignation in
which the subordinate is always the person asked to move or leave.
Such a policy can have an unequal effect, systematically requiring
more women than men (or vice versa, depending on workforce
makeup) to leave. And this by itself could be a potential violation of
Title VII.

When deciding to enact a dating policy, remember that individual
state laws differ as to what privacy rights workers enjoy in particular
situations, whether it involves coworker dating or chain-of-command
situations. Although these statutes can specifically involve the right
of employees to smoke off-duty, amendments and court decisions can
broaden the application of these laws.

Although it is clear businesses shouldn't snoop, it's reasonable to require that problems be promptly brought to a designated person's attention. Whether employees comply or not is less important than the fact that the business has opened up clear channels of communication, including ones that can eliminate potential harassment and other employee-related complaints.

Stephen Sheinfeld is the head of the Labor and Employment Law Department of New York City's Whitman, Breed, Abbott & Morgan. He observes:

> The swings in this area have been momentous over the past, let us say, fifteen years. The law and attitudes regarding sexual harassment evolved from "ignoring the boss having his way with the secretary" to "we'll have to fire that one" after the Clarence Thomas hearings. It wasn't until just a few years ago that the pendulum began to swing from ending those relationships at any cost to let's "manage them and not ban them."
>
> Now, there is recognition that people work long hours at work and romance may be found in the workplace. The law on sexual harassment is enforced much more strictly now than before—although there are many gray areas—and the workers are generally educated now as to what's "proper" or not. Although the courts continually try to define the gray areas between where is the line drawn in the "touching—off-color joke" areas, the boss-subordinate relationship is a particularly sensitive area. Since soured romances can make for messy lawsuits, the question is what can a company do? And to correctly balance the rights to privacy of all its workers?
>
> A starting point is that what happens outside the workplace is nobody's business—but what happens inside is the firm's business. So, if no one sees or knows about an outside romance, then the company generally has no right to interfere. However, if two workers report to one another, have long lunches and time off together on work time, or personal arguments occur at work, then this becomes the company's business.
>
> Companies should have a written policy as to relationships in the workplace, if anything to let employees know what those policies are and that they are being fairly and equally treated. And these policies usually don't allow relationships that are supervisorial in nature, give rise to conflicts of interest, or otherwise adversely affect the workplace. Once these policies are in effect, it is important that the company effectively communicates them to its employees.

A Strong and Enforced Sexual Harassment Policy

This goes almost without saying. As emphasized throughout this book, a reasonable policy with regard to workplace dating can exist only with a strong sexual harassment policy as one of its underpinnings. Although a broken romance by itself isn't evidence of harassment, nor if there are complications, true harassing conduct is not to be tolerated. When employees violate the trust the company has placed in them by disrupting the work environment with unreasonable, unwelcome conduct, the company must take action. If the firm has a well-considered sexual harassment policy, discipline measures should be taken in accordance with it.

A sexual harassment policy should include the following:

- Statement of policy to create a harassment-free workplace;
- Definition of sexual harassment (unfortunately, it will be vague, but try to use clarifying examples);
- Policy of nonretaliation for making complaints;
- Specific procedure(s) for preventing harassment (such as training programs and management "awareness" seminars);
- Clear and thorough investigation and remedy procedure;
- Reporting procedure on who reports to whom under this policy;
- Timely reporting requirements (there can be statutory time limits by when charges must be completed);
- Definition of the scope of the investigation (how wide or selective);
- Selection process for the "right" investigator (so no conflicts of interest are present);
- Policy that treats the accused fairly (to avoid later wrongful termination or defamation lawsuits);
- Impartial review of all files, circumstances, and facts;
- Efficient and fair interviews that balance the rights of the accuser and the accused;
- Reasonable time by when an investigation is to be completed;
- Reasonable discipline measures, depending on the proven severity of the conduct; and
- Written summaries of the findings and discipline, placed in the appropriate company and employee files.

And this is only a start.

However, a distinction must be made between sexual harassment and reasonable behavior within the bounds of a consensual relationship. Companies should keep in mind that the use of more mediation techniques and quicker intervention can minimize their "harassment" exposure. Further, if a company doesn't have a written sexual harassment policy, it should develop one and soon. Contact your chamber of commerce, industry or trade group, or an experienced attorney to put one in effect.

Communicate, Communicate, Communicate

Regardless of industry or size, all companies need to communicate their work policies to their employees, including their guidelines on work romances. Businesses must precisely describe what their formal policies are, what the corporate climate is, whom to contact for confidential advice, and what procedures are to be followed when a reporting relationship or conflict-of-interest situation exists.

Communication should not be limited to the businesses' formal or informal policies. It should also include what happens practically with work couples, the pros and cons of these relationships in that workplace, and the dynamics of coworker relationships—in short, practical advice for the expected involvements that will occur. "It needs to address a central point that a personal relationship between coworkers or those in reporting lines will change the nature of their work relationships. You need to bring this out into the open," advises Tom Davidow, a principal with Genus Resources of Needham, Massachusetts.

Discussion groups should cover what might happen if the romance doesn't work out, what might happen if it does, and how the couple should relate to each other and their coworkers. The firm should assure its workers that it doesn't want to stop people from seeing each other (even if it could); it simply wants the opportunity to head off possible trouble, including with supervisorial relationships.

In short, the company must coax work relationships up from the depths where people by instinct try to hide them. It has a duty to manage office relationships with dignity and flexibility, just like any other aspect of the employment relationship. "As part of this, it appears that companies with open communication lines and a relaxed environment seem to do better in the areas of romances and accompanying low sexual harassment problems," concluded Tom Davidow.

Harley King, the director of human resources development for Health Care & Retirement Corp. (a large nursing home operator and diversified health care company with 20,000 employees), instituted a program for the company called the "Circle of Care" in 1988. This eleven-hour training program was created so that its employees would learn to be helpful, caring, and responsive to its patients, families of patients, and coworkers. All workers, from executives to nursing aides, learn how to compliment others, be kind, and respond correctly to upset workers and clients, including learning how to hug properly. The company endorses hugs, or friendly embraces, as part of its corporate policy for everyone. To short-circuit the inevitable sexual harassment concerns, the policy requires that the hugger secure the "huggee's" permission before an embrace can begin.

What's important is not just the hugging and kindness policy (which also motivates workers to treat its elderly nursing home patients with care), but the overall training concept and approach. This corporate program trains its "trainers," who then work at its subsidiaries training new employees in their program. There are seven modules in the program:

- Who are the company's "guests" (patients, the families of patients, and HCR's employees);
- You're only responsible for your own behavior ("it starts with me");
- Families: what makes people tick;
- The art of active listening;
- Saying the right thing at the right time;
- Interpreting body language; and
- Learning how to deal with the angry guest or customer.

Harley King observes:

You can run this program with modifications for any industry. We're talking about basic corporate communication here, including telling your employees what your corporate culture is. One reason for adopting this approach at HCR was that we had a number of different cultures at the company in the late eighties due to various acquisitions we had made. Our Circle of Care reinforces our vision statement. It teaches how we want to interact with each other, how we should relate to our customers, and how we should work together as a company.

The key is that a company communicate its culture and policies in a positive, upbeat way to all of its employees. Any business can adopt this approach to bring positive messages to its employees of a "kinder, gentler" workplace, including what employees can expect from their personal relationships at work and the firm's pro-interactive approach. This is just good management practice.

Mediate, Mediate, Mediate

The magnitude of the relationships that occur in the workforce is staggering. According to the BNA study, one-third of all romances start at work. However, keep in mind that we're now dealing with broken work affairs that subsequently cause problems, not the numbers of relationships that work out. Or, if they do end, don't cause problems. As we've seen, a small proportion of broken romances result in extended problems that management must deal with, and even fewer wind up in the hands of an attorney.

Mediation is a powerful tool to use when relationship difficulties arise. There's little room for an apology in the courtroom or during an official investigation, but this empathy can be used to transform conflict into resolution by the parties and mediator when working together. Work issues can be separated from the nonwork issues of a personal relationship.

For example, one coworker was bothered when another employee continually pestered her for a date. Lucy complained to her supervisor, who talked, in turn, with the worker, Ron. He asked Lucy for a date the next day; she refused again and marched immediately into her supervisor's office. Instead of writing up Ron for sexual harassment under their "one warning and you're out" policy, the supervisor asked Lucy to consider talking it over with Ron under a trained facilitator's supervision. She accepted. Ron agreed also but was advised he would be written up—at best—unless he worked this out to her and the company's satisfaction.

The facilitator (or mediator) developed that Ron kept catching the wrong signals from Lucy. He was misinterpreting her friendly nature for romantic intentions, and this was a communication problem on his part. During the mediation, Lucy admitted that Ron was a good worker, but she didn't want to become romantically involved with him. Ron just wasn't her type. Lucy, in turn, discovered that she was giving off mixed signals by the words she was using, including after the supervisor first intervened. It took two sessions, but the communication problems were worked out. Ron didn't ask her out again, and Lucy could compliment him (which he liked) on his work habits.

Mediation is especially useful when a broken romance spills over into the workplace. If the ex-lovers can't work out their differences (as Beth did with "Dufus" in Chapter 1), they can choose anyone both respect to help them sort out the problems—perhaps a coworker both trust or a friend who knows them well. Before a manager says "work it out, or decide who leaves," try this approach. The mediator can be a trained facilitator, the company's appointed "ombudsman," or just someone both ex-lovers will listen to.

Let's take the example of Russell and Dana. Russell was the manager of a software product, and Dana managed another—both worked in the same small office and made joint marketing decisions. They had engaged in a torrid love affair for two months (unknown to management) before Dana decided to call it quits over Russell's "quirky, little habits" that drove her nuts. The ex-lovers couldn't decide on how to continue working together, and a supervisor's intervention didn't help either.

Before arbitrarily assigning fault and transferring or firing one (or both of them), their boss suggested having a trained work relationship specialist intervene before he took unilateral action. The mediator talked to Dana and Russell together, then separately over a weekend. He first determined that neither had an imperfect motive, such as power, getting ahead, or just sex. The affair simply didn't work out. If either had dishonest motives, the mediator's job would have been more difficult.

Dana said she could work with Russell, if he would just put their differences behind them. Russell said he could, but their experience was that he really couldn't. Eventually, they hammered out an agreement, subject to their boss's concurrence. Dana would arrive in very early in the morning to get her work done; Russell would arrive later and stay into the evening. They would have limited interaction, and for the first few weeks, their marketing interaction would be in front of their boss. Dana would have the option to transfer out when a suitable opening came up. If this didn't occur in one month, then Russell would have that transfer option. In the event that problems resurfaced that affected the company's operations, management would step in and make its decision.

As it turned out, Russell met a woman outside the company, and his interests headed off in that direction. Dana worked in the department for three months, then transferred to a better position. Both of them continued with the company. Russell's supervisor still isn't sure what he would have done if the intervention hadn't worked.

Requiring mediation or intervention is easy. If one or the other ex-lover refuses, what has the company lost? It simply takes the action it was planning to all along (or removes the worker who refused to try mediation). Employing mediation simply places a step between the parties' inability to work out their difficulties and management's unilateral decision.

Mediation won't work in all cases, as you would expect. People who are used to seizing power in situations will find it difficult to give that away in a mediation. As Michael, an experienced Ph.D. specializing in mediations, stated: "My responsibility is to balance the perceptions of power, to create a level playing field. Mediation won't work where one party refuses to give up in a given situation what he or she perceives to be power. It also doesn't work where one party, or the other, is convinced that they have the superior bargaining position, one-sided facts, or everything is clear-cut. Or when the offender's behavior is so outrageous as to require immediate discipline or termination.

"The process is particularly beneficial when the parties are simply not able to understand or communicate with one another. Regardless of the type of case, mediation is generally effective in 70 to 80 percent of all situations where the parties sit down and try to work it out. That's the key.

"If someone agrees to using mediation or an intervention, then you know that they're leaning toward trying to work something out. Even if the process isn't successful in arriving at an agreement, one advantage is that the discussions are heading in a positive direction. It's ideal for starting towards an acceptable solution, at least in part, for all parties."

Keep the Channels of Communication Open

Employees should be encouraged to "speak their piece" openly and confidently, regardless of the type of problem, and this approach shouldn't be limited to office relationships and harassment complaints. The human resources executives interviewed put a premium on keeping a free, open, and positive environment at work, aside from their formalized policies and procedures. Such an environment encourages the airing of problems and potential solutions before it becomes too late. Without these channels, senior management runs the risk of only learning about employee problems from an attorney's threatening letter.

Follow Basic Concepts of Fairness

A progressive company is one that values fundamental concepts of equality and fairness. This means, for example, that the lower ranked employee isn't automatically given the ax when romance problems spill into the workforce. This approach can not only be used legally against a company, it's inconsistent with a fair disclosure and intervention policy.

Fairness means a neutral investigation of complaints that's fair to both parties, regardless of gender, and in which the firm isn't trying to take the easy way out. Fairness doesn't mean that the company tries to address every employee's complaint—only those reasonable and legitimate ones that most workers would agree should be accommodated. More broadly, fairness means that all employees earn the same amount of money for similar performance of the same job responsibilities, regardless of gender, age, sexual orientation, or other distinctions. Hiring, promotion, and advancement decisions are based on who does the best job and how, not on any other factor. Fairness is fairness.

Respond Promptly and Reasonably to Problems

Whether an organization uses mediation or not, it must respond promptly to the reasonable concerns of its employees. In the sexual harassment area, the words used are that "the company will make a prompt investigation of any worker's grievances and take reasonable, appropriate action." This timely reaction should be used to investigate fairly the legitimate complaints of its employees.

Employees will be encouraged to communicate their problems when they know they will be treated fairly, confidentially, and promptly. A company can't decide the way every complaining worker wants, but it can respond promptly and reasonably to the problems brought to its attention.

Balance Employee Privacy With the Company's Interests

Employee Privacy Rights

We've discussed before the rights of privacy as they apply to employee dating in Chapter 5. Remember that workplace privacy issues fall into two basic categories: off-the-job and on-the-job behavior.

Off-the-job behavior ranges from smoking and dating to political and recreational activities (nudist camps, right-wing and left-wing militias, and even sexual freedom groups). On-the-job issues range from drug testing and property searches to the use of video surveillance and locker searches. A variety of federal and state laws and court decisions apply, depending on the particular issue; consequently, this is a complicated legal area.

Employees insist that employers have no right to concern themselves with off-the-job conduct. The employers contend that they have legitimate interests in policing business interests, such as preserving trade secrets, maintaining quality control, and controlling health costs (by regulating smoking, for example). The guiding principle applied will be that organizations should only be interested in activities that are directly related to a worker's ability to perform his or her job properly—and any prohibitions on these activities must be limited in scope.

Regardless of the law, the controlling concept should always be how employees will react to a proposed rule. Pro-interactive companies basically should only be interested in what employees do on company time and to meet corporate goals.

A Reasonable E-Mail Policy

The law on E-mail is easy to describe—there isn't much now. However, legal experts maintain that businesses should draw "lines in the sand" between what's okay and what's not okay. Generally, these policies should state that voice mail, employees' computers, and E-mail are the company's property (which physically they are) and subject to monitoring. Further, they should provide that these systems aren't for personal use, and that the employer has the right to intercept, review, and retransmit all communications sent over its systems. The company should state that its systems cannot be used for illegal, obscene, defamatory, or other inappropriate communications. As one technology litigator said, "Companies need to have formal policies in place on the proper uses of E-mail and other vehicles to protect themselves. Otherwise, they're going to get into trouble, and employees won't know the ground rules."

On the other hand, employers need to state that any disclosure of information obtained through this monitoring will be strictly limited and only for business-specific reasons. Additionally, employers need to enact protections on when this auditing can and cannot be done; clearly, it can't be allowed on a general basis or without a specific business reason such as intercepting the passing of trade secrets or obscene E-mail messages.

Because the law in this area is undeveloped and raw, it will take time for the courts and legislatures to define what's permissible. Given this, lovers will need to be discreet with their E-mail communications. You're better off being careful than sorry.

Arbitration Clauses

As we've seen, jury trials can result in higher dollar judgments than trials before a judge. Juries can be inflamed by a good lawyer's argument, whereas arbitrators and judges usually aren't. Consequently, it is to a company's legal advantage usually to arbitrate contested cases (although there are exceptions).

A 1991 Supreme Court decision (*Gilmer v. Interstate/Johnson Lane Corporation*) held that the plaintiff in a discrimination lawsuit had to use the securities industry's standard arbitration procedures, having signed a standard agreement containing a clause that required arbitration to be used in employment disputes. As a consequence, companies are increasingly requiring new employees to sign agreements that they will arbitrate rather than litigate disputes with the company. For example, the securities business has used an industry-wide mandatory arbitration policy for years—which the *Gilmer* decision upheld. Court challenges have been filed when arbitration is mandated to be used in resolving legal disputes, but most courts have interpreted the *Gilmer* decision as providing broad support for mandatory arbitration.

Supporters of mandatory arbitration argue that this process provides for a prompt resolution of employment disputes without the time, cost, and negativity typically associated with litigation; reduces the legal expenses of both parties; allows experts in that field to make the decision, as opposed to judges who have general expertise; reduces inflammatory jury awards; and, as a private proceeding, allows "dirty laundry to stay hidden."

The drawbacks are argued to be, among other factors, that employees are relinquishing their rights to a trial before a jury; appeals are limited from any arbitrator's decision; any awards for punitive damages are strictly limited; and there's no deterrent effect when the proceedings are kept confidential. Litigators argue that such an agreement cannot be voluntary when it's made a condition of the employee's hiring.

An employer may require that both mediation and arbitration be used to solve employment-related disputes. If the mediation proves unsuccessful, then the legal dispute is resolved through arbitration, rather than litigation. As individual states differ in the required wording to mandate arbitration, an owner or executive should consult with his or her legal counsel for assistance. Whether arbitration is contractually mandated or not, mediation is still the preferred alternative to use first.

Effectively Training Supervisors

Many books and articles go into great detail about properly training supervisors to recognize and deal with sexual harassment claims. The same approach should be taken in teaching them to know the difference between office romance problems and sexual harassment ones. Managers should be trained in a positive approach to dealing with office relationships, learning how to talk confidentially with employees about relationships before there's a real harassment complaint. Supervisors should know whom they should call to mediate or solve problems that are more relationship based. Trust your workers; they'll conduct themselves properly when you create an open and trusting work environment.

Employment Practices Liability Insurance

Traditional business insurance policies specifically exclude coverage for sexual harassment and other employment practices liabilities. The insurance industry developed in turn employment practices liability insurance to cover these areas. Coverage is offered for both defense costs and settlement payments.

If a company can afford the premiums on this insurance, it has plugged one gap, no matter how it runs its workforce. A business can have a harassment liability, even if it's done everything right. For example, even if a supervisor's actions in requiring sex for a promotion are clearly prohibited by a company's policies, that business still has a liability for those actions whether or not it has any knowledge of them. As with any insurance policy, there are deductibles, limits, and "fine print" exclusions. Be careful, there can be exclusions for willful or intentional acts, so read the policy closely before making a final decision.

Many companies find such insurance coverage too expensive, especially in today's cost-conscious environment. However, it may be possible to negotiate a discount on the premium if the firm provides education, training, and seminars on harassment.

Office Romance Agreements

Another line of defense for companies is using office romance agreements, signed by both parties, whereby they agree that the relationship is: (1) welcome, voluntary, and consensual; (2) on an equal basis; (3) not affecting any term or condition of the other's employment; and (4) not in violation of the firm's sexual harassment policy. The company's attorneys' can draft these agreements, employing a letter form that's signed at the bottom by the recipient. These documents can later be a defense against harassment charges if the affair breaks down.

The agreements do not have to be formal; in fact, they can simply be handwritten letters that are countersigned at the bottom by the other partner. The goal is for both parties to agree that their affair is consensual without any work-related influences. The company and the supervisor benefit by using these statements, provided the subordinate in a boss-subordinate relationship signed the agreement knowingly and voluntarily. It may be necessary in unusual cases for the subordinate to be represented by an attorney, as with prenuptial agreements to avoid later "lack of legal representation" or "undue influence" charges.

The Best Company Defense

Hands down, the best defense is how a company works and interacts with its employees. Does it create a stimulating, open work environment, emphasizing communication and solving problems? Or does it rely on rules, "no-nos," and punitive, restrictive policies?

Is the company more interested in how its employees socialize, get along, and work together in a positive humane way? Or is it command conscious and rigid? Pro-interactive companies enjoy the best legal defense and a more productive work environment. They just don't have the problems that others do.

Chapter Seventeen

The Twenty-First Century

The demographic and sociological events that have taken place over the past fifteen years have been unprecedented. Women hold 46 percent of jobs, with the clear trend toward 50 percent and even more over the next several years; when managerial and professional specialties are considered, 48 percent of all the positions are filled by women (up from 40 percent in 1983).

The studies previously discussed show that women contribute one-half or more of the money in 45 percent of two-income families (with some surveys indicating 50 percent), and this proportion is expected by the experts to continue climbing. Two-thirds of American families have two wage earners (up from 42 percent in 1975), and this proportion is also expected to increase, given the need for two incomes in today's economy simply to make ends meet.

At the same time, the proportion of women never married by their late twenties tripled in just three decades to one-third of that age group by the mid-nineties, and 4.5 million unmarried couples now are choosing to live together. The average age before a woman marries has been increasing, and the experts believe that all of these statistics will continue to climb.

Why? The long hours expected at work are not going to diminish for either sex, and the positive impact of women on the workforce will spread. Men have been pushing for equality, because it's in their interest, especially with the vast number of married men who have working wives. Given the now-expected contribution by women to household income, it's natural that they'll continue to push aside whatever barriers are in their way, including the "glass ceiling."

A Different Workplace

These unprecedented trends have created a different workplace. Pro-interactive companies support day care and after-school facilities for children, flextime, work at home, married employees, and easier social integration and dating between workers. We have seen that the flood of women into the workforce resulted in a tightening of sexual harassment policies, along with the decline of antinuptial and anti-fraternization policies.

Organizations that once didn't allow married couples even to work together at the same place, or tolerate adultery, have done an about-face to encourage married spouses to work there and turn a deaf ear to what goes on between consenting employees (provided there isn't a complaint). Businesses are on record as supporting social interaction among workers due to the contentment this brings; they are also recognizing that if the company demands so much of its employees' time for work, it should also allow employees to meet, match up, and mate at work.

Antinuptial romance policies are nearly out for the count. As Fraser, the human resources specialist who's trying to change his company's policy, said: "Like most firms, we don't prohibit dating, since you couldn't even if you wanted to. What this means is that it's okay to date discreetly, but that if you marry, then one of you has to leave. To me, that doesn't make any sense, and most companies clearly agree."

The Competitive Pressures

Companies are trying to retain workers who meet and marry there. They realize it makes no sense to recruit the best who are married, then turn away the best "homegrown" couples for getting married. Organizations, whether they're businesses, professional firms, universities, or police and fire departments, need to recruit the best workers—and the best want to bring their spouses with them. At the same time, these same organizations have had to liberalize their policies on employee interactions and dating because that's what their single workers are demanding.

Human resources executives echo this position. Given the investment companies are making in their workforce (including women who are being groomed for higher positions), these businesses want these workers to stay. They have a sizable stake in their employees, and this doesn't disappear when two employees become involved with one another. It makes no sense to force well-trained employees to leave for the wrong reasons.

As Rob, a principal in a human resources consulting firm, said: "Where the demand for workers outstrips the supply, companies have to do more to get the good people, especially in industries such as high tech, info, and communications. It's a competitive necessity. These companies must provide child care, flexible hours, part-time jobs, telecommuting, as well as allowing, even encouraging dating. And this demand for well-trained workers exists, regardless of the state of the economy."

Workplace relationships include third-party ones between employees and customers, vendors, clients, and suppliers, since a romance outside the company at times can be easier to handle than one in it. Companies with less progressive rules soon discover that their workers go underground or look outside the company and leave. These companies are having to change their policies to more pro-interactive ones over time.

The New Rules of Romance

One-third of all relationships start at work, and given the ruthlessness with which American businesses have seized on ways to increase income, they are changing their rules to accommodate this development. We have seen that companies are providing more facilities where their employees can work out, play softball, swim, or even dance. At the same time, these interactions are leading to relationships in which the partners have equal decision-making powers and responsibilities: if someone is your equal at work, then that carries over into your marriage. And one-half of all these office liaisons result in a long-term relationship or marriage.

Office romances are a fact of modern American life, and organizations are being forced to recognize and legitimize their existence. Where companies now look the other way, in essence saying that it's okay to date because their policies don't prohibit it, businesses will formalize these informal understandings just as they do for married workers.

The Law of Romance

Organizations do not now as a rule view relationships and consensual conduct separately from their fears of sexual harassment complaints (although they cause problems by using a one-size-fits-all harassment policy to deal with most relationship problems). However, employees can ask coworkers out, be refused, and not be guilty of committing harassment. They can try to maintain a relationship without being responsible for committing sexual harassment. The key is that reasonable behavior is to be accepted as part of a relationship, and unreasonable sexual behavior is not—and the difference can be defined.

This isn't different from what the law already provides. However, companies in the future will handle relationship complaints as problems involving a romance, not as potential crimes to be covered by their sexual harassment policies. The two are different, and in recognizing that fact, companies will become even more "couple rights" oriented.

Meeting and becoming involved with someone at work (including marriage) is being decriminalized. This change has accelerated in the past few years. A parallel change has been occurring in attitudes about workplace romances, and companies will enact guidelines that will bring these relationships up from the darkness. These policies basically will recognize that (1) office romances exist naturally in the workplace; (2) the company has no interest in them, provided the partners remain professional with no excessive public displays of affection; (3) the firm will manage reporting or conflict-of-interest relationships, striving to keeping both workers but eliminating the conflict; and (4) romance problems won't be treated as sexual harassment issues, but as relationship problems (unless unreasonable conduct is clearly present), among other provisions.

Pro-Interactive Companies

As trusting employees and supporting couples (whether dating or married) becomes a competitive necessity, companies over time will become more pro-interactive and less afraid of falling into the "sue-and-be-sued" legal quagmire. Businesses following these commonsense "self-interest" approaches will continue to multiply, understanding that social friendships at work, especially among higher profile, "long-workweek" committed employees, cannot help but support their goals. Employees will note these firms, and more will choose companies that are so pro-interactive to be their employers.

Bankers Trust Company

Peter Gurney, managing director of employee relations for Bankers Trust, said:

> "Bankers Trust is family friendly. We have emergency day care, vacation camps, variable workweeks, telecommuting, flextime, and paid child care leave. We don't have any rules that say you can't date.
>
> "We don't say spouses or significant others can't work at the firm—that would be unrealistic and could adversely affect the individuals as well as the business. We say you can't supervise the other half of the team, and if both are in the same department, or if a conflict of responsibilities exists between departments, we'll try hard to transfer or realign the responsibilities of one employee. If this isn't possible, then the employees will have to choose which one works for another company. If there is a problem in a relationship that's affecting performance, then we will endeavor to work it out so both people can continue to be productive.
>
> "We do this because we want to preserve and develop our talent. We have a high investment in our employees, and the way to keep the best is to foster a committed environment."

Romance vs. Harassment

The one-size-fits-all application of sexual harassment policies will change to accommodate the law of romance. As companies liberalize in the next decade, affirming their commitment as pro-interactive organizations to their employees from competitive necessity (and regardless of the economy) and to employee education, sexual harassment will become less of a legal concern. Although more and more relationships will start at the workplace, actual sexual harassment complaints and litigation will lessen. Employees will understand clearly what's acceptable behavior, companies will fairly enforce their sexual harassment policies, and office romances won't be subject to the chilled climates in effect at various organizations now.

Harassment vs. Gender Discrimination

Gender discrimination will replace sexual harassment as the cause célèbre—so the attorneys need not worry about the decline in their harassment litigation. As women climb up the corporate ladder, they will consult lawyers more when they aren't promoted to CEO, chief financial officer, treasurer, vice president of human relations, or whatever job they've targeted. The glass ceiling will eventually be shattered, although it may take strenuous litigation to bring this about. A strong support for these tactics will come from the women's partners, their husbands who also are in that workforce and will benefit from these advances in equality.

Ford Motor Company

Ford Motor Company is one of the huge number of firms that have changed over the years to become in tune with the times. Nancy, the senior manager at Ford with thirty years experience there, observed: "A picture of Ford managers thirty years ago would be males dressed in the same dark navy-blue suits, white shirts, and conservative ties with no mustaches or beards. They all looked the same. Today, the dress is more casual where women can wear slacks and men can wear Dockers with sports shirts and Sperry Topsiders.

"The company's response to office romances has changed similarly. Thirty years ago, people kept their relationships hush-hush and to themselves. If it was discovered, then one of you had to quit or was fired. Period and end of story. Today, managers and lower level employees don't have to hide it at all, although they can't continue to supervise one another. The attitude is that 'if they're going to sleep together, so be it.'

"Another example of this cultural and organizational flexibility is seen with gays and lesbians. Thirty years ago, homosexuals had to cover up—they had no choice, and gay women had to act as if they were with a male. Today, it's an entire new world. At Ford, there is a GLOBE bulletin board for gays—or the 'Gay, Lesbian, and Other Bi-Sexual Employees' where they can post meetings, comments, and other information. Although there is still a sensitivity on the part of gays on how 'open' they can be on their sexual orientation and relationships, there is no question that this is quite different today. Some years ago, they couldn't even afford the suspicion that they were different.

"All of this has happened in the last five years, and I believe the climate changed dramatically when Ford 2000 happened along. We must think globally now, women are being groomed for managerial and executive positions, minorities are advancing, and Ford has definitely become pro-interactive."

Other examples of pro-interactive companies have been discussed before. Employment benefits such as flexible work schedules, job-sharing arrangements, telecommuting programs, flexible benefits, child care credits and arrangements, elder care, gender equality, and positive affirmation of workplace romances will become standard. As we saw in Chapter 6, these trends won't be limited to just the large companies—they will be embraced by small and medium-size companies, as well. This philosophy and corporate culture will become the norm in the twenty-first century.

It's About People

Ann Landers printed a sweet "how-we-met" story about a woman who sat in the row behind a soldier in church at the end of World War II. Since he knew all the lyrics to the songs, she figured this man couldn't be all that bad. Later, she learned that he was a doctor. Three months later, she slipped on an icy walk and injured her arm. The doctor who treated her was the same man who sang in church that day. He insisted that she stay in the infirmary, and he visited her twice a day. When she was discharged, he asked her to go to the movies in celebration. They subsequently married in the same chapel where they had first met singing.

The letter writer then imagined how that same story would go now:

> Last week, I attended church services and noticed that the soldier sitting behind me knew all the words to every song. I figured anyone who knew those lyrics was probably a member of the religious right.
>
> I bumped into him a month later. After cussing him out and telling him to watch where he was going, I learned he was a doctor. Three months later, I slipped on an icy walk and injured my arm. After suing the property owner for all I could get, this same doctor treated me and insisted that I stay in the infirmary. He then made

twice-daily visits to see how I was doing, which made me suspicious. I complained to his supervisor and filed a sexual harassment suit.

I was discharged in January, and the doctor asked if I would like to see a movie and celebrate. I told the police he was a stalker and applied for a restraining order. When the doctor asked me to marry him in the same chapel where we first met, I called the FBI. They searched his apartment to make sure there were no shrines built to me and bodies hidden under the floor-boards.

I married the guy anyway, because after all, doctors earn six-figure incomes. Signed, Tuned In and Turned Off in La Jolla, California*

What amazes the experts is that despite these politically correct and sometimes chilling times, people continue to meet, fall in love, and enjoy relationships at work—and this phenomenon is measured in the millions of people each year. *Romance is alive and well today, despite the opposition and fears. Workplace affairs of the heart will take a quantum leap into the twenty-first century.*

*Permission to reprint granted by Ann Landers and Creators Syndicate.

Appendix 1

Sample Office Romance Guidelines

Once a company and its managers decide to establish and implement office romance guidelines, the actual provisions are straightforward. The following form may need to be modified depending on a firm's workforce, environment, philosophy, and specific problems in the past. An attorney should review these written guidelines and any applicable federal, state, and local laws prior to their use.

Our Office Romance Guidelines (Long Form)

1. *Sexual Harassment.* Sexual harassment will not be tolerated at this Company (the words "Company," "we," and "our" are used interchangeably; "you" refers to our employees), and this is treated specifically by our harassment policies. Although sexual harassment and office romances are treated here as being mutually exclusive, unreasonable dating or relationship conduct may cross into the area of harassment, and these situations will be treated under our standard harassment policies and procedures.

2. *Office Romances.* It is our policy to ensure a mutually supportive, open, and interactive workforce. All workers shall be free to date or not to date, at their option and regardless of marital status, but subject to our guidelines and decisions. Dating means a social occasion or relationship (as opposed to primary work motives) that occur between two employees, whether off or on our work premises. These guidelines will apply to all of our workers, regardless of seniority or level of responsibility and whether they are full time or part time.

These guidelines further will apply to our employees, whether they have dated or are dating another employee, customer, client, vendor, independent contractor, or some person in any other business relationship with this Company.

Our employees shall use common sense when they date with an eye to preserving the integrity and professionalism of our workplace. What happens between two consenting workers outside the workplace will usually be their business—but what happens inside the workplace is our business. So, if no employee or third party perceives a negative effect on work efficiency, cordiality, or productivity, there usually will be no reason for this Company to intercede. However, if two workers report to one another, have long lunches and time off together on work time, or have personal arguments in the workplace, for example, this conduct then becomes the Company's business.

3. *Supervisor-Subordinate and Conflict-of-Interest Positions.* Should a consensual romantic or sexual relationship occur between a supervisor and a subordinate (or any other conflict-of-interest situation, such as where one of the partners has access to sensitive personnel, medical, or financial data), then *both workers* have an immediate duty to coreport their relationship to their immediate supervisors, as part of their job responsibilities. Conflict-of-interest reporting requirements include, but are not limited to: *<Insert Your Company's Specific Concerns When Relationships Must Be So Reported>*. A supervisor-subordinate relationship also includes "unequal power" working arrangements such as when a lower ranking worker from one department works with a higher ranking worker from another and that work could affect a term or condition of the lower ranking worker's employment.

4. *Confidentiality.* All Company employees (whether in management or not) and any third parties employed by this Company who receive information pursuant to these guidelines shall treat all such data gained as confidential and personal. Provided, however, that such person(s) may disclose this to other Company personnel for bona fide business and decision-making purposes.

5. *Procedures.* When a reporting or other conflict-of-interest situation is discovered, we shall as a general rule: (1) encourage communication and problem resolving between all concerned parties; (2) meet with the lower ranking worker to determine and record that the relationship is truly consensual; (3) eliminate the reporting to and/or performance reviews by the superior (including matters existing at the time of disclosure) by assigning one or both employees to different

departments and/or projects, reassigning performance reviews, or as otherwise determined by the Company at its sole discretion (including deciding if one or both employees stay, leave, or transfer); (4) enforce the supervisor's withdrawal from any further decision making that could affect any condition of the lower ranking worker's employment (and for a time period as the Company determines); and (5) try, but not as a promise, to accommodate the interests of both workers to retain their present levels of responsibility (including balancing the rights of coworkers and the Company's interests) by modifying work schedules, restructuring jobs, or other work modifications—but all being subject to the Company's total discretion. We will listen to the involved employees' reasonable input on which employee is best suited for a transfer or any other suggested arrangement; however, any final decision is the sole and complete responsibility of this Company.

6. *Marriage.* Any employees who marry at this Company shall be treated no differently than any other married couple that we employ here as new employees. We welcome married couples, partners, and "significant others" who always work toward meeting our Company's goals in a professional manner.

7. *Be Discreet.* All dating is to be maintained in a discreet manner with an eye toward maintaining professionalism and our overall working environment decorum. All employees who are dating should work toward keeping public displays of affection to a minimum, as well as keeping their personal relationships separate from all work responsibilities. Although our employees are free to be romantically or personally involved as they choose (but for supervisor-subordinate or other conflict-of-interest relationships), this doesn't mean that exercising this privilege may interfere with our right to maintain a professional, stable, and productive workplace.

8. *Complaints.* Any employee who has a complaint owing to a friendship or personal relationship in our workforce is encouraged to make an informal complaint to the Human Resources Manager or any other supervisor as designated by the Company. The lower ranking employee in any personal relationship is encouraged to meet with the most senior officer or supervisor available to discuss a workplace issue. Complaints may be of any type, whether it's receiving unwelcome pressure to date, the ending of a relationship, or having problems simply in working together. All complaints shall be handled confidentially, and coworkers or outside third parties in a business relationship

with us are encouraged to make reasonable complaints owing to inequities or unfairness resulting from personal relationships involving Company personnel.

A. *Investigation.* The Company shall investigate the complaint, including meeting with the concerned individuals (both separately and together), not only to ascertain the facts, but to work toward finding a reasonable and acceptable solution.

B. *Unreasonable Conduct.* "Unreasonable" dating practices shall not be tolerated, such as a superior placing unwanted pressure on a subordinate to date; any employee making persistent, unwanted advances; or any worker making continued, unwelcome social contacts aimed at restoring a broken relationship. These actions may also be treated under our standard sexual harassment policy, depending on the severity of the unreasonable conduct.

C. *Mediation/Intervention.* This Company encourages the use of mediation and conflict-resolving intervention to resolve workforce problems created by an employee's dating practices or office romance. This mediator may be your supervisor, any other designated or acceptable Company personnel, or a professional hired from outside our workforce. The Company may suggest or condition professional counseling for one or both parties as part of this process.

9. *Existing Policy.* These guidelines do not constitute a contract of employment, nor do they alter, change, or modify other Company employment policies. Each employee of the Company acknowledges that he or she has received, has read, and understands these Office Romance Guidelines, as well as all other employment policies, as indicated by their signature below. *<Date and Signatures by Company Representative and Employee Follow>*

Note: The company should maintain an "open door" policy, including using informative seminars and discussion panels to talk about these guidelines, the pros and cons of a workplace romance, and the available offices for confidential discussions. Open communication channels allow problems to be solved before "irreconcilable differences" can occur between the partners and even management. This includes talking with coworkers who may be worried about an office romance, as well as gaining the input of the participants. What's important is that these relationships should be managed—not banned.

The presence of this policy by itself, and together with maintaining and enforcing reasonable sexual harassment procedures, will provide a very helpful defense against hostile environment harassment claims, although not necessarily against quid pro quo claims. However, the procedure described in these guidelines can produce evidence that a workplace romance was indeed voluntary and cut down on the risk that reporting relationships will spill over into sexual harassment complaints. The fact that both workers have a duty to report their relationship (which may or may not happen) gives an additional element of protection. The company should ensure that its office romance guidelines are consistent with all its other policies and neutral in their application to all employees.

The following short-form office romance guideline may need to be modified depending on a company's workforce, environment, philosophy, and specific problems in the past. An attorney should review these written guidelines and any applicable federal, state, and local laws prior to their use.

Our Office Romance Guidelines (Short Form)

<Name of Company>'s policy is to maintain a professional, efficient, and productive work environment, consistent with the rights of its employees to their privacy for off-work conduct that doesn't involve this Company. We recognize that our employees have, desire to, and will form personal relationships with other employees, clients, vendors, and other people associated with *<Name of Company>*'s business. However, as we state in our policy handbook, we will not tolerate sexual harassment, discrimination, or other illegal conduct.

We will not interfere with our employees' personal relationships, regardless of whom they are dating or in a relationship with, provided both workers continually maintain a professional image, efficient work level, and no excessive public displays of affection. However, we discourage personal relationships between supervisors and subordinates or other conflict-of-interest situations.

The conflict-of-interest situations discouraged at this Company are: *<List Discouraged Specific Conflict Situations Particular to this Company>*. We do not encourage relationships in these conflict situations, owing to the potential work disruption, sexual harassment concerns, and favoritism perceptions by coworkers. We will try to accommodate any reasonable alternative, consistent with this Company's goals and objectives, to retain all involved workers at their existing responsibilities. However, the reporting or objectionable work element in that relationship will be eliminated by transferring people and/or their supervising responsibilities over their partner to other employees. However, any final decision is the sole and complete responsibility of this Company, including the termination of one or both workers.

Any employee with a complaint due to a personal relationship, unwelcome pursuit, or relationship breakup is encouraged to work out those difficulties with the other worker on non-Company time. If that isn't or wouldn't be successful, than that employee should contact <Name of Supervisor or Office to Be Contacted> for immediate assistance on a confidential basis. Depending on the circumstances, we encourage communication (both between employees and this Company), mediation, and/or outside professional counseling to resolve these problems.

Depending on the severity or intensity of the conduct, the Company's policies that prohibit sexual harassment may be invoked, including their provisions for a fair investigation, prompt decision, and fair punishment if warranted under the circumstances. The purpose of this office romance policy is not to unreasonably interfere with the rights of privacy that our employees should enjoy with their personal relationships, provided that they don't interfere with the Company's absolute right to maintain a professional, positive, and efficient work environment at all times.

These guidelines do not constitute a contract of employment. Each employee of this Company acknowledges that he or she has received, has read, and understands these Office Romance Guidelines, as well as all other employment policies, as indicated by their signature below. <Date and Signatures by Company Representative and Employee Follow>

Appendix 2

Working Mother's 1998 "100 Best Companies for Working Mothers"*

Allstate Insurance Co.
American Management Systems
Amgen
Amoco Corp.
Arnold & Porter
AT&T Corp.
Avon Products
Bankers Trust New York Corp.
Barnett Banks
Eddie Bauer
Bayfront Medical Center
Ben & Jerry's Homemade
Benjamin Group
Beth Israel Deaconess Medical Center
BP Exploration (Alaska)
Bureau of National Affairs
Leo Burnett Company
Calvert Group
Chase Manhattan Bank
CHP Media

Chrysler Corp.
Cigna Corp.
Cinergy Corp.
Citicorp/Citibank
Computer Associates International
Coopers & Lybrand, LLP
Corning
Dayton Hudson Corp.
Deloitte & Touche
Dupont Co.
Dupont Merck Pharmaceutical Co.
Eastman Kodak Co.
Fel-Pro Incorporated
First Chicago NBD Corp.
First Tennessee Bank
Ford Motor Co.
Gallup Organization
Gannett Co.
Genentech
General Motors Corp.

*First appeared in *Working Mother,* October 1997. Written by Milton Moskowitz. Reprinted with the permission of MacDonald Communications Corporation. Copyright 1997 by MacDonald Communications Corporation.

Glaxo Wellcome
Hallmark Cards
John Hancock Mutual Life Insurance
   Co.
Hewlett-Packard Co.
Hill, Holliday, Connors, Cosmopulos
IBM
Johnson & Johnson
S. C. Johnson Wax
KPMG Peat Marwick, LLP
Lancaster Laboratories
Life Technologies
Eli Lilly and Co.
Lincoln National Corp.
Lotus Development Corp.
Lucasfilm Ltd., Lucas Digital Ltd., and
   Lucasarts Entertainment Co.
Marquette Medical Systems
Marriott International
MassMutual
Mattel
MBNA America Bank, N.A.
Mentor Graphics Corp.
Merck & Co.
Merrill Lynch & Co.
Millipore Corp.
3M
J. P. Morgan
Motorola
Nationsbank Corp.
Neuville Industries
Nike

Northern Trust Corp.
Owens Corning
Patagonia
Plante & Moran, LLP
Price Waterhouse
Proctor & Gamble Co.
Promega Corp.
Quad/Graphics
Rex Healthcare
Ridgeview
Rockwell International Corp.
St. Paul Co.
St. Petersburg Times
Salomon Brothers
Salt River Project
Sara Lee Corp.
SAS Institute
Seattle Times
Sequent Computer Systems
Texas Instruments
Tom's of Maine
TRW
United Services Automobile
   Association
Universal Studios
University of Pittsburgh Medical
   Center
UNUM Life Insurance Co. of America
USA Group
VCW
Wearguard
Xerox Corp.

Selected Bibliography

Adelson, Joseph. "Splitting Up." *Commentary,* September 1996, 63–66.

Adler, Jerry. "Adultery: A New Furor." *Newsweek,* September 30, 1996.

Alderman, Lesley. "Surviving an Office Romance Without Jeopardizing Your Job." *Money,* February 1995, 37–40.

"Are Office Romances OK?" *Training & Development,* May 1994, 38.

Associated Press. "Chain Must Pay Male Sex-Harassment Victim." *New York Times,* November 24, 1995, A-28.

Associated Press. "Army Settles Harassment Suit for $60,000." *New York Times,* November 26, 1996, A-16.

Bamford, Janet. "Changing Business as Usual." *Working Woman,* November 1993, 63.

Barash, Douglas S. "God and Toothpaste." *New York Times,* December 22, 1996, 6-27.

Barlow, Wayne E. "Do Employees' Electronic Messages Spell Trouble for You?" *Personnel Journal,* October 1995, 135–38.

Bickner, Mei L., Christine Ver Ploeg, and Charles Feigenbaum. "Arbitration." *Dispute Resolution Journal,* January 1997, 9–12.

"Bill Paxon & Susan Molinari." *People Weekly,* February 13, 1995, 81.

Bloch, Gerald D. "Avoiding Liability for Sexual Harassment." *HR Magazine,* April 1995, 91–96.

Bordwin, Milton. "Containing Cupid's Arrow." *Small Business Reports,* July 1994, 53–57.

Brady, Lois Smith. "Vows: Ann Pluemer and Christopher Barber." *New York Times,* December 25, 1994, 1-49.

Brady, Robert L. "Workplace Searches: Avoid Legal Problems." *HR Focus,* April 1995, 18.

Braiker, Harriet B. "The Etiquette of Love." *Working Woman,* November 1988, 148–51.

Brocklehurst, Ann. "When Two Is Company." *McLean's*, November 6, 1995, 40–41.

Brown, Helen Gurley. *Sex and the Office*. New York: Avon Books, 1983.

Brown, Theresa J., and Elizabeth Rice Allgeier. "Managers' Perceptions of Workplace Romances: an Interview Study." *Journal of Business and Psychology*, winter 1995, 169–76.

Brown, Theresa J., and Elizabeth Rice Allgeier. "The Impact of Participant Characteristics, Perceived Motives, and Job Behaviors on Co-Workers' Evaluations of Workplace Romances." *Journal of Applied Social Psychology*, April 1996, 577–95.

Bryant, Adam. "Companies Watch Scandal for Clues to Own Policies." *New York Times*, February 16, 1998, A-11.

Bureau of National Affairs, Inc. *Corporate Affairs: Nepotism, Office Romance, and Sexual Harassment*. Washington, D.C., 1988.

Bureau of National Affairs, Inc. *Fair Employment Practices*. Washington, D.C., 1995.

Caldwell, Mark. "Fishing off the Company Pier." *Men's Fitness*, January 1996, 45–47.

Case, John. "Corporate Culture." *Inc. Magazine*, November 1996.

Chase, Brett. "Risk Management: Dating Subordinates Is Widely Prohibited." *American Banker*, June 17, 1997, 5.

Clinebell, Sharon, Lynn Hoffman, and John Kilpatrick. "Rights and Liability." *HR Focus*, March 1995, 19.

Cohen, Roger. "Over There, Different Rules on Sex." *New York Times*, June 7, 1997, 1-9.

Cole, Nicola. "Firms Shrug at Office Romance." Gemini News Service, London, May 30, 1995; as reported in the *World Press Review*, September 1995, 34.

Collins, Gail. "The Bold and the Unemployed." *Working Woman*, February 1993, 92.

Coren, Michael. "Office Romance." *National Review*, February 21, 1994, 63.

Coyeman, Margorie. "Isn't It Romantic?" *Restaurant Business*, October 15, 1997, 51–52.

Cropper, Carol Marie. "That Unwritten Code Against Fraternization." *New York Times*, October 26, 1997, 3-14.

Curtis, Liz. *"Making Advances: What You Can Do About Sexual Harassment at Work."* London: BBC Books, 1993.

Deadrick, Diana L., Scott W. Kezman, and R. Bruce McAfee. "Harassment by Nonemployees: How Should Employers Respond?" *HR Magazine*, December 1996, 108–12.

Dirk, Johnson. "A Sexual Harassment Case to Test Academic Freedom." *New York Times*, May 11, 1994, D-23.

Disenhouse, Susan. "Workers in Love, With the Boss's Blessing." *New York Times*, April 24, 1996, C-1.

"The Divorce Dilemma." *U.S. News & World Report*, September 30, 1996, 58–60.

Dold, Catherine. "Office Romance in the Age of Sexual Harassment." *Glamour*, March 1996, 234–37.

Dowd, Maureen. "Liberties: Cosmic Girl." *New York Times*, April 28, 1996, 4-13.

Egler, Theresa Donahue. "Five Myths About Sexual Harassment." *HR Magazine*, January 1995, 27–30.

Eyler, David R. "Far More than Friendship." *Psychology Today*, May/June, 59–60.

Feder, Barnaby J. "Agee Leaving Morrison Knudsen." *New York Times*, February 2, 1995, D-1.

Federico, Richard F., and James M. Bowley. "The Great E-Mail Debate." *HR Magazine*, January 1996, 67–72.

Ferraro, Cathleen. "Love at Work." *Sacramento Bee*, February 14, 1995.

Fisher, Anne B. "Getting Comfortable with Couples in the Workplace." *Fortune*, October 3, 1994, 139–43.

Fisher, Anne B. "Is the Office the Right Place for Romance?" *Cosmopolitan*, May 1995, 253–55.

Ford, Robert C., and Frank S. McLaughlin. "Should Cupid Come to the Workplace?" *Personnel Administrator*, October 1987, 100–109.

Furchgott, Ray. "Earning It: Workers Who Signed Away a Day in Court." *New York Times*, July 28, 1995, 3-9.

Gelder, Lawrence van. "Love Potion No. 9. in the Water Cooler." *New York Times*, February 2, 1997, 3-11.

Gill, Brian W. "The Gray Areas of Sexual Harassment." *American Printer*, November 1995, 66.

Goldner, Diane. "Third-Party Harassment: When a Client or Customer Oversteps the Line." *Glamour*, October 1995, 132.

Goodrich & Sherwood Co. "Valentines at Work—Courting Trouble." *Supervision*, February 1996, 13.

Goodman, Ellen. "Lewdness Alone Isn't Harassment." *Mail Tribune*, February 26, 1997, 8A.

Greenfield, Meg. "The Last Word: Sexual Harasser?" *Newsweek*, October 7, 1996, 90.

Gross, Jane. "Now Look Who's Taunting: Now Look Who's Suing." *New York Times*, February 26, 1995, 4-1.

Guarino, Vicki. "Mercy Flights Prevails in Sex Harassment Trial." *Mail Tribune*, May 15, 1996, 3A.

Haas, Carol. "No Fraternization Policies Help Keep Romance Out of the Office." *Atlanta Business Chronicle*, May 19, 1995, 6A.

Hardman, Wendy, and Jacqueline Heidelberg. "When Sexual Harassment Is a Foreign Affair." *Personnel Journal*, April 1996, 91–97.

Harris, Lynn. "Sexual Ethics." *Glamour*, December 1996, 156.

Haskell, Milly. "Managing Your Sexuality." *Working Woman*, August 1994, 29–33.

Henderson, Stephen. "Sexual Harassment: America Re-Examines the Issues." *Chicago Tribune*, May 23, 1996.

Hequet, Marc. "Office Romance." *Training*, February 1996, 44–50.

Hoenig, James K. "Mediation in Sexual Harassment: Balancing the Sensitivities." *Dispute Resolution Journal*, December, 1993, 51–53.

Holcomb, Betty. "How Families Are Changing." *Working Mother*, July 1994, 29–36.

Hollway, Wendy, and Tony Jefferson. "PC or Not PC: Sexual Harassment and the Question of Ambivalence." *Human Relations* 49, no. 3 (1996): 373–93.

Howard, William M. "Arbitrating Claims of Employment Discrimination." *Dispute Resolution Journal*, October–December 1995, 40–50.

Huebner, Janice Anderson. "Business Management: How to Avoid Sexual Harassment Traps." *HR Focus*, March 1995, 15–16.

Hymowitz, Carol, and Ellen Joan Pollock. "Corporate Affairs." *Wall Street Journal*, February 4, 1998, 1.

Jay, Susan. "SOU Redefines Policy on Sexual Misconduct." *Mail Tribune*, May 16, 1997, 4A.

Jeffrey, Laura S. "The Office Romances: Foolish or Fabulous?" *Federal Times*, February 12, 1996, 1.

Jenner, Lisa. "Office Dating Policies: Is There a Workable Way?" *HR Focus*, November 1993, 5–6.

Johnson, Kirk. "On-Line Romance: Office Workers Feel Cupid's Byte." *New York Times*, March 26, 1994, 1-21.

Judson, George. "Egalitarianism Invades a Shrine of V.I.P. Privilege." *New York Times*, May 17, 1996, B-1.

Karpeles, Michael D. "Set Guidelines for Workplace Romance." *Human Resource Professional*, January/February 1998, 26–28.

Keenan, Denis. "A Good Working Relationship?" *Accountancy*, November 1995, 90.

Kent, Margaret, and Robert Feinschreiber. *Love at Work*. New York: Warner Books, 1988.

Kilborn, Peter T. "Backlog of Cases Is Overwhelming Jobs-Bias Agency." *New York Times*, November 26, 1994, 1-1.

Klein, Jeffrey S., and Nicholas J. Pappas. "Sexual Harassment: Analyzing Severity, Persuasiveness." *New York Law Journal*, April 7, 1997.

Laabs, Jennifer J. "Sexual Harassment." *Personnel Journal*, February 1995, 36–43.

Laabs, Jennifer J. "What to Do When Sexual Harassment Comes Calling." *Personnel Journal*, July 1995, 42–53.

Landers, Ann. "'How-We-Met' Tale Turns Contentious in the '90s." *Chicago Tribune*, May 24, 1997.

Leibovich, Mark. "Sleepless in Silicon Valley." *San Jose Mercury News*, June 21, 1996.

Lewin, Tamar. "New Guidelines on Sexual Harassment Tell Schools When a Kiss Is Just a Peck." *New York Times*, March 15, 1997, 1-8.

Loftus, Mary. "Frisky Business." *Psychology Today*, March/April 1995, 34–41.

Loftus, Mary J. "Romance in the Workplace." *USA Today*, November 1995, 28–30.

Losey, Michael R. "Manage the 'Personal' in Interpersonal Relations." *Managing Office Technology*, November 1993, 25–29.

"Love in the Office." *Newsweek*, February 15, 1988, 52.

"Love at Work: Readers' Advice on Office Romances." *Glamour Magazine*, November 1994, 95.

Lowndes, Nell. "Dangerous Office Liaisons." *Legal Assistant Today*, September/October 1993, 64–73.

MacFarquhar, Neil. "Denying Sex Harassment, Haytaian Sues His Accuser." *New York Times*, January 31, 1996, B-5.

Mainiero, Lisa A. *Office Romance: Love, Power, and Sex in the Workplace.* New York: Rawson Associates (MacMillian Publishing Company), 1989.

Marelich, William D. "Can We Be Friends?" *HR Focus*, August 1996, 17.

Maremont, Mark. "Astra USA Settles Harassment Suit; To Pay $9.9 Million." *Wall Street Journal*, February 6, 1998, B (6:6).

Massengill, Douglas, and Donald J. Peterson. "Legal Challenges to No-Fraternization Rules." *Labor Law Journal*, July 1995, 429–35.

McDermott, E. Patrick. "Survey: Using ADR to Settle Employment Disputes." *Dispute Resolution Journal*, January 1995, 8–13.

McGuire, Powers. "*Harris v. Forklift Systems, Inc.* and Hostile Work Environment Harassment." *Labor Law Journal*, May 1995, 314–20.

McNerney, Donald J. "New Legal Worry: Third-Party Sexual Harassment." *HR Focus*, July 1996, 3–6.

Michael, Robert T., John H. Gagnon, Edward O. Laumann, and Gina Kolata. "Sex in America." *Glamour,* November 1994.

"Mom, the Provider." *New York Times,* May 14, 1995, 4-14.

Moskowitz, Milton. "Twelfth Annual Survey: 100 Best Companies for Working Mothers." *Working Mother,* October 1997, 18–96.

Murray, Kathleen. "At Work: A Backlash on Harassment Cases." *New York Times,* September 18, 1994, 3-23.

Nelton, Sharon. "Sexual Harassment: Reducing the Risks." *Nation's Business,* March 1995, 24–26.

"The New Providers." *Newsweek,* May 22, 1995, 36–38.

Nobile, Robert. "Sexual Harassment: Do You Know How to Respond?" *HR Focus,* January 1996, 13–14.

Nuffer, David. "Adversarial or Conciliatory? What Litigators Should Know About Mediation." *Dispute Resolution Journal,* January–March 1996, 24–27.

"Office Romance Requires Restraint, Discretion." *Cincinnati Business Courier,* December 18, 1995.

Olson, Walter. "The Long Arm of Harassment Law." *New York Times,* July 7, 1996, 4-9.

Onishi, Norimitsu. "Georgie Porgies and Other Outlaws." *New York Times,* October 6, 1996, 4-2.

Peak, Martha H. "Cupid in a Three-Piece Suit." *Management Review,* April 1995, 5.

Pierce, Charles A. "Factors Associated With Participating in a Romantic Relationship in a Work Environment." *Journal of Applied Social Psychology,* (in press).

Pierce, Charles A., and Herman Aguinis. "Bridging the Gap Between Romantic Relationships and Sexual Harassment in Organizations." *Journal of Organizational Behavior,* 18 (1997): 197–200.

Pierce, Charles A., Herman Aguinis, and Susan K. R. Adams. "Effects of a Dissolved Workplace Romance and Rater Characteristics on Judgments and Responses to Sexual Harassment Accusation." Manuscript submitted for publication, March 1998.

Pierce, Charles A., and Herman Aguinis. "Workplace Romances: Implications for Your Career." *Career Magazine.* January 3, 1997.

Pierce, Charles A., Donn Byrne, and Herman Aguinis. "Attraction in Organizations: A Model of Workplace Romance." *Journal of Organizational Behavior,* 17, (1996): 5–32.

Pimentel, Benjamin. "Former Oracle Worker Charged With Perjury." *San Francisco Chronicle,* April 20, 1996, D(1:5).

Prorok, Robert F. "Employer Liability Extends to Customers, Clients, and Vendors." *HR Magazine,* November 1993, 4.

Reuben, Richard C. "The Lawyer Turns Peacemaker." *ABA Journal,* August 1996, 54–62.

Robinet, Jane-Ellen. "Companies Turn Attention to the Bloom of Office Love." *Pittsburgh Business Times Journal,* September 16, 1996, 11.

"Romance in the Office: One Court's View." *Supervisory Management,* July 1994, 4.

"Romance in the Workplace: Corporate Rules for the Game of Love." *Business Week,* June 18, 1984, 70–71.

Schmitt, Eric. "Military Maneuvers: War Is Hell. So Is Regulating Sex." *New York Times,* November 17, 1996, 4-1.

Sciolino, Elaine. "Air Force Lieutenant Given Discharge for Fraternization." *New York Times,* July 12, 1997, 1-6.

Segal, Jonathan A. "The Unprotected Minority?" *HR Magazine,* February 1995, 27–33.

Segal, Jonathan A. "The World May Welcome Lovers . . ." *HR Magazine,* June 1996, 170–79.

Segal, Jonathan A. "Sexual Harassment: Where Are We Now?" *HR Magazine,* October 1996, 69–73.

"Sex Harassment Case Draws Swift Action." *New York Times,* January 10, 1995, A-1.

Shafer, Ronald G. "Romance Blooms." *Wall Street Journal,* March 28, 1997, 1.

Shaner, Dean J. "Romance in the Workplace: Should Employers Act as Chaperons?" *Employee Relations Labor Journal,* summer 1994, 47–71.

Siwolop, Sana. "Earning It; When Americans See Bias and the Boss Is Foreign." *New York Times,* May 5, 1996, 3–11.

Spiegel, Jill. *Flirting for Success.* New York: Warner, 1995.

Stickler, K. Bruce. "Viewpoints: For Job-Bias Suits, Ballooning Costs." *New York Times,* July 17, 1994, 3-11.

Sunoo, Brenda Paik. "Business Etiquette Makes or Breaks Employee Relations." *Personnel Journal,* June 1996, 173–74.

"Survey Results: Personal Relationships in the Workplace." *Erdlen Report,* February 1996.

"Survey Results: Personal Relationships in the Workplace." *Romac Report,* February 1997; February 1996.

Symonds, William C., Steve Hamm, and Gail DeGeorge. "Sex on the Job." *Business Week,* February 16, 1998, 30–31.

Tamminen, Julie M. *Sexual Harassment in the Workplace: Managing Corporate Policy.* New York: Wiley, 1994.

Tannen, Deborah. *Talking from 9 to 5.* New York: Morrow.

Thacker, Rebecca A. "A Descriptive Study of Situational and Individual Influences Upon Individual's Responses to Sexual Harassment." *Human Relations* 49, no. 8 (1996).

Thompson, Rebecca. "Office Romances: Are They a Bad Idea?" *Legal Assistant Today,* September/October 1993, 80.

"Ticklish Questions." *Across the Board,* April 1996, 46–52.

Townsend, Anthony M., and Harsh K. Luther. "How Do the Men Feel?" *HR Magazine,* May 1995, 92–96.

Trexler, Stephen H. "Extra Insurance." *HR Magazine,* September 1996, 128–32.

"Wanna Date? The Office May Not Be the Place." *HR Focus,* April 1995, 14.

Wareham, John. "The Rules of the Game." *Across the Board,* October 1997, 49.

"For Water Cooler Paramours, The Ties That (Legally) Bind." *New York Times,* February 22, 1998.

"When It's Harassment, and When It's Not." *Washingtonian,* August 1993, 152.

Williams, Andrea. "Model Procedures for Sexual Harassment Claims." *Arbitration Journal,* September 1993, 66–75.

Williams, Lena. "A New Level of Tolerance for Adultery." *New York Times,* January 4, 1996, C-8.

Williams, Lena. "What's in a Wink?" *New York Times,* November 24, 1996, 13-1.

Winograd, Barry. "Men as Mediators: In Cases of Sexual Harassment." *Dispute Resolution Journal,* April 1995, 40–43.

Woolfolk, John. "Oracle Boss Named in Termination Lawsuit." *San Francisco Chronicle,* October 21, 1993, A(21:1).

Index

alternative dispute resolution (ADR)
  in ABA survey, 260
  see also arbitration; mediation
American Management Association (AMA) survey
  (1994), xvi, 1, 6, 11–12, 21, 32, 63, 270
antidiscrimination laws, 249
antifraternization policies, 15, 76–78, 102–3, 112
antinepotism policies, *see* married couples
arbitration, 252–53, 259, 262, 284–85
armed forces, 75–76, 140, 254
attorneys
  hourly rates for sexual harassment cases, 248
  relationships with clients, 38, 72
  for sexual harassment cases, 16, 258–59
Autodesk, 103–4, 107, 110

Bankers Trust, 107, 267, 292
boss-subordinate relationships
  as affecting productivity, 36
  changes in handling, 273
  companies avoiding, 9, 10, 12, 19, 20, 112
  conflict of interest in, 38, 297
  coworker complaints about, 190
  dating the boss as watch-out area, 37–38
  fairness in reassignment or resignation, 274
  favoritism in, 37, 50–51, 80–81, 143
  going public about, 180
  knowing your intentions are serious, 166
  opportunism in, 142
  quid pro quo harassment committed only by those
    in power, 46
  reasonable policies for, 270–71
  sample office romance guidelines on, 297
  standard of reasonableness for, 59–60
breakups, *see* ending relationships at work
Bureau of National Affairs (BNA) study (1988), xvi, 1,
  279

careers, 24, 26, 41–42, 145–47
Civil Rights Act of 1991, 45, 244
Civil Rights Act of 1964, Title VII of the, 44–45, 249
clients, 38–39, 72, 82–84, 126–28
communication
  of company policy, 277–79
  creating safe channels of, 171–72
  keeping the channels open, 281–82, 299
  miscommunication between men and women,
    134–37
  misinterpretation of sexual interest, 156
  starting at the beginning, 14, 164
  variety of methods of, 153–54
company liability for sexual harassment, 46, 51–52,
  81–82
compliments, 8, 59, 136
confidentiality, 297
conflicts of interest, 26, 38–39, 297, 300
consent, 85
corporate climate, 93–117
  changes in, 10
  checking out before beginning a relationship,
    144–45

communication of, 277
couples adapting to, xvii, 97–102
employee dating policies, 11–12
as varying over time and by department, 96–97
see also pro-interactive companies
corporate game playing, as watch-out area, 39
Council on Families in America report (1995), 6
coworkers
  backing up sexual harassment complaints, 258
  consult with a work buddy, 173
  dealing with, 178–96
  favoritism as grounds for harassment case by, 50–
    51, 80–81
  as hostile to boss-subordinate relationships, 143
  keeping the relationship a secret from, 35, 145,
    148–49, 178
  reactions of as watch-out area, 35–36
  recognizing the signs of love, 179
  the reporting and complaining coworker, 190–92
  restraining yourself in front of, 179–80
  when to go public, 166–67, 180–86
  working with, 189
cultural differences, regarding sexual harassment,
  91–92, 132
customers, 38–39, 126–28

damage control, for breakups, 238–39
dating etiquette, 133–34
defamation, counterclaims of, 89
Delta Air Lines, 106
dispute resolution, alternative, *see* alternative dispute
  resolution
divorce, 116–17, 198–99, 272

educational institutions, 54–55, 74, 84–85
EEOC, *see* Equal Employment Opportunity Commission
E-mail
  company monitoring of, 79, 283–84
  keep messages discreet, 149
  meeting via, 154–55
  a reasonable policy for, 283–84
  sexual harassment concerns, 79, 155
employee privacy rights, 77, 112, 274, 283–84
employer liability for sexual harassment, 46, 51–52,
  81–82
ending relationships at work, 14–15, 224–46
  the company's approach to, 241–44
  a cooling-off period, 235–36
  damage control, 238–39
  discussing bail-out strategies, 168–69
  "exit routes" for, 35, 151, 186
  as fact of life, 120
  at first, 234–35
  if it's interfering with work, 236–38
  mediation for, 236, 279–81
  more than work is involved, 227–29
  nonwork considerations, 240–41
  as not having to be earth-shattering, 229–32
  not taking "no," 239–40
  potential legal problems, 62, 80

ending relationships at work (*continued*)
    sexual harassment litigation resulting from, 8, 40,
        237–38, 239–40
    as watch-out area, 41
    who loses more, 244
    why did it end, 232–34
    working it out, 236
    you can't hide, 225–27
entertainment industry, 94, 95
Equal Employment Opportunity Commission
    (EEOC)
    Del Laboratories suit, 8
    as having no enforcement power, 248
    procedures for sexual harassment cases, 249–51
    sexual harassment definition, 53
    statistics on sexual harassment litigation, 17, 63,
        251–54
    on third-party harassment, 81–82
"exit routes," 35, 151, 186
extramarital affairs
    in the armed forces, 140
    companies as in a bind over, 72–73
    company responsibility for, 81
    the injured spouse, 192–95, 198
    percentage of work romances as, 139–40
    as watch-out area, 40

favoritism
    affairs increasing possibility of, 32
    boss-subordinate relationships and, 37, 143
    companies dealing with, xvii
    coworker complaints about, 190
    friendships raising concerns about, 28
    as grounds for harassment case by coworkers, 50–
        51, 80–81
    mediating claims of, 116
    prohibiting married couples for preventing, 25
financial institutions, 38, 113
flirting, 130–31, 135, 136
Ford Motor Company, 26, 107, 211, 293–94
Fortune magazine
    "100 Best Companies to Work for in America," 108
    survey on office romances, 9, 32
friendships, 6, 28, 112, 128, 141–42, 233, 236

gender discrimination, 51, 80, 293
Gilmer v. Interstate/Johnson Lane Corporation, 284
gossip (rumors), 116, 143, 178, 182, 242

Harris & Associates survey, 212–13
Harris v. Forklift Systems, Inc., 48
high-tech industry, 22, 113
hostile working environment, 46–48
    the actions must be unwelcome, 49–50
    affairs as not indicating, 8
    companies attempting to prohibit, 18
    the company's liability for, 51
    in EEOC definition of sexual harassment, 53
    persistent ex-lover creating, 239–40
    presence of a policy as a defense, 300
    "reasonable woman" test for, 50
    for women managers, 81
Human Resources Management survey (1991), 11

Inc. Magazine poll (1992), 100
independent contractor relationships, 83

"Jenny Craig Eight," 88
Johnson and Johnson, 106–7
Johnson Wax, xvii, 105–6, 267
joint partnering, 164–77
    act the same as before, 172
    consult with a work buddy, 173
    create a mutual partnership, 147–51
    creating safe communication channels, 171–72
    if the romance dies, 168–69
    keep love separate from work, 172–73
    maintaining a professional image, 170–71
    in new rules of romance, 13–14
    as not meaning you stay together, 167–68
    starting at the beginning, 148, 165–67
    think ahead, 173–74
    in today's relationships, 213
    when to go public, 166–67
    work considerations, 170–75
jokes, 53, 55, 104, 137

liability insurance, 285–86
litigation for sexual harassment, 16–18, 247–64
    about attorneys, 258–59
    average award for, 247, 251–52
    cost of, 248, 250
    defense costs for, 253
    don't make the decision when you're upset, 256
    examples of, 17–18, 254–56
    favoritism as grounds for suit by coworkers, 50–51,
        80–81
    have you done all that you can do, 256–57
    if you want to go further, 256–63
    making the final decision, 263
    mediation compared with, 259–62
    overview of, 262–63
    procedures for, 248–54
    proving your case, 258
    the statistics are against you, 17, 63, 251–54
    as taking years, 17
    what do you really want, 257
    who's the real winner, 264
living together by unmarried couples, 6, 115, 288
"locker room" talk, 135–36

married couples, 210–33
    already married versus meeting at work, 213–14
    changing policies on, 289–90
    policies not treating differently, 19
    prohibiting from working together, 25
    reasonable policies for, 270
    regulation of, 78–79, 213
    sample office romance guidelines on, 298
    transition from dating to marriage, 214–23
    trend toward employee-sensitive policies, 111
mediation
    after a breakup, 236
    company's using for relationship problems, 116,
        241, 242
    effectiveness of, 281
    limitations of, 281
    in reasonable policy for office romances, 272
    in sample guidelines for office romances, 299
    for sexual harassment, 259–62
Meritor Savings Bank v. Vinson, 47–48

miscommunication, 134–37
Mobil Europe survey, 24

National Association of Female Executives (NAFE)
    poll (1992), 8
nepotism
    extended to include domestic partners, 243
    see also married couples

ombudsman, 270, 273, 280
one-night stands, 60, 74–75
open door policies, 56

persistence
    as creating a hostile environment, 239–40
    versus sexual harassment, 62, 67–71, 130
Personnel Journal survey, 115
Personnel magazine survey (1986), 5
physical relationships, 60
preventive action, on sexual harassment, 132
privacy rights, 77, 112, 274, 283–84
productivity changes, as watch-out area, 36–37
professional image, maintaining, 170–71
professional reputation, damage to as watch-out
    area, 35
professions, 38, 72, 82–84
pro-interactive companies, xvii–xviii
    balancing employee privacy with company inter-
        ests, 283
    on breakups, 241
    company climate of, 267–69
    continue monitoring policies of, 111
    dealing with coworker complaints, 190
    developing, 109–10
    discussing problems openly, 115–16
    emphasizing problem solving not punishment,
        116–17
    as enjoying the best legal defense, 287
    evaluate the company before accepting an offer,
        110
    examples of, 104–8
    husband-wife teams in, 25
    as profiting from pro-interactive policies, 7
    reasons for pro-interactive policies, 9–12
    rituals as pro-interactive, 96
    sexual harassment policy, 52
    trend toward, 111, 291–92, 294
public displays of affection, 11, 150–51, 216, 298, 300
public sector employees, 78

quid pro quo harassment, 45–46
    the actions must be unwelcome, 49
    the company's liability for, 51, 286
    opportunism leading to complaints of, 143, 144
    presence of a policy as a defense, 300

real estate industry, 39, 125
reasonableness, standard of, 59–60
"reasonable woman" test, 50
rejections, 155–58
relationships at work
    affairs contrasted with, xvi, 5–6
    agreements on, 286
    in the armed forces, 75
    benefits of, xv, 29–30, 199–200
    "benign neglect" policy for, xvii, 11, 109, 294
    bringing them into the open, 20

challenges to, 198–99
the chances people take for love, 137–38
company policies for, 18–20
continuing, 15–16, 210–23
and the corporate climate, 93–117, 144–45
coworkers against the company, 80–81
dealing with coworkers, 178–96
decision to get involved depending on your situa-
    tion, 33
enduring relationships, 206–8
evaluate career pros and cons, 145–47
examples of, 2–5
an ex-lover against the company, 80
ex-lovers against each other, 80
factors in the decision, 42–43
as flourishing, 1, 12, 57–58, 295
as friendships, 6
friendships ripening into, 28
as here to stay, 31
knowing what you want, 139–41
the law of romance, 58–62
legal rights regarding, 76–87
long form guidelines on, 296–300
love happening in strange places and ways, 162–63
the lovers against the company, 76–80
major "watch-out" areas, 34–42
marriage or long-term relationship resulting from,
    xvi, 6, 21, 32, 290
meeting and getting to know one another, 118–38
motives as important in, 33–34, 142–44
new rules of romance, 12–13, 139–51, 290
no-fraternization policies, 15, 76–78, 102–3, 112
one-night stands, 60, 74–75
other legal considerations, 49–51
people choosing relationships over jobs, 24
prevalence of, 5
problem situations, 155–58
a reasonable policy on, 269–75, 291
relationship advances treated as sexual harass-
    ment, xv–xvi
reporting, 19, 271, 297, 300
rigid approach as driving people underground,
    115
risks of, 7, 31–43
in the same department, 140, 151
same-sex relationships, 24, 293
samples guidelines for, 296–301
the secret of successful couples, 201–6
selling the boss and the company, 186–92
sexual harassment distinguished from, 58–63, 291,
    292
short form guidelines for, 300–301
starting off, 152–54
starting out as friends, 141–42
statistics on, 21
surveys on management views on, 32–33, 269
the test of time, 208–9
third-party relationships, 81–82, 290
in the twenty-first century, 288–95
ups and downs of, 200–201
using the policy on, 274–75
variety of, 24–25
when love's in full bloom, 197–209
when to go public, 166–67, 180–86

why companies don't crack down on, 9–12
why romance thrives, 6–7
working out the problems, 85–87
as worldwide, 24
written policies on dating, 11–12
written versus informal policies, 113–14
see also ending relationships at work; extramarital affairs; joint partnering; married couples; sexual harassment
Rulon-Miller v. IBM, 78

same-sex harassment, 49–50
same-sex relationships, 24, 293
secrecy
    from the company, 212–13
    from coworkers, 35, 145, 148–49, 178
    rigid policies driving people underground, 115
"*Seinfeld* verdict," 88
sexual harassment, 44–92
    arbitration for, 252–53, 259
    in the armed forces, 75–76, 254
    asking for a date as not, 157
    Autodesk policy on, 104
    client charges against professionals, 72, 82–84
    company size and policies on, 100
    the company's liability for, 46, 51–52, 81–82
    conduct must be primarily sexual in nature, 156
    cultural differences regarding, 91–92, 132
    as depending on the person, 75–76
    in educational institutions, 84–85
    EEOC as having no enforcement power, 248
    EEOC definition of, 53
    by E-mail, 79, 155
    favoritism as grounds for suit by coworkers, 50–51, 80–81
    fear factor in policies on, 56–57
    flirting distinguished from, 130
    gray areas regarding, 275
    horror stories of, 73–74
    impact not intention in defining, 55
    Johnson Wax policies, xvii, 106
    liability insurance for, 285–86
    major points in policies on, 273
    media's sensationalizing of, 247–48
    mediating claims of, 116, 259–62
    of men, 87–88
    men and women responding differently to cases of, 90
    men fearing charges of, 128
    men fighting back against charges of, 88–89
    as negative side of office romance, 7–9
    Office for Civil Rights guidelines on, 131–33
    office wolves made extinct by laws on, 26, 158
    one-size-fits-all approach to, 64–67, 265–66
    people's reactions as different, 55–56
    persistence versus, 62, 67–71, 130
    preventive action for, 132
    prompt response to, 282
    regulating romance with policies for, 114–15

relationship advances treated as, xv–xvi
relationship problems distinguished from, 271–72
romance distinguished from, 58–63, 291, 292
same-sex harassment, 49–50
sample office romance guidelines on, 296, 301
soured affairs resulting in charges of, 8, 40, 237–38, 239–40
statistics on, 8
a strong policy on, 276–77
by third parties, 81–82
what is illegal, 44–45, 53–55
zero tolerance policies, 132
see also hostile working environment; litigation for sexual harassment; quid pro quo harassment
sexual preference, 104
signed contract disclaimers, 76–77
slang, 59
socializing
    changing policies on, 289
    as fringe benefit, 12
    line between work and, 140–41
    long hours leaving little room for outside, 21–22
    policies against, 15, 76–78, 102–3, 112
    Springfield Remanufacturing's activity committees, 108–9, 268
standard of reasonableness, 59–60
supervision
    effective training for supervisors, 285
    putting yourself in the boss's shoes, 188
    selling the boss and the company, 186–92
    see also boss-subordinate relationships
surveillance techniques, 77

third-party dating, 123–24, 290
third-party sexual harassment, 81–82
Title VII of the Civil Rights Act of 1964, 44–45, 249
Training & Development survey (1994), 5
travel, xvi, 115–16, 126
two-income families, 212

"unequal power" working arrangements, 297
unmarried couples living together, 6, 115, 288

valentines, 8, 59

work-dates, 124–25
Working Mothers "100 Best Companies for Working Mothers" survey, 12, 107–8, 302–3
workplace, the
    changes in, 10, 289
    line between socializing and work, 140–41
    as meeting and dating place of choice, xvi, 7, 22–23
    office protocol, 157
    people as at their best in, 23
    propinquity in, 22
    what happens inside is the firm's business, 275, 283, 297
    women as peers in, 13, 288
    see also coworkers; relationships at work
wrongful termination lawsuits, 88

zero tolerance, 132